Developing
Caring Relationships
Among Parents, Children,
Schools, and Communities

*I dedicate this book to the memory of my parents, Dan and Rose McDermott,
for whose unconditional parenting I am filled with immense gratitude,
and to my wonderful children, Dan, Erin, and Matthew, who have been
very patient with my own efforts to do the same for them.*

Developing
Caring Relationships
Among Parents, Children, Schools, and Communities

Dana McDermott
DePaul University

SAGE Publications
Los Angeles • London • New Delhi • Singapore

For information:

Sage Publications, Inc.
2455 Teller Road
Thousand Oaks, California 91320
E-mail: order@sagepub.com

Sage Publications India Pvt. Ltd.
B 1/I 1 Mohan Cooperative
  Industrial Area
Mathura Road, New Delhi 110 044
India

Sage Publications Ltd.
1 Oliver's Yard
55 City Road
London EC1Y 1SP
United Kingdom

Sage Publications Asia-Pacific Pte. Ltd.
33 Pekin Street #02-01
Far East Square
Singapore 048763

Printed in the United States of America

Library of Congress Cataloging-in-Publication Data

McDermott, Dana, 1945-
Developing caring relationships among parents, children, schools, and communities/
Dana McDermott.
    p. cm.
Includes bibliographical references and index.
ISBN 978-1-4129-5408-2 (cloth)
ISBN 978-1-4129-2786-4 (pbk.)
  1. Parent-teacher relationships—United States. 2. Home and school—United States.
3. Community and school—United States. 4. Adult learning—United States. I. Title.

LC225.M39 2008
371.19′2—dc22

2006103540

This book is printed on acid-free paper.

07   08   09   10   11   10   9   8   7   6   5   4   3   2   1

Acquisitions Editor:	Diane McDaniel
Editorial Assistants:	Erica Carroll and Ashley Plummer
Permissions Editor:	Karen Ehrmann
Production Editor:	Melanie Birdsall
Copy Editor:	Bonnie Freeman
Typesetter:	C&M Digitals (P) Ltd.
Proofreader:	Cheryl Rivard
Indexer:	Ellen Slavitz
Cover Designer:	Janet Foulger
Marketing Manager:	Nichole M. Angress

CONTENTS

LIST OF APPENDICES

The Appendices are available online at www.sagepub.com/mcdermottappendices.

APPENDIX A: SAMPLE QUESTIONNAIRES

A1: The Parent-Teacher Role Checklist
A2: Getting to Know Our Parents

APPENDIX B: WORKSHOPS

B1: Parents as Adult Learners Workshop—Deconstructing Parent Involvement
B2: "You Can't Sit at My Table" Workshop—Scenarios
B3: Advocacy in Schools and Communities Workshop

APPENDIX C: NEWSLETTERS

C1: Resiliency Newsletter
C2: Resiliency Notes for Professionals
C3: Communication Newsletter—Enhancing Effective Communication in Home,
      School, and Community
C4: Friendship Newsletter—Some Thoughts on Friendship
C5: Transitions Newsletter
C6: Parenting for Prevention Newsletter

APPENDIX D: MODEL DEVELOPMENT MATERIALS

APPENDIX E: RESOURCES FOR PARENTING EDUCATION AND SUPPORT

PREFACE

This book is written for those of you who will work with parents and families in schools and communities or who are currently doing so. It is an essential supplement to graduate and upper-level undergraduate courses in home, school, and community involvement in schools of education or human development and related courses in psychology, family studies, family and consumer sciences, early childhood education, health sciences, or social work. It is an essential addition to training for professionals in Head Start, home visiting, and Strengthening Families programs and in community development. My approach is different from that of other texts on parent-child-school-community relations. I focus in more depth on the developmental tasks and perspectives of the adults in children's lives. I wrote this book because as a developmental psychologist, I feel most books and disciplines spend too little time understanding parents, teachers, and other caregivers as developing persons hoping and needing to form caring relationships with others in their lives.

This book follows a theory-to-practice format so the reader can "see" how an understanding of theories of development and relationships enhances practice. Part I focuses on the current rich and informative theory and research about how parents and other adults of diverse backgrounds grow, learn, and competently fulfill their parental and caregiving roles. Helpful charts, diagrams, and sample tools for use with parents are provided in Chapters 2, 3, 4, 5, and 6 and in several appendices for the reader to see the progression of work in the field and to organize the information for understanding and immediate application. Large amounts of information (such as a narrative of a focus group with middle school parents or questions about parents' and professionals' unique cultural perspective in this process of caring for others) are classified and boxed for easy reading.

Inspiring quotations and questions, posed at the beginning of each chapter and answered throughout, guide the reader to the important issues to be addressed, and questions at the end of the chapter promote experiential learning, critical thinking, synthesis, planning, evaluation, and action. From the beginning, I suggest ways theories should inform practice. Through the use of appreciative inquiry, the reader "sees" in each chapter examples of parent-child-school-community relationships that have succeeded and understands why.

The second, more application-oriented part of the book describes how practitioners have used the comprehensive theory and research from Part I to develop best practices models for parent-child-school-community relationships that differ from many models used today in schools and community-based agencies. The Parent Education Initiative is described in Part II and in more detail in Appendix D1 as an exemplary model.

WORKING FROM A FAMILY STRENGTHS PARADIGM

A few decades ago, when I began teaching "parenting in cultural context" courses to undergraduates and graduate students, I found child development and community psychology and sociology students, special education students, early childhood education students, future principals and policymakers, nurses, future school counselors, pastoral counselors, social workers, and future teachers taking the course. This course and the learning and conversations among students from different disciplines resulted in a richer understanding of parents and themselves, as well as of complex social contexts. Tools for relating to parents in a variety of situations were presented in those classes and are provided in Chapter 6. The hope of instructors of these kinds of courses then and now is that professionals embrace an approach to working with parents and families that is grounded in an understanding of the parents' developmental challenges and potential as well as the societal challenges they face. With its focus on adult developmental and learning issues that parallel child developmental issues, this book also provides an opportunity and a guide for the professional and personal development of the practitioner, most specifically in Chapter 8. I have also included useful information throughout to inform policy making and educational and societal reform.

A problem with traditional books on parent or family involvement is that they tend to be written within the paradigm of top-down relationships (Graue, 1998; Shirley, 1997). Even in books that view parents as partners, parents are often referred to in stereotypical terms and as teacher "assistants" rather than as colearners and coconstructors of knowledge and action plans (Drummond & Stipek, 2004; Lareau & Shumar, 1996). Parents are encouraged to be involved to enhance student success. Little attention is focused on understanding a parent's thinking capacities or feelings of self-efficacy, although these topics are analyzed in their children. New professionals still come out of these traditional courses braced for coping with parents as member of groups (e.g., single parents, minority parents, affluent parents, "difficult parents," etc.).

I wrote this book to provide an alternative and to give readers an opportunity to reflect on their beliefs about the professional role, the parent role, and child and family needs, as well as school and community needs. This opportunity is often missing and is sorely needed by professionals working or planning work with parents (Graue & Brown, 2003).

The first purpose of this book, then, is to fill a knowledge gap. What do we need to know about parents before we ask them to fulfill certain roles? This book does not review or describe every existing parent involvement program. It describes the journey of professionals working to understand theories of optimal parent-teacher-child development and then to apply them to the design of programs.

CONSIDERING PARENTS AND TEACHERS AS LIFELONG LEARNERS

This book offers another unique proposal. Ideally, each school should have a parenting educator (McEwan, 1998) to support parents, families, and teachers as parents-caregivers themselves. This professional is still rare in schools. Just as we have been learning about the complexity of infant development, so educators have been learning about the complexity of the parenting role, and indeed the adult role (Kegan, 1994). Experts (Brazelton & Greenspan, 2000; Comer, 2001) are calling for teachers to better understand human development in order to facilitate children's growth socially, emotionally, and intellectually. This book also addresses human development for professionals and parents as adults who are growing socially, emotionally, and intellectually. While schools, understandably, have been structured to focus on students, the time is right to find a way to better understand parent and teacher contexts (Comer, Ben-Avie, Haynes, & Joyner, 1999).

Principles of adult learning are very important tools to accomplish this task. This book describes the development and implementation within a school setting of a center for parent growth and development consistent with all the information on adult learning and human development put forth in Part I. In Part II, I share lessons learned in implementing this paradigm shift in thinking about parents, teachers, and others who care about and for children: We need to think about them as adults who are learning and growing in different and unique ways along with the students in their care (McDermott & Segal, 1998).

This book also fills a research gap regarding one group of parents. Books on parent involvement tend to be based on work with so-called at-risk parents or to assume that all parents who have middle-class values and goals are not at risk. Having also studied parents of higher socioeconomic status, I can firmly suggest that parents and caregivers of children of all socioeconomic backgrounds are at risk of not growing and often do not help children grow. The reasons include the ways society defines and supports parents, the ability or willingness of adults to fulfill their roles, and the narrow way in which society defines school support and student success, as well as adult success.

Because of the dawning emphasis on schools as learning communities; because of the new challenges facing parents, teachers, schools, and community agencies; because of all that is known about the complexities of the parent and caregiving role; and because of what is known about adult learning and development, this book provides new guidelines for parent-child-school-community relationships. As a North American author, I also feel a responsibility to provide opportunities for readers to learn from professionals around the world. The reasons we lack adequate parent involvement in schools and communities cannot be understood until we step back and gain a broader view of the adults in children's and students' lives.

I have chosen to use *we, us,* and *our* rather than *this author* because I want to remind the reader and myself that I was part of a larger community of lifelong learners involved in researching and writing this book, and I continue to be part of that community. Consequently, my personal reflections have been separated from other material in the text. The book is both a synthesis of scholarly literature and an opportunity for the reader to apply and extend the topic. It has been designed to also be a useful opportunity for learning and dialogue beyond the United States. To that end, the Appendices, containing various questionnaires, workshops, newsletters, model development information, resource material, and other exemplary projects and resource sites here and abroad, are not bound into the text but are posted to the Sage Web site at www.sagepub.com/mcdermottappendices. This format not only provides opportunities for updating the information but also allows for easy use, adaptation, and suggested improvements by the readers. Feedback and recommendations from readers are most welcome.

ACKNOWLEDGMENTS

I would especially like to thank Joy F. Segal, my collaborative partner in planning, designing, implementing, and assessing the Parent Education Initiative project shared in this text. Her vision, creativity, and commitment to supporting parents and teachers as lifelong learners were essential to the success of this project. I also wish to thank Harriet Heath for her support and collaborations and for her extensive body of work on caring and parenting, which has contributed so positively to the practice of many educators and family-serving professionals.

I would like to thank the founding members of the National Institute for the Study of Parenting Education (NISPE), launched in Clayton, Missouri, at the Clayton Family Center. Special thanks to Carol Kaplan-Lyss and Debbie Reilly at the center and to all NISPE members for creating this way to support the work of parenting educators in schools and communities across the country. I also thank my colleagues of Prepare Tomorrow's Parents for their commitment to preparing the next generation of parents. Thanks to the National Parenting Education Network for its work to elevate the field of parenting education and support.

In Chicago, I have been especially inspired by Bernice Weissbourd, founder of Family Focus and the Family Resource Coalition. I could not have done my work without the support of the Irving Harris Foundation, the George Clemens Foundation, the John D. & Catherine T. MacArthur Foundation Minority Women's Leadership Grant, the Fund for School Reform Planning Grant, research funding from Loyola University and DePaul University, and funding from the Anne E. Liebowitz Foundation.

I wish to thank the parents, teachers, staff, and students of the schools in which I have had the privilege of working collaboratively over the years. Special thanks to the Latin School of Chicago, Saint Ignatius School, and St. Peter's School and to the following Chicago public schools: McKay, Morrill, Saucedo, White Career Academy, and Haugan School. I would also like to thank the students at Loyola

University–Chicago and DePaul University, who have taught me so much as we work to understand and support parents and families. Thanks also to my colleagues at DePaul's School for New Learning for their support.

Special thanks to educators Julia Gippenreiter, psychology professor at Moscow State University in Russia, and Peter Turner, former director of the Southern Region of the Catholic Archdiocesan Schools in Sydney, Australia, for collaborating with parent educators like myself to find better ways to support parents and teachers around the world. Thanks to the many educators and leaders I met in Russia in 1993 in Moscow at the Kavchek School, the Gymnasium High School, and innovative community organizations and parent centers such as Yablaka, who were all seeking more-effective ways to work with parents. Thanks to parent and community educators in Sydney, Australia—Sister Loreto McLeod, RSM, Caroline Benedet, and Grainne Norton—and to school parents and staff in both countries for their commitment to working in more-caring and collaborative ways.

I also wish to acknowledge the following reviewers for their reading of and helpful suggestions for the text:

Joel Nitzberg, Cambridge College

Helen Marks, Ohio State University

Phyllis M. Garcia, Arizona State University, Tempe

Lee Shumow, Northern Illinois University

Judith R. Mayton, Oral Roberts University

Jaesook Lee Gilbert, Eastern Kentucky University

Regina Miller, University of Hartford

Janet S. Fields, Mercer University

Beth Nason Quick, Tennessee State University

Saigeetha Jambunathan, New Jersey City University

Gloria Wenze, University of Scranton

William McInerney, University of Toledo

Natalie Kennedy Beard, Harris-Stowe State University

Tunde Szecsi, Florida Gulf Coast University

Barbara Foulks Boyd, Radford University

Lesley J. Schoch, North Idaho College

Elizabeth J. Sandell, Minnesota State University, Mankato

Sandra Saucedo Scott, Eastfield College

Grace Hui-Chen Huang, Cleveland State University

I would like to especially thank my Sage editor, Diane McDaniel, for her continuing support and guidance, editorial assistants Erica Carroll and Ashley Plummer, production editor Melanie Birdsall, and copy editor Bonnie Freeman for their eagerness to support my efforts throughout.

Finally, I would like to thank colleagues and friends Idy Gitelson, Donna Newton, Barbara LeBlanc, Ann Ellwood, Rae Simpson, Glen Palm, Joan Comeau, Nancy Kelly, Carol Coughlin, Carol Lewke, Andrea Schuver, Joan Barbuto, and Marilyn Swierck, who have inspired and supported me over the years. Their support in thinking through our roles and the needs of children, families, schools, and communities has sustained me on my journey in spite of challenges along the way. And it goes without saying that I could not have done the research and work without the support and encouragement of my entire family, especially my children and my sister Therese Tetzner.

INTRODUCTION
Thinking Mindfully About Parents

In his wonderful poem "The Road Not Taken," Robert Frost described two roads in a woods and how choosing the less traveled one had "made all the difference" for him. This book asks you the reader to take a less traveled road as well, one that I hope will make a positive difference in relationships with families. It asks you to look at parents, families, and yourself in a new way. It draws on the scholarly work on the concept of *mindfulness* and specifically *mindful learning* (Langer, 2000), which asks educators to approach teaching in a very different way as well. Langer asks educators to avoid delivering information as absolute fact and to help students avoid forming mind-sets about any subject they study, because such mind-sets often place limitations on their learning. Langer describes mindfulness as "a flexible state of mind in which we are actively engaged in the present, noticing new things and sensitive to context" (p. 220).

I ask you, thinking mindfully, to notice new things about parents and parent involvement in this book. Rather than give you a definition accepted as fact, I will ask you to think about five ways parents in very different situations might view parent involvement. I also ask you not to take in the information shared here as if it were new facts but to question it, reflect on it, and test it against your experience. I don't ask you to replace old facts with new facts but to be open to new possibilities and new ways of understanding the issues.

In each chapter in this book, you will find a variety of ways to view parents. Part I reviews theories and research on parent involvement and engagement, the parenting process, adult learning, and cultural diversity. Case studies and narratives are interspersed to connect concrete experiences to theoretical frameworks. To date, the ideas for this book have been explored with teachers from the United

States and from Mexico, Canada, Russia, Australia, Africa, England, Japan, and Germany who are also working for change to strengthen schools and families. The research and examples from international sources, though not representative of all countries worldwide, are interspersed throughout. I hope that an even larger international community of educators and parent- and family-serving practitioners will join this ongoing dialogue.

PART I. UNDERSTANDING PARENTS WITHIN THEIR CULTURAL CONTEXT

Chapter 1 poses the question, why are parents and teachers resisting school and societal expectations for parent involvement? A description of some past and current parent-teacher experiences in schools reveals that some parents feel they are told what to do, and teachers feel they do not have time to solve parent-school-child problems, which seem to be escalating. Parents and teachers are expected to "fix" children (Turnbull, Blue-Banning, Park, & Turbiville, 1999). Both parties resist this expectation without looking at the larger systems affecting children's lives as well. So the mindful question might be, how could people approach parent involvement if they understood more about how it is viewed by families and teachers?

The chapter also describes typical standards and guides for parent involvement that in themselves explain why many parents and teachers might be resistant and recommends that the diverse needs of teachers and parents be considered in setting these standards. The book provides a historical glimpse of the changing view of the role of parents by theorists and researchers over several decades. Almost all models of parent involvement in the past suggested that the school or agency should define and provide a role for parents and provide parenting education and skill development as well if they were needed. But we must ask whether what the models usually provide is adequate for the complex society in which we live.

Few books describe the kind of programs that are appropriate based on current theory and research on the parenting process and the ideal parent-child relationship. What we now understand about good parenting provides a clue to why parents do not always want to spend their time on homework. Elias and Schwab (2004) reviewed all the expectations of parents today—all they must do to support their children's growth within a society that seems to thwart their efforts—and suggested that just supporting parents in being parents will in the long run help children succeed academically as well as socially and emotionally. Of course, part of being parents would involve being interested in what children do in school and other settings. What you might ask is, don't parents know what to do? And if they don't, isn't the solution just a matter of teaching them some skills?

Understanding Theories and Research on Parenting

Chapter 2 reviews the progression of theories about the ideal parent-child and adult-child relationships to encourage. What should parents and teachers be doing to support a child's growth and development? The way "experts" have evolved in their theories about parents' roles and tasks over time has affected the way society thinks about parents and about school relationships with parents and with children. This thinking has moved from unidirectional theories of parents' effects on children to theories describing the impact of children on parents and teachers. It has also shifted from a view of the child as a passive recipient of parenting or teaching to efforts to understand how children might each perceive and relate to each adult in their lives very differently.

Here are just some of the factors to think about in understanding parent-child and adult-child relationships today: behavioral genetics; cognitive-developmental processes; social relationships; children's effects on adults; attachment and interpersonal neurobiology; personality and trait theories; social-cognitive perspectives; parental self-understanding, awareness, and identity; family systems theories; bioecological systems theories; and family empowerment models. There is so much to know about parents and children, and it is often missed in traditional courses on parent involvement or child development.

In Chapter 3, I discuss a particular developmental and ecological theory of parenting that focuses on parental competence (Heath, 1998, 2006) to give order to the large amount of information in Chapter 2. This theory describes the internal characteristics or ego processes of parents and caregivers of children and the external factors that facilitate or impede their and their children's growth. It puts the parent back into parenting theories. To work effectively with parents and caregivers, it is essential to understand their beliefs and their capacity for thinking; feeling; perspective taking; decision making; problem solving; coping; anticipating, planning, and appraising situations; nurturing; advocating; communicating; and their level of parental awareness. Finally, we have to consider all the additional factors, such as physical and mental health, gender, temperament and goodness of fit with the child, developmental level, previous experience, social support, and current cultural and societal impact. So when we think about parents, I suggest that a focus on these topics and a sensitivity to context, as Langer (2000) has suggested, guide our thinking.

Understanding Parents and Teachers as Lifelong Learners

The goal in Chapter 4 is to move from theory to methods, review current models and goals of parent involvement and parent-teacher relationships, and describe these models' obstacles to success in light of what is known about parents as adult learners and as lifelong learners. Current texts on parent, school, and community are missing the large body of theories and information about parents in Chapters 1 through 3, about adult learning principles in Chapter 4, and about the importance of using this information to inform and assess current school practices. So we must ask, what could it mean to our practice if we think of parents and teachers as lifelong learners?

In Chapter 4, I suggest that there is a disconnection between the message in current parent involvement guides and the information on principles of adult learning and development. I also provide examples of programs that are addressing adult needs. Adult learners appreciate diverse approaches to learning. Successful adult learning focuses on relationships; inquiry and process; joint problem solving; self-direction; the rich experiences adults bring to learning; the critical thinking–dialogue–action process; an adult's readiness to learn and act; the importance of filtering information through a parent's values, beliefs, and feelings; and the importance of allowing parents and teachers the opportunities to use successful adult learning strategies suggested by Taylor, Marienau, and Fiddler (2000), such as assessing situations, collaborating, experimenting, imagining, inquiring, performing-simulating, and reflecting on how they work together. If this is how adults learn best, can we provide parents and teachers better opportunities to do so?

I have added the dimension of adult development to adult learning because the fact that parents, teachers, and other professionals working with children should be growing over their lifespan is often missed or seen as a zero-sum, with any focus on them being viewed as a loss of time to focus on the child. Adult self-care is needed for ultimate student success (First & Way, 1995; Smith, Cudaback, Goddard, & Myers-Wall, 1994), as is time for self-correction and self-generation (Flaherty, 1999). A caring school model of relating and some parent development initiatives described in Part II illustrate how this information can be incorporated into program development.

Understanding Culturally Diverse Parents and Teachers

In Chapter 5, I address in detail culture as it affects how parents view parent involvement and their role (though culture is addressed throughout the book). The way in which parents receive information from a school depends on how that information is filtered through their cultural beliefs and values. Knowledge about culture is effective if it speaks not in terms of group stereotypes but in terms of answering a broad range of questions about individual parents' ideas, goals, and beliefs about children and themselves, the school, and other issues. Stereotypes imply mindlessness, or doing things without thinking. As Langer and Moldoveanu (2000) note, "Negative intergroup attitudes can (also) be the result of mindless categorization" (p. 6). I recommend that professionals dealing with cultural diversity ask themselves a broad list of questions in dealing with cultural diversity. Experts (Graue & Brown, 2003) strongly encourage asking future and current professionals some similar questions to help them explore where they stand and the cultural perspective they hold.

Once we have addressed how parents think and learn best, we must also understand how culture and social class interact. Irrespective of socioeconomic status, certain parents are more supportive of the school-as-expert approach because it is consistent with their cultural experience. Therefore, they may take a passive, hands-off approach to school interactions even though they are quite actively involved in other areas of their children's lives. Some parents have language challenges, and some consider themselves to have little to offer their children. Is it better to try to change people, to accept where they are and what they can or are willing to contribute, or to explore different perspectives, as mindfulness would imply?

As Goodnow and Collins (1990) asked several years ago, what do we know about the content and quality of parents' ideas? Consistent with their research, this chapter asks, what might they believe about the direction of child development, or about how parenting conditions affect families? What are their beliefs about children's, parents', and teachers' roles? What are their goals for children and their ideas about the nature of children and even of their own situations? Asking these guiding questions makes more sense than studying what particular cultural groups do.

PART II. FROM THEORY TO PRACTICE: FOSTERING CARING AND CULTURALLY SENSITIVE PARENT-CHILD-SCHOOL-COMMUNITY RELATIONSHIPS

Chapter 6 and Part II move from theory to practice, although practical applications are referred to throughout. Readers will learn about a model for institutionalizing caring and culturally sensitive parent-school relationships in a school. A parenting educator often facilitates this process, and the model emphasizes building better human connections. The model is unique in that it was developed in light of the theory discussed in Part I to account for the complexity of parenting. Whether readers are teaching preschoolers, special education students, or adolescents, whether they are working in community schools or family support agencies, the model is a heuristic that can facilitate caring and successful parent-child-school-community relationships. The model promotes caring in terms of how teachers and other professionals relate to students, families, and each other; how students are encouraged to relate to adults and to each other; and how families, children, and schools relate to each other and their community.

The model introduced in Chapter 6 takes theories of parenting, adult learning principles, and culture into consideration. Heath's (2001) "parenting process," which is used as a guide, takes everyone's situations, goals, beliefs, cultural background, needs, feelings, developmental level, learning style, social context, temperament, time, energy, and resources into consideration in making decisions. It is a way to deal with issues related to child rearing, school discipline, parent-professional conferences and planning, home visits, and school and community challenges.

Understanding Parents' and Teachers' Concerns

Chapter 7 describes the range of issues of concern to parents and teachers across grades and social class, such as discipline, peer pressure, and assessment of student success, both academically and from a social-emotional perspective. I present data from educators and family support professionals about the issues parents of all social backgrounds have in common and the areas where parents might differ. Some themes occur across age groups, and there is clearly a learning curve for all adults, not just parents. This chapter discusses the themes of control, autonomy, communication, and threats from the environment. How to approach these topics with adult learning principles and a caring process of decision making is also shared. Some of the topics affect adults of all cultures, educational levels, and socioeconomic backgrounds most strongly in terms of their sense of powerlessness. In addition, Chapter 7 includes diverse methods of presenting material on these topics based on parents' learning preferences and sociocultural background.

Chapter 8 demonstrates that the same theories of adult development and adult learning that underlie the parent-engagement model will effectively support teachers and all adult caregivers as well. I describe teachers and other professionals serving families in a preK–12 school who successfully enhanced their own learning and reflective practice at school through faculty development and engagement in a parent education initiative. Readers will also find descriptions of other successful tools for professional development (writing, storytelling, etc.) that relate to similar support initiatives for parent and teacher development.

Specifically, this chapter highlights a parallel learning experience of teachers and parents within one model development school to demonstrate that teachers and parents can and should be on a similar learning journey, both for their own benefit and for the benefit of the children in their care. As a member of both a teacher group and a parenting group at this school, I was in a unique position to see parent and teacher-staff learning and reflection (McDermott, 1999). Without the opportunity to take time off from university work to share in the experience of parents and teachers for 5 years, I could never have adequately appreciated the potential for adult growth that this model offers.

Ensuring That the Next Generation of Parents Is Prepared for Their Role

In Chapter 9, readers will learn how to build, within a caring school model, a way to teach parenting so that students will be even better learning partners with teachers, better parents in the next generation, and better classmates, as well as more well-rounded academically, socially, and emotionally. The theory, research, and rationale for teaching parenting education from preK to Grade 12 indicate that among many good outcomes, parents in the next generation will be better prepared to partner with teachers competently and confidently (Brazelton & Greenspan, 2000; Eisler, 2000; Zigler, 1999; and countless others). The parenting skills taught to children and youth are linked to the parental and teacher competency needs discussed in Chapter 3. Thus, these programs not only make students well-equipped future parents but also help them improve their current relationships with peers, parents, teachers, and others. The courses emphasize the importance of relationships and of providing the right environment, from infants' earliest days, to maximize their potential for future development.

The caring process of relating and decision making described in Chapter 6 is central to this curriculum. School parents have the opportunity to learn an adult version of the student parenting program as well. It is often easier for parents to come into a parenting curriculum when it is tied to what their children are learning and, more important, tied to family issues that have more face validity to many than learning the new math does.

The Epilogue reviews the rationale for using the approach to parent and professional engagement described in this text (focusing on relationship more than involvement and on being more than doing). Readers are advised to take a thoughtful approach to a complex situation such as parent-teacher relationships. The Epilogue also reviews the successes and challenges of the theory-to-practice models put forth in the text and notes challenges, such as an institution's anticipated resistance to change, and pressures to focus on student performance in academics. Nevertheless, I recommend staying on this "road less traveled."

Bonnie Benard (1996) summarizes it this way:

Ultimately research on resilience challenges the field to build the connectedness, this sense of belonging by transforming our families, school and communities to becoming "psychological homes" wherein youth can find mutually caring and respectful relationships and opportunities for meaningful involvement. . . . Creating belonging for youth means we must also do this for ourselves. (pp. 5–6)

Something must be done to improve parent-school-community relationships, so even though the task seems daunting, we must move forward. That something includes designing a model demonstrating collaboration from all systems in parents' and families' lives, including neighborhood and community service agencies, medical services, religious institutions, government policies, and so on. We cannot focus on just the home or school and expect adults in these two institutions to solve all problems without the support of their entire community and society.

In addition, borrowing from the work of appreciative inquiry (Cooperrider, 2001), I suggest throughout this book that we move from identifying problems to thinking about what could be possible. In the decades I have spent listening to parents, teachers, and professionals working with families, I have heard abundant stories of collaborations that have worked well. I have included some of these stories, and I apologize for omitting so many others. I have included as many as I could to fulfill the goals of appreciative inquiry (Barrett & Fry, 2002, pp. 6–7), which involve the four Ds: *discovering* times when adults have provided nurturing environments for children, *dreaming* together to envision what the future might hold for our children and ourselves, *dialoguing* with each other within environments of safety and trust, and *designing* better spaces for all of us to live and grow. Appreciative inquiry might pose questions such as these: When have parents and all the adults in children's lives felt successful in caring for children? What supports and strengthens our ability to care? What conditions need to be in place for these successes to happen more in the future? Let the inquiry begin.

Part I

UNDERSTANDING PARENTS WITHIN THEIR CULTURAL CONTEXT

Part I outlines the principles of adult learning and cultural competence that will be illustrated in Part II. The theories and research on parenting and caring presented in Part I lay an essential groundwork for the unique approach to home-school-community relations that will be presented in Part II. Whenever possible, examples of applications are included to bring the theoretical concepts alive in practice.

Chapter 1

Understanding Parent Involvement and Engagement in Schools Today

"The process is simple," says Dan Rothstein. . . ."It requires a shift from the habit of delivering information to parents towards facilitating inquiry."

—Cushman, 1998, p. 2

Some of the questions this chapter addresses:

- How have people thought about parent involvement in the past?

- What might be a new way to think of parental involvement and parent-teacher relationships?

- How might goals differ in past and current conceptions of parent-teacher relationships?

- How are educators from other countries thinking about this issue? What recommendations are they making?

- What are some challenges of implementing this new, engagement-focused approach to parent-teacher relationships?

FRAMING THE ISSUES

Parents and teachers often struggle with the rising expectations for parent involvement today. Parents are sometimes reluctant to get involved in the way schools expect them to, and administrators and teachers sometimes hesitate to interact with parents (Graue & Brown, 2003). This reluctance is at odds with the current thinking about involvement, which is almost always that more is better. Furthermore, little is known about the meaning of this involvement to the various parties involved. Many believe teachers and parents want children to succeed, and there is evidence to support this belief (Drummond & Stipek, 2004). Parents and educators are bombarded with research studies reminding them that involvement is related positively to academic success (Henderson & Mapp, 2002; Jeynes, 2005). Yet their conscious and unconscious resistance does not really surprise anyone. We have only to look at our own situations, history, and the components and principles of parent-teacher involvement and adult learning to find some reasons involvement remains problematic. Take a moment to consider your own experiences and expectations of parent involvement in schools. What comes to mind for many of us are often-dreaded parent-teacher conferences, a teacher calling a parent about a child's failures or misbehavior, a room mother who organizes the holiday party for an elementary school class, or a parent prodding a child to do homework. In addition, many educators have experience with parents' advocating for special needs children or getting involved in fundraising.

■ How Have People Thought About Parent Involvement in the Past?

The theme that generally emerges is parent involvement in association with overcoming obstacles to the academic success of a child or the school or with "extra," fun things. The reason parents appear in these scenarios is, according to many, their desire to be a positive influence within the system, but their actual influence has been limited. Even with the No Child Left Behind parent involvement mandate, many feel the parents' role is confusing and limited. As Wendy Puriefoy (2005), president of the Public Education Network, noted, "Rather than bringing people closer to their schools, the No Child Left Behind law is causing many Americans to feel increasingly distrustful of and marginalized by professional educators" (p. 1).

Not surprisingly, theories, research, and writing in the field have focused on themes of parent involvement in specific areas, such as academics. As a developmental psychologist studying the growth and development of parents, I was frustrated while teaching in a school of education to find that the typical texts focused not on parents as individuals but on parent involvement or what parents should do or not do. When you type *parents* into a search engine, you often find *parent involvement,* which almost always focuses on children's academic success. Added to helping with homework, volunteering in the classroom in the early school years, or advocating for a special needs child, I found topics such as dealing with illiteracy and other parental limitations. The theme was frequently that educators had to "deal with" parents and "get them" to support the school and their child. If parents did not do what the school wanted them to do (usually to help with academics), it was the parents' fault if their child did not succeed.

Promoters of parental involvement have often been early childhood or special education teachers who realize the importance of parent support to their own efforts on behalf of children. Other parent involvement promoters include federal agencies and state departments of education, whose involvement guidelines, posted on their Web sites, talk about adult learning, two-way communication, and decision making, but the learning is still described in terms of parents' learning about the child or the school in order to support school goals. The State of Iowa Department of Education (1994) description of parent involvement is typical of many state definitions of parental involvement: "receiving ideas from the school, learning about school programs, becoming confident in terms of helping children learn and having more positive views of teachers" (p. 1). All this is good, and the state of Iowa is in fact exemplary when it comes to supporting parents and teachers, but many teachers, principals, and supporters of initiatives like the Comer School Development Project, the School of the 21st Century, the Coalition for Community Schools, and the Institute for Responsive Education believe it is time for a "new frontier" in parent involvement. How can government agencies think about parent involvement in a new way?

TRADITIONAL DEFINITIONS OF PARENT INVOLVEMENT

Government agencies promote parent involvement and are clear in their goals. The U.S. Department of Education Web site (www.ed.gov/parents/academic/help/partnership.html) indicates that the focus of parental involvement is primarily academic success even though the materials for parents are described as "preparing children for the 21st century." There is no opportunity to question school goals or too narrow academic standards or for all stakeholders to react to the goal of academic success. What of all the parents who think the main goal of education has to do with the moral and social development of children, as Reese (2001) has found to be the case with immigrant Latino parents?

For years, Epstein (1995; Epstein & Sanders, 2002) has been educating and supporting schools and parents as they think about and define parent involvement and home-school partnerships. The Guides for Parent Involvement (Epstein & Salinas, 2004) are roughly as follows:

1. Parenting ("assist families with parenting skills" and human development, understand families' background, culture, and goals)

2. Communicating (via parent-teacher conferences and school-home mail)

3. Volunteering in the school (recruit parents as identified by individual school need to support students in school)

4. Learning at home (encourage parents to help with homework, support student goals, and encourage children to involve parents in homework activites)

5. Decision making (involve parents as leaders, e.g., in parent-teacher associations and school committees and advocacy activities)

6. Collaborate with community groups, including businesses, organizations, and universities (to provide family and school services and to work together to improve the community)

These components provide ample room for a growth-enhancing role for parents, though it is often not addressed in schools. In Part II of this text, I will discuss many of the components above, though in a more parent-focused and developmental way than is often the case.

The Parent Teacher Association (PTA) has delineated similar national standards and also allows for parent development. Its Web site notes,

1. "Communicating between home and school is regular, two-way, and meaningful.

2. Parenting skills are promoted and supported.

3. Parents play an integral role in assisting student learning.

4. Parents are welcome in the school and their support and assistance are sought.

5. Parents are full partners in the decisions that affect children and families.

6. Community resources are used to strengthen schools, families and student learning." (PTA, 2000–2006)

Many parents feel that they are not involved in decision making and that the language of school policies and mandates is often unnecessarily difficult to understand

PTAs work with schools on a variety of projects, such as planting trees, monitoring playgrounds and classrooms, and organizing afterschool activities for students.

SOURCE: Reprinted with permission from PTA/Michelle LaFond.

(Puriefoy, 2005). How has the school identified the skills parents need? Are those skills related only to tutoring? The PTA Web site (www.pta.org) is filled with helpful information for parents. It also has information on the research pointing to the significant and positive relationship between parent involvement and student academic success. Some critics of this research (Levine & Weins, 2003; Mattingly, Prislin, McKenzie, Rodriguez, & Kayzar, 2002; White, Taylor, & Moss, 1992) have concluded that given the methodological flaws in many studies, the impact of parent involvement in schools may be overstated. They note that definitions and measures of involvement remain difficult to isolate from everything else going on in students' lives. (This criticism is the reason groups that promote the involvement of communities and businesses to support, strengthen, and advocate for families are so important.) While terms like *decision making* and *collaboration* are often mentioned in connection with *parent involvement,* one still wonders what this involvement looks like in typical schools. Many researchers have pointed to the power discrepancies within most school systems as obstacles to ideal partnerships (Cervero, Wilson, & Associates, 2001; Graue, 1998; Sarason, 1995; Vincent, 1996).

POLITICAL, PHILOSOPHICAL, SOCIAL, AND CULTURAL ISSUES

Political, cultural, and philosophical forces come into play in the dilemma of parent and teacher resistance to school expectations for parent involvement. To understand this resistance, we must understand what parents have expected from schools in the past, what is expected now, and what will be expected in the future. How is this resistance related to government policies and today's culture, economics, and politics? And how is it related to the way educational institutions were and are currently structured?

Lareau (1989, 2003) has suggested that parental actions related to education are still built into school philosophies of an appropriate role for parents, which is to do what is good for children—and the school defines what that is. Graue and Brown (2003) also found this attitude in new education majors in a Midwestern university setting. The 130 future teachers who participated in their study seemed to think family involvement should come in response to school directions. They were somewhat suspicious of parents, whom they viewed as caring more about themselves than their children and unwilling to admit their children had problems. These future teachers described the ideal parent as attentive and deferential to teachers and their expertise. The study participants were preoccupied with needing to establish their authority as teachers and saw the relationship between schools and parents as asymmetrical. Graue and Brown suggested that future teachers needed to reflect on how their own experiences and their own positions of privilege shape their views of parents.

McConchie (2004), in an issues paper prepared for Australian educators and communities concerned about involvement, cites other barriers to family-school partnerships, including fears that partnering with families in decision making will diminish the principal's authority. Some teachers in this review felt that because parents did not understand the school or the system, they likely would not know how to get involved in those types of roles. McConchie also suggested that teachers felt their professionalism was threatened when parents were involved in pedagogical issues, and this fear led in turn to parents' being excluded from any efforts to rethink educational practices. The paper concluded that parent initiatives often succeeded or failed based on teachers' perceptions (p. 8).

■ What Might Be a New Way to Think of Parental Involvement and Parent-Teacher Relationships?

Most educators may not realize that parental noninvolvement in school activities such as homework can be a parent's personal and political statement that what a school does is not always a good thing. In other words, parents may define good involvement as refusing to help a child do 4 hours of nightly homework, because that much homework interferes with family life. Such a refusal is usually seen as a deficiency in parents because doing homework is rarely questioned by society. (See Kohn, 2006, for a thoughtful and well-researched critique of homework.) If one were "thinking mindfully," students, parents, and teachers might meet to reflect on homework together and look at it in a new way.

Palmer (1998) suggests that the way to get at the truth of a matter is not to have an expert talk down to stakeholders but to put the subject in the middle and let all stakeholders provide insights into its meaning (p. 102). One might ask, what are a school's goals in giving homework? Are there different kinds of homework? What about relationship "work" at home and school and in the community? Thus, parents would not react by just assisting with homework without question but could take "critical actions" (Calabrese Barton, Drake, Perez, St. Louis, & George, 2004), in which they evaluate the school's assumptions, policies, and beliefs about homework. Or in the case of No Child Left Behind, parents could critically evaluate what it is really doing for poor and disadvantaged children and how the focus on test performance to assess learning is in effect "dumbing down classrooms" (Kohn, 2004, as cited in Meier, Kohn, Darling-Hammond, Sizer, & Wood, 2004, p. 91).

Graue (1998) has introduced the informative concept of *answerability,* which complicates the situation even further. Most middle-class parents feel they are answerable primarily to their own children and must advance their children's achievement in society rather than advance society by questioning the amount of homework, competition, and individual achievement promoted in the United States and the lack of focus on caring, cooperation, citizenship, and life skills many feel are so important in adult life. They rarely question the funding of education, which leaves poor children with fewer resources than their own children enjoy. Our schools and governments have a responsibility to ensure equality for all. Do all U.S. schools "overcome the differences in starting point of children from different social groups" (Coleman, 1966, p. 72), as they were originally designed to do? If not, why not? Certain parents are rewarded more than others by an institution that has not been asked enough by parents, society at large, and policymakers to critically review the emphasis on homework, competition, and other school structures and goals. Almost a century ago, Winship (1912, p. 517) questioned this emphasis, believing homework disadvantaged poor children.

On the other hand, many teachers who choose to focus on cooperation feel a push from some parents to be more competitive. Thinking mindfully, we can look at competition and cooperation in a different way. Langer and Moldoveanu (2000) describe people mindlessly learning the basics about something. One of the things many people mindlessly accept as fundamental is the belief that homework, like competition, is good. Another is that reading, writing, and math are what children need to succeed. Langer and Moldoveanu note,

> Having mindlessly accepted this information, it rarely occurs to us to question who determined what the basics are. . . . Once we learn the basics mindlessly so that we no longer have to think about them, we are not in a position to vary them readily as we get more information about the task. (p. 3)

Some of the most thought-provoking suggestions for viewing the situation differently and relating to parents come from de Carvalho (2001), an educator who grew up in South America but did her graduate work in education in the United States and reared her own children here. She suggests that how schools involve families is a political and cultural issue with some negative ramifications for families. She questions the use of the school culture as the starting point (a top-down approach) for learning and suggests the home culture should be more influential in this regard.

Like Graue, de Carvalho (2001) concludes that "the main contradiction of parental involvement in schooling as a policy is that, albeit wrapped as grassroots, it is really top down" (p. 110). She too might praise the parent who refuses to help with homework without questioning its need or value. She notes, "Although families basically exist for children, they have their own needs, obligations, and policies (goals and practices), including children's house chores, sleep time, and family activities (not family math!), with which school homework interferes" (p. 128).

Calabrese Barton et al. (2004) also noted the danger of schools' seeing parents through the lens of a deficit model simply if these parents do not do what schools value. This concern has also been voiced by educators in Australia in a position paper compiled after several meetings with diverse stakeholders and much research:

One of the disturbing but common research findings is that school views about families are often predicated on a deficit model, which sees parents and their children in terms of having particular needs since they lack particular desirable attributes. Teachers and other professionals are charged with providing skills and knowledge to compensate for these deficiencies. This view can then lead to paternalistic practices whereby the views of parents and their children are neither sought nor valued when they are known. . . . Further, parents may be classified as either "good" or "bad," based on generalizations that are simply not supported by research such as:

- single, supporting mothers are assumed to be both poor and bad parents;
- low income parents are assumed to be both disinterested and unsupportive of schools, have low literacy skills and unable to support their children with reading or other homework;
- parents whose first language is not English cannot help with homework;
- when children are poorly behaved their parents must be deficient in some way;
- good parents come to the school when invited or are required to do so. (McKeand, 2003, as cited in McConchie, 2004, pp. 6–7)

This research is cited because in my experience in Australia and review of its department of education findings and recommendations, I found much to commend these researchers' honest look at these macro issues. Being mindful, teachers will not accept myths such as those listed above as fact but will try to get to know and understand all parents and their sociocultural contexts. Teachers will also try to learn from parents (Turnbull, Blue-Banning, Park, & Turbiville, 1999, p. 168).

To support child, family, and teacher development within a cultural context, we would need a great deal of change, especially in the way the relationship between the school and the family is defined.

■ How Might Goals Differ in Past and Current Conceptions of Parent-Teacher Relationships?

Everyone, not just students, needs to be thought of as part of a learning community. A learning community is not just about fixing parents or children who are deficient or who complain about teachers. If people are always learning, then they need not criticize each other for sometimes getting things wrong. There also needs to be room for people to discuss the how, what, and when of children's learning (Calabrese Barton et al., 2004). This is a concern regarding the No Child Left Behind mandate. As Puriefoy (2005) noted, many parents believe that schooling should be done at local community schools rather than moving children outside their communities. These parents also believe important course content should not be eliminated so that instruction can focus only on passing tests. Parents also feel they should not have to fill all family hours with homework (Kohn, 2006). De Carvalho (2001) elaborates as follows:

This movement towards family educational accountability can be interpreted in terms of a redefinition of the scope and functions of schooling within cultural politics, as a movement that extends the reach of the school and its knowledge . . . in order to encompass domestic education and community cultural life. Through the formalization of homework within the family-school partnership, educational policy is regulating family life and socio-cultural life, an interesting case of extending the *disciplinary power* (Foucault, 1977) of the school to children's homes and to parenting activities. (p. 132)

Thus, homework becomes a "basic" and a case of family education and cultural politics, and parents who do not help unquestioningly are considered, in a way, bad children. Perhaps this kind of treatment is why so many parents resist involvement in their children's schools. Thinking mindfully, we could ask, what are some things parents do in their family and community activities to support their child's learning? What can children learn from the relationships between their parents and others in their community, such as senior citizens, neighborhood groups, and others? What are some ways teachers could integrate into school learning activities those things children do and care about in their out-of-school lives?

NEW PARADIGMS AND NEW SOLUTIONS: FOCUS ON ENGAGEMENT

To summarize thus far, though there is some sensitivity to family context in various guidelines, in reality parent involvement is primarily still a matter of the school and the government, as experts, reaching out to families who need support to help their children or to get assistance to help their children. Official learning about children's familial and community contexts is still limited.

■ How Are Educators From Other Countries Thinking About This Issue? What Recommendations Are They Making?

In Australia, schools are attempting to revise curricula ("Essential Learnings" and "New Basics") in some states where "greater value [is] being placed on the knowledge and skills that children bring to the classroom as a result of family and community influences" (McConchie, 2004, p. 1). Similar initiatives in the United States are cited later in this text.

Graue and Brown (2003) suggest that field experiences with parents should be an essential component of teacher training. Calabrese Barton et al. (2004) suggest that schools use the word *engagement* rather than *involvement,* as this book will do from now on, emphasizing the parents, not just in what they do but in who they are and what relationships they form with people in schools and communities. Calabrese Barton et al. see engagement as "a desire, an expression, and an attempt by parents to have an impact on what actually transpires around their children in schools and the kinds of human, social and material resources that are valued within schools" (p. 11). Their research allows others to view parents as authors and agents in schools and not as passive recipients of unexamined directions.

Just as some parent education programs focus on understanding children so that parents can "manage" them, understanding families often seems more a means than an end in itself. The many schools and community organizations that are sensitive to family needs today are clearly an improvement over schools that focus on children and disregard their family context. Williams (1998), for example, describes a context-sensitive approach. This School Reform Project focused not just on needs but also on family culture as a dynamic resource.

Principals took the lead. Other exciting programs to be described in later chapters include Libros y familias; the Tellin' Stories Project (teachingforchange.org); the Parents Write Their World Project, affiliated with the Big City Program of the University of Illinois at Chicago College of Education; the Study Circles (study-circles.org); and appreciative inquiry projects in schools. Other exciting programs are highlighted in the MetLife's Teacher-Parent Engagement through Partnerships resource (MetLife Foundation, 2002). Head Start and the School of the 21st Century (Finn-Stevenson & Zigler, 1999) also focus on this strengths-based approach to understanding parents.

Photo by Stacy Mitchell.

Grandfather is interviewed by his grandson as part of a school effort to make family history topics an integral part of the curriculum.

■ What Are Some Challenges of Implementing This New, Engagement-Focused Approach to Parent-Teacher Relationships?

Many parent involvement models are in transition today. Just as people question the likelihood of success of a so-called new FBI or CIA without real changes to the system, they also question new ideas about parent involvement that don't critically analyze current school structure, philosophies, and policies that might affect their own situation. Lopez (2003) describes many community actions to enhance the power of parents for system reform and school accountability: Community education organizing "focuses on 'relational power' which is the power to act collectively in order to make system change" (Cortes, 1993, as cited in Lopez). Lopez goes on to say,

Organizing counters this individualized trend by bringing people into relationships with one another so that they can identify and act on school issues. Through one-on-one conversations, group dialogue, and reflection, parents and other residents develop a strong sense of community, and learn how to use their collective power to advocate for school change. In contrast, parent involvement approaches that focus on individual skill building rarely provide opportunities for dialogue about common problems. (p. 3)

The discussion that many hope we can eventually have would address the following questions:

- How are current school policies and approaches to parent involvement viewed by prospective teachers, current teachers, students, and families?
- How do many current school practices and guidelines impact children and the adults in children's lives, who are also growing and learning human beings with their own experiences, beliefs, needs, goals, ideas, and feelings?

Answering these questions encourages the development of the adults in children's lives and benefits children academically and personally as well.

So while government agencies mention the need for schools to better understand families, they do not usually mean truly changing the school system or having family life inform school life to a great degree. Not-for-profit agencies like Family Focus and some of the school reform programs (Comer et al., 1999; Williams, 1998) have supported new ways of working with parents, but much of this work still originates in or refers to agencies or special grants or focuses primarily on child outcome—a failing not only of schools but also of many of the helping professions.

Leaders in higher education today complain that future teachers are not required to take a course in understanding family dynamics and culture. See, for example, Shartrand, Weiss, Kreider, and Lopez (1997). If family engagement is needed for success, then teachers need to be prepared to do it well. However, few states incorporate family engagement into teacher training and certification. Shartrand et al.'s study of 60 teacher certification programs in 22 states showed that when these programs existed at all, they tended to be in preschool teacher training. Some of the reasons they were not included elsewhere were resistance in attitudes of teachers and administrators and a lack of external pressure, funding, or other support. In addition to this book, the Family Involvement Network of Educators is an excellent resource to help teachers better understand families, as is the new text *Preparing Educators to Involve Families,* edited by Weiss, Kreider, Lopez, and Chatman (2005).

SUMMARY

I have described parent involvement guidelines for the purpose of background, not criticism. They are consistent with the way schools are currently construed and structured. Their authors presumably have the good of children in mind and can point to philosophical and empirical work to justify their conclusions. But these conclusions must continue to be reevaluated as educators think mindfully about the issues of today's society, the best practices in school settings, adult development and learning, and what children need in order to survive and thrive.

In spring 2002, *60 Minutes* did a telecast about the high quality of parent involvement in military base schools. Much of that involvement had to do with a system in which equal opportunity and democracy were key goals for the military culture and for their schools. Teachers were encouraged to involve parents in planning and were required to involve them in decision making. This situation turned out to be win-win. An educator in an institution of higher learning noted on the show that this degree of parent involvement is still rare and that in general, teachers are not prepared adequately to work effectively with parents as equal partners, which implies that parents play some role in decision making. Cuttance and Stokes (2000) describe effective parent involvement as comprising (a) different but equally valued roles for parents and educators and (b) mutuality, including listening to each other and maintaining a responsive dialogue.

What does *partnership* really mean? Vincent (1996) says, "Like 'participation,' 'partnership' is a diffuse concept. It implies a broad spectrum of ideas embracing equality, consensus, harmony and joint endeavor" (p. 3). Achieving partnership between parents and educators in our schools would take time and a huge paradigm shift within school cultures. This book will demonstrate how this shift can be accomplished through a comprehensive, caring school decision-making model and other parent initiatives being implemented nationally and internationally.

Some Activities and Questions for Investigation, Reflection, and Action

In this guided action process, I ask you to think, reflect, and plan on the basis of ideas and findings from this chapter:

Think

1. How do people mentioned in this chapter suggest educators rethink parent involvement?

(Continued)

(Continued)

2. Think about one issue in this chapter that might be new to you, such as the relationship between power and the expectations of parents with regard to homework or the concept of answerability. Read more about the topic from the authors cited or other sources or perspectives and evaluate their analysis of the topic. How might your own experiences inform your analysis?

Reflect

3. Reflect on your own experience of parent involvement as a student in school or as a teacher now. What would you like to see remain the same? What might you like to see change? Discuss how your own experience might shape your views of parents today.

Plan

4. Plan on journaling as you use this text. See Appendix E1: Journaling Guides (www.sagepub.com/mcdermottappendices) for more information on journaling. Write about the following: As a professional, what are your hopes and fears regarding your relationships with parents? How might they relate to what you read in this chapter?

5. Role-play a discussion between someone who supports a more traditional view of parents and someone who uses mindfulness to look at parents in a new way. What kind of questions might the second person ask? Reflect on the results of this process. What questions might you now have for others when some of these conversations happen in real life?

Chapter 2

UNDERSTANDING THEORIES
AND RESEARCH ON PARENTING

More and more child-rearing researchers are beginning to recognize, appreciate and explicate the dynamic, changeable nature of parental behavior.

—Holden and Hawk, 2003, p. 189

Some of the questions this chapter addresses:

- How has the understanding of parenting changed over the years?
- What place does the concept of relationships have in developing theories?
- What place does sociocultural context have in developing theories?
- How do current ecological and developmentally based theories affect the way professionals understand, view, and engage parents?

In her home-school involvement model, Epstein (1995; Epstein & Sanders, 2002) includes parenting education, home visitations, and communication as important for schools to provide parents. This chapter looks more deeply at parents in preparation for that work. In this way, we will take a different road from most parent-involvement books, which seldom regard parents as more than a conduit for a child's development. If parenting education should be provided by schools, a number of questions require attention: What should the subject matter of that parenting education be? What are the theories on which an education model should be based? Do all the theories over the past century regarding parents prepare us to assess what school programs typically offer parents today? Do all parents need education? Shouldn't they know what to do? Is there consensus on the best methods of providing parenting education and support and which professionals should provide it? How much should future teachers know about parents? What theories adequately explain the roles and needs of all the other people who provide caregiving to children, such as grandparents, foster parents, aunts, uncles, older siblings, baby-sitters, professional caregivers, and so on? Why is it also very important for professionals to understand the context in which parents and caregivers of children attempt to fulfill their roles?

Much preservice training focuses on an understanding of the professional role. This chapter sheds light on parents and the parent role as studied from the early 20th century to the present. These theories also inform an understanding of ideal adult-child roles. This historical overview of parenting, and the parenting education and support methodology flowing from these theories, discussed in Chapter 4, will help you appreciate the progression to today's emphasis on nurturing adult-child and adult-adult relationships, which are key for parents, teachers, and all adults who care for and about children. My summary is necessarily brief and differs from other summaries in both content and emphasis; see Bornstein (2002), Kuczynski (2003), Luster and Okagaki (2005), and Van der Pas (2003) for in-depth looks at theories and research on parenting and child development. I have highlighted the theories I believe to be especially pertinent for educators. These theories are cited throughout the text, but I ask you to take a historical look at all of them first to understand how they have evolved.

■ How Has the Understanding of Parenting Changed Over the Years?

Parenting is no longer viewed as a bag of skills but as being about a person growing and learning along with a child and others. It is about bidirectional relationships, differently supportive social contexts in which parenting takes place, and the need for society to support parents and caregivers of children in their difficult tasks. In Chapter 3, one integrating theory of parenting is put forth to aid your understanding and to give you a guide for this book and for your practice. But before that happens, it is important for you to see (a) why that theory makes sense and (b) how schools and other institutions often have not changed their views even though theorists and researchers have advanced our understanding of what parents need to fulfill their role. This review of theories of parent-child relationships will be thematic rather than chronological because certain early theorists have conceptualized parenting in ways that theorists are able to build on today.

EARLY-20TH-CENTURY THEORISTS

In their early training in many fields, students learn of the classical theories of parent-child relations. They learn that the *behaviorist Watson* (1928) believed that children could be acted on by their environment, including their parents, who, with help, could turn those children into whatever the parents wanted them to be. Children were seen as blank slates, and experts would instruct parents as to how to rear them. Little room was left for the children's impact on their own development or on the parents' thinking and experience. For Watson, what was in the child's or adult's mind was scientifically unknowable and therefore unimportant.

Freud (1936) saw parents (usually mothers) as mainly responsible for gratifying their children's psychosexual needs and being responsible for how their development evolved. Freud's was a unidirectional model of parenting and influenced many early parenting programs. *Psychoanalysts* of the time focused on parents who had not had their own emotional needs met as children and on how this lack would negatively affect their own children.

Deutsch (1945) believed that healthy women did not need any help to learn how to parent, because they should know it instinctively. *Benedek* (1970) believed that in addition to parental instincts, how one was parented, what one learned from that parenting, and how one parented did matter. While parenting, parents should reflect on their own relationships with their parents, consider how their own parent-child relationship was working in the present, and use that information to develop their evolving parental identity. Parents' self-confidence in parenting depended on their successes in meeting their child's needs. The bidirectional interplay between parent and child was at last being considered.

Adler (Dreikurs, 1989) broke away from Freud and focused not on the inner conflicts and drives of a person but on the interpersonal dimension. The founder of *individual psychology,* Adler believed that each child was born unique and with an innate social interest in others. He felt children were born with a need to belong to the human community, to move forward, to succeed in accomplishing their life goals, and to feel secure in the world. He focused less on individuals' past than Freud did and more on their purposive behavior. He did not believe children were blank slates and focused very much on the attitudes or views people might have toward each environmental input they received. He felt children needed to be treated with respect and encouragement within a democratic environment. His writings were geared to the lay public, and his theories inform many current parent education programs.

At this same time, the *behavioral genetics theory* of *Gesell* (1946; Thelan & Adolph, 1992) suggested that the course of development was within the child and that the parents' role was simply to support the unfolding of their child's inherited predispositions and provide an environment that was appropriate for the child's maturation level. Parents needed to provide food, clothing, and shelter, of course, but Gesell did not focus on parents' thinking about their role and insights regarding how to help a particular child. Children would develop if parents just let them do so without interfering. Gesell provided detailed observations of the course of development in children. However, the thinking that predominated in his time was either-or thinking: Was the crucial factor environment, as Watson suggested, or heredity, as the behavioral geneticists thought?

Genetics-versus-environment arguments continue. A beneficial by-product of this debate is that researchers focusing on the importance of environment in child development are more careful to take genetic influences into consideration, and socialization researchers (Maccoby, 2000) continue to make a strong case to geneticists that environment affects child development even before birth (Williams, 1998), in utero. The danger of focusing on just heredity is that parents might think it is not worth the effort to try to influence their children positively. Ignoring genetics in the case of gender has also caused much pain and misinformation in families. Thinking mindfully, one would deal with the ambiguities involved in sex and gender.

Sutherland (1983) found that many parents she studied were in transitional states regarding the way they viewed children's needs and the parental role. Many of the Mexican American mothers she studied were transitioning from the Gesell model, focusing on the natural unfolding of development, to an American culture, where parents generally are more active than traditional Mexican mothers are in thinking about and shaping a child's development. Lareau (2003) reports that many working-class families in the United States also tend to believe in the "accomplishment of natural growth," in which a child's development unfolds as long as basic comfort, food, and shelter are provided by caregivers (p. 3). This belief affects the way a parent's perceived role meshes with school expectations. In contrast, Lareau describes middle-class parents as focusing more on "concerted cultivation," in which their role is to do all they can to advance their children. This approach, she suggests, meshes much better with the way U.S. schools are structured than does the natural growth perspective (pp. 2–3).

THE INTERACTIONSISTS

Chess, Thomas, and colleagues (Thomas, Chess, Birch, & Hertzig, 1961) are characterized as *interactionist theorists.* They did not focus on just nature or nurture but on the interaction between one particular parent and one particular child in one particular environment. They believed that "behavioral phenomena are considered to be the expression of a continuous organism-environment interaction from their very first manifestations in the life of the individual. This overall approach may be designated as interactionist" (p. 723). Optimal development occurs, they noted recently in a review of their important body of work on temperament and good-ness of fit, "when there is a consonance between environmental opportunities and expectations and the organism's capacities" (Chess & Thomas, 1999, p. 14). This theory will be discussed in more detail in Chapter 3. Certainly discussions about a child's potential not being maximized due to a poor fit with a teacher or parent or within environments of large school classrooms, crowded homes, unsafe neighbor-hoods, and so forth conform to this approach of looking at parents and children or teachers and children within their environmental context.

Similarly, *Erikson's theory of psychosocial development* (1963, 1968) placed more emphasis on a child's biological characteristics and the environmental fac-tors affecting children's growth and development than on unidirectional parental influences. Parents were to provide the environmental context for children and introduce them to society. Erikson's concept of the ego as an organ of mastery whose capacities may increase during parenting recognizes also that parents, like children, have the potential to grow as they adapt to changing infants and chang-ing societal contexts. He spoke of the "cog-wheeling" of development, which can apply to parent-teacher or parent-child relationships. Parents and teachers, as well as other professionals working with children, are not solely givers meeting the needs of everyone else; rather, each person gives and receives from the others, and each changes and develops as a result of the interchanges between them (Erikson, 1963, p. 231). He took parents' thinking and feeling into consideration, as well as their culture and context. His theory will be explored further in Chapter 3 as it is one that many believe has a broad enough framework to incorporate all our new information about parents and children. His *stage of generativity* highlights human beings' need not only to be cared for but to care for others as well, something Adler (Dreikurs, 1989) also believed was innate in humans.

Theorists and researchers have also believed that if practitioners were to under-stand the impact of parents on children, they needed to understand not only a parent's developmental history and personality but also how parents thought about their role and about children. *Piaget's* research (Flavell, 1963) on children's different stages of *cognitive development,* with which teachers are very familiar, began informing theories of parenting and parental social-cognitive thinking and awareness in particular. Piaget believed that parents needed to understand how children think in order to facilitate children's cognitive development over time. He also talked about the interactions of the child and the environment by using the constructs of assimilation (taking in from the outside) and accommodation (look-ing at that input within one's own thinking). While Piaget focused on just cogni-tion, his theory and research have done much to inform theories about the parent role, and parents were no longer seen as just a mass of personality limitations or as somewhat irrelevant. *Sameroff* and *Feil* (1985) and *Newberger* (1980; Newberger & Cook, 1983) studied and theorized about stages of parental thinking and concepts of development, paralleling Piaget's cognitive stages for children. Both lines of research are discussed in detail in Chapter 3.

We have also learned from *Vygotsky*'s work (1978) that *social interactions* between active, thinking children and their active, thinking caregivers were essential for a child's development. The *zone of proximal development* has to do with adults' taking an active role in facilitating children's maturation by being with them as they are challenged by more-advanced tasks. It has been defined as the distance between what the child can accomplish alone (the level of actual development) and what the child can do when helped (the level of potential development). The image is the scaffold (Rogoff, 1990; Wood, Bruner, & Ross, 1976): A parent erects a structure (parent support and guidance) around a child's behavior. As children gain more skills, the parents dismantle the scaffold. Thus, the role of parents was coming to be seen as intentional rather than instinctual or learned. In this view, parents need to be sensitive to times when their children are open to more learning.

TRAIT THEORISTS

Some theorists and researchers have focused on various *traits* (fundamental units of personality) or parental styles more than on parent-child interactions and thinking. Critics of these personality or trait theories feel it is more important to look at the interaction of a parent adjusting to different children of different ages, genders, and temperaments over time than to look at just the parent's traits. Personality theorists have answered that the ability to adjust to change might itself be a trait (Johnson, 1997). Belsky and Barends (2002) have asked that one not throw out a consideration of a parent's personality in favor of a focus on the impact of the child or a focus on parent-child thinking and interactions. They have noted that some parents respond differently to the same child or to a similar situation, which implies that the parents' own personalities are in fact involved. They also note that a parent's having a personality trait such as neuroticism, sometimes called negative affectivity (implying possible psychological distress, such as depression, anxiety, hostility, or unrealistic ideas), does not mean the parent will always treat a child in ways consistent with that trait. A lot depends on other contextual factors. So a number of theorists (Belsky & Barends, 2002; Vondra, Sysko, & Belsky, 2005) encourage others to continue to focus on parental personality as one way of understanding parents and parent-child relationships. Personality and all the psychological resources of adults caring for children are worthy of study and understanding, as are the ways these personality theories relate to parents and teachers.

Parents and teachers with certain personality factors may find that these factors make their role difficult to fulfill. For example, an extroverted parent or teacher often draws energy from interacting with children, whereas introverted parents and teachers may often feel drained or overwhelmed by the same interaction and need to recharge their batteries in a quiet setting. What if they don't have an opportunity to recharge? If they do not think about the fit of their personality with their role and their context, they may doubt their abilities and give up. Chess and Thomas's research (1999) on goodness of fit provides very important information regarding such situations.

Personality, according to recent reviews by Belsky and Barends (2002) and Vondra, Sysko, and Belsky (2005), often involves the Big Five personality factors of neuroticism, extroversion, agreeableness, openness to experience, and conscientiousness. In other terms, personality involves one's self-esteem; locus of control; and the psychological maturity to take another's perspective, control one's impulses, feel secure in one's own life, and be able to get one's needs met (Belsky, 1984). Heinicke (2002) adds to the complexity of this construct by including within a parent's personality the factors of adaptation competence (a parent's efficient, calm, persistent, and flexible approach to problem solving), capacity for sustained relationships (e.g., empathy and positive mutuality in an ongoing relationship; see also Jordon, Kaplan, Miller, Stiver, & Surrey, 1991), and self-development (an ability to establish autonomy in relation to others and to feel self-confident).

Understanding the importance of all these factors to parents makes it hard to imagine teens' taking on the parental role without support. With the right kind of relationships and support, caregivers can become more psychologically mature and effective over time. Of course, many serious medical and mental illnesses add complications and challenges (see Zahn-Waxler, Duggal, & Gruber, 2002). As one might guess, research on parental personality, as summarized by Vondra et al. (2005, pp. 38–43), has shown that parents who possess the following qualities care for children in ways that are more supportive, sensitive, responsive, and intellectually stimulating than do parents who lack these tendencies: low in psychopathology, low in neuroticism (calm, relaxed, hardy, secure, and self-satisfied), high in extroversion (with positive affect toward their children and sensitive and cognitively stimulating), high in agreeableness (soft-hearted, good-natured, trusting, helpful, forgiving, and straightforward), open to experience (tending to enjoy new experiences, having broad interests, and very imaginative), conscientious (organized and having high standards; always striving to achieve goals), high in self-esteem and internal locus of control, and psychologically healthy and mature.

Seligman (2002), like Maslow (1970), has asked psychologists to focus more on positive personality traits than on negative ones. In Seligman's *positive psychology,* the focus is on "the capacity for love and vocation, courage, interpersonal skill, aesthetic sensibility, perseverance, forgiveness, originality, future minded-ness, high talent and wisdom" (2002, p. 3). He also encourages schools, families, and other institutions to focus on nurturing a person's strengths rather than being preoccupied with fixing people. He has found in his research that when parents and children were trained to enhance their learned optimism, future mindedness, interpersonal competence, and persistence, those qualities acted as a buffer to men-tal illness, decreasing depression and anxiety significantly, regardless of socio-economic status. This research will be discussed further in Chapter 7, when we address ways parents and teachers can help children think about themselves and situations more positively.

Parents and professionals come in all levels of psychological health and matu-rity. Thus, expecting the same thing from all of them is not realistic. Parents are on a continuum of maturity and ego development when they have children. They may also have different physical and mental illnesses. The foregoing discussion of traits should not be interpreted as a focus on deficits but as a growth approach that guides us to look at someone's status not as weakness but as an indication of where that person needs to grow and mature. We contribute to that growth when we ask, what are this parent's positive traits and how can they be strengthened? I hope that schools collaborate well with family support agencies to support parents and teachers as they learn and mature personally.

Belsky and Barends (2002) describe maturity in terms of *ego strength* (capacity to cope with life's challenges; Grossman, Pollack, & Golding, 1988), *psychological integration* (extent to which people are warm and secure in themselves and enjoy inti-mate relationships with the important people in their lives; Brunnquell, Chrichton, &

Photo by Debrah Clark.

Teacher and parent talk at the end of the school day in the school child-care center.

Egeland, 1981), and *ego resiliency* (the resourceful adaptation of a person to changing circumstances; Block & Block, 1980). Most researchers have concluded that having these abilities is positively associated with effective parent-child and adult-child relationships and growth. Just as there is wide diversity among teachers in terms of the psychological resources listed above, there will be wide diversity among the parents with whom we work, but most parents and teachers can grow in all these areas. A newsletter prepared for parents (see Appendix C1: Resiliency Newsletter) and a handout for teachers on the topic of resiliency (Appendix C2: Resiliency Notes for Professionals), available on the Sage Web site for this book, www.sagepub.com/ mcdermottappendices, elaborate on this important quality.

In addition, the Comer School Model (Comer, 1989, 2001), which focuses on the development of the whole child, emphasizes helping young children develop positively so that they can mature and form and sustain strong relationships throughout their lives.

For the educator, the most popular trait-based approach to parents was derived from *Schaefer* (1959), who discussed the familiar parenting traits of warmth and control, and *Baumrind* (1989, 1996), who has generated a body of theory and research on authoritarian, permissive, and authoritative parenting styles (of which the authoritative style is considered the most desirable and effective and encompasses warmth and firm control). However, some researchers have found that more positive effects are associated with parental warmth (Lewis, 1981) than with parental control.

Today, theorists make a distinction between "parental structure/predictability" and the construct of control (see Kohn, 2005, p. 234). Baumrind's research found that children of either authoritarian or permissive parents tended to be goalless and less confident and competent than are children of authoritative parents. Here, Kohn and others would have wanted to distinguish between permissive parents who were confused, did not care about their children, or neglected them and those who carefully deliberated and then chose more democratic, child-centered interactions (p. 234). Today the positive effect of authoritative parenting is often more strongly associated with being warm and very aware of and involved in one's children's lives than with being controlling (p. 235). Children of authoritative parents are often more goal- and future-minded and more self-confident than other children are.

While understanding personality theories and parental styles may help us better understand parents and teachers, parental styles often need to vary with different children and at different times. If the trait approach is the only thing we teach parents and teachers in school workshops, it can lead to the erroneous conclusion that parents and caregivers are effective only if they behave similarly at all times regarding all children and all situations (Holden & Miller, 1999). In spite of some questioning of these constructs as described originally and some changes in how they are thought about (Baumrind, 1996; Kohn, 2005), parental style remains a popular topic in parent or teacher workshops.

BIDIRECTIONAL AND TRANSACTIONAL THEORIES

■ What Place Does the Concept of Relationships Have in Developing Theories?

R. Q. Bell's *child effects approach* (1968) found that parents and children actually regulate each other's behavior. This finding contrasts with Freud's parent effects approach, which proposed a unidirectional effect, from adult to child. Child effects theories, focusing on children's behavior affecting parents, differed from popular trait theories focusing more on parent personality styles. Bell's child effects perspective and the parent effects perspective might be more helpful if considered as parts of a larger transactional model rather than as competing theories. As Holden and Miller (1999) note in describing Bell's important work on the effect of children on parents, parenting should be thought of as a *relational* rather than an *individual difference construct,* and therefore, child-rearing strategies will vary from one child (and one time) to another within a family.

Related to this bidirectional parent-child interaction approach is *attachment theory* (Ainsworth & Bowlby, 1991; Cassidy & Shaver, 1999). Research demonstrates that the attachment relationship between parent and child reflects a system promoting survival and competent functioning in children. Attachment theorists focus on the parent and suggest that caregivers need to establish a secure base for infants during the first year of life by being sensitive to the cues emitted by infants, addressing their needs, and supporting their emotional regulation. Where do parents learn how to do this? Understanding attachment and the process involved is important for educators.

The attachment process has been described as *contingent communication:* "The signals of a child are perceived, made sense of, and responded to in a timely and effective manner. . . . When parents generally provide a sense of predictable contingency, the child feels understood, joined, and a sense of communion between parent and child is established" (Siegel, 2005, p. 7). Infants learn to trust that caregivers will take care of their needs. That trust develops into *secure attachment,* facilitating the exploration of the environment and supporting the development of social and cognitive competence and the important feeling of efficacy. The hope is that their securely attached children—the next generation—will be able as parents to adapt to changing environments and changing children. With this secure sense of well-being, children will be able to cope well with stress and to mature.

Some children one encounters in schools have experienced noncontingent communication, in which these important trusting relationships between parents and

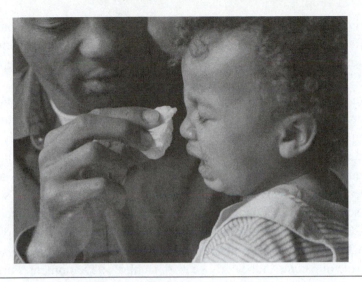

A father provides love, security, and comfort for his daughter.

children have not occurred as described above. Siegel and Hartzell (2003) link these problems of attachment with the work of early theorists who looked at parents' own childhood experiences for clues to parents' difficulties in rearing a securely attached child. Siegel (2005) concluded that "it is not what happened to you that matters most in determining how you raise your children; instead it is how you have come to make sense of your early life experiences that is the most robust predictor of how your children will become attached to you" (p. 2). Thus, for many parents, making sense of their own early experiences may have to take precedence over helping their child with homework.

Siegel (2005, pp. 10–11) theorizes that if parents have not reflected on how their own childhood experience affects their parenting, they may be dismissive toward their own child, and an *avoidant attachment* may result. Parents whose unresolved issues and strong emotions from their own childhoods intrude into their own parenting may be so preoccupied with those issues and emotions that they may have *ambivalently attached* children. Finally, Siegel suggests that parents with unresolved experiences of trauma or loss often rear children with *disorganized attachment*.

The good news is that many believe these problematic attachments can be resolved. "By offering the opportunity to deepen self-understanding, to make sense of one's life, our hope is that parents could make the choice to enhance the security of attachment of their children while at the same time creating coherence and vitality in their own lives" (Siegel, 2005, p. 11). The importance of self-understanding will be addressed shortly. It is often not included in preservice teacher training. Yet if teachers do not study and understand these issues, how can they succeed in engaging diverse parents in schools? Thinking mindfully, we can ask, could parents be more effective in their role if they were given the opportunity to better understand the impact of their past experience on their current role perceptions and behavior?

Although attachment is an important piece of information, Chess and Thomas (1999) assert that attachment is not the only factor to consider in supporting parents and children. These researchers suggest that in addition to exploring early life experiences and attachment issues, people can understand current relationship challenges by understanding the *goodness of fit* between parents, children, and others in their lives in terms of temperament, personality, relationships, and social contexts. Few school programs focus on these areas with teachers, let alone parents.

Siegel (2005, p. 3) contends that research on the brain and the whole field of interpersonal neurobiology emphasizes the need for understanding and supporting the crucial role of parents in the early years of a child's development. Furthermore, this research is partly responsible for the movement to teach parenting to students before they become parents. Exciting programs for preK to Grade 12 around the world teach parenting to the next generation of parents. The students have an opportunity to observe parents and infants and learn what is needed to form strong relationships between parents and children. These programs often include opportunities for students to reflect on their own experience of being parented (Heath & McDermott, 2006; McDermott, 2003–2004, 2006; Schiffer, 2002; Tomison, 1998; see also Chapter 9 of this text). This is a much better strategy than dealing with the many students who have not formed strong attachments with their caregivers. These programs focus on goodness of fit between parents and infants as well.

HUMANISTIC THEORISTS

Sensitive feedback and communication between parents and their infants and children were also encouraged in the *humanistic and reflective theory* of *Carl Rogers* (1973). He suggested parents use "therapeutic skills" of empathy to understand a child's needs and feelings. *Maslow*'s detailed list of human needs (1969, 1970) is also very helpful for parents. Unfortunately, Maslow's thinking about people's strong need to care for something or someone beyond the self (*self-transcendence*) did not receive much attention until after he died. It is being discussed now (Koltko-Rivera, 2003) and will be elaborated on in Part II.

In a humanistic approach, parents are taught to reflect their children's feelings back to the children to help them grow in self-awareness and understanding, thus facilitating their children's psychological maturity. Many parenting programs that used this approach focused not on just individual parent deficits or on a child's dispositions but on the various attitudes, information, and skills, such as empathy, that parents need in order to have good relationships with children (and that therapists need in order to be effective with clients). Ironically, even though these programs were supposed to be therapeutic for parents, they used the transmission model of education in that the "experts" had the skills and taught them to parents (as noted in Thomas & Footrakoon, 1998).

The popular parenting program of Thomas Gordon (Parent Effectiveness Training; 1975, 1991) expanded on this theoretical perspective. Healthy development for children was closely related to their ability to identify and communicate their feelings. With the proper parent support and caring environment, children would be able to solve their own problems and deal with change, which personality theorists considered key to psychological maturity. Thomas's program emphasizes accepting the child and wanting to understand the child's viewpoint. The assumption is that with this respect and nonjudgmental approach, a child will be more open to self-reflection, which is also related to effective higher-order thinking and mature parenting in the future.

Ginott (1965/2003) also believed in working with parents so that they learned the skills that would allow them to communicate with their children in nonjudgmental, caring ways and to understand their children's feelings and their own feelings as well. He cared about the emotional lives of children, as do Greenspan and Greenspan (1985). They helped parents see *discipline* as more about sharing and modeling values such as respect than about punishing or rewarding children. They too would appreciate the recent work on mindfulness. Today, work in emotional intelligence (Elias, Tobias, & Friedlander, 1999; Goleman, 1995) and emotion coaching (Gottman, 1998) reflects this approach.

The parenting model of Dreikurs (1969), reflected in Dinkmeyer, McKay, Dinkmeyer, Jr., & McKay's Systematic Training for Effective Parenting program (1987) and in Popkin's Active Parenting Now program (activeparenting.com), builds on the work of Alfred Adler (described in Dreikurs, 1989) and focuses on respecting, understanding, and encouraging children. In these programs, children, in addition to being respected as individuals, are expected to contribute to the family and be responsible members of a democratic society. Dreikurs believed in understanding children's feelings to decipher their goals and guide them from misbehavior to social integration within the family and society. The focus of these programs is on the active parent (as described earlier by Erikson), who focuses on the child's strengths, on effective parent-child communication, and on encouraging responsibility. Dinkmeyer et al. are also clear that their focus on discipline (e.g., logical consequences) is very different from a behavioral approach of using rewards and punishments to motivate children.

Behavioral parent education programs and some classroom management programs minimize the importance of emotions, thoughts, and motivations of the child
and adult and focus instead on observable behavior that can be changed by rewards
and punishment and positive and negative reinforcement (see, e.g., Patterson,
1986). Of course, changed behavior in children does not always persist when adults
are not present. For some children at some ages and in some situations, behavior
modification may "work" in the short term. The question is, How does it affect the
parent-child relationship and the development of each person in the long term?

In addition to facilitating a child's self-awareness, *Kohut's self-psychology
theory* (1977) helps us understand how to facilitate adult self-understanding as
well. Recognition of parent developmental needs is often seen as a prerequisite to
interventions with abusive parents (Shanook, 1990). Brems, Baldwin, and Baxter
(1993) compared the effectiveness of a traditional Parent Effectiveness Training
and behavioral parent education program and some classroom management programs, on the one hand, with a program focusing on the self-psychology model
with built-in mechanisms for self-understanding, on the other. While all had about
the same effect, there was lower attrition and more parental enthusiasm for the
self-psychology model. Siegel (2005) also focuses on how parents' deeper self-
understanding leads to a deeper understanding of their own children, which in turn
can facilitate growth and development for both the children and the parents.
Unfortunately, schools offer few programs of this sort.

Newberger's construct of parental awareness and thinking (1980; Newberger &
Cook, 1983) influenced current parenting approaches such as the Reflective Dialogue
Parent Education Design, implemented by Thomas (1996; Thomas & Footrakoon, 1998;
Thomas, Cooke, & Scott, 2005). These programs show that with professionals' facilitating parental self-development, parents reach a higher level of ego development
and "have a wider repertoire for dealing with, and more complex ways of understanding their children, their parenting role, and their parent-child relationships than
parents who have not reached these levels (Upshur, 1988; Weiss, 1988)" (Thomas &
Footrakoon, 1998, p. 8). Thomas has parents view videos of parent-child behavior and
think about what they might do and why. An essential element of mindfulness is
allowing someone to become an observer of others and of their own behavior in order
to gain new insights about the self and the relationship.

Since the 1970s and McBride's (1973) classic book *The Growth and Development of Mothers*, theorists and researchers have forcefully demonstrated the value of
supporting parents' growth needs in order to enhance their and their children's development (Galinsky, 1987; Jordon, Kaplan, Miller, Stiver, & Surrey, 1991). As many
researchers (Belenky, Bond, & Weinstock, 1997; Belenky, Clinchy, Goldberger, &
Tarule, 1986/1997; Belenky & Stanton, 2000; McBride, 1973; and others) have
found, mothers who acknowledged their own needs and were listened to and validated

by others were more effective with their children than were mothers who lacked this support. Interventions could indeed help mothers develop higher levels of thinking and often resulted in higher self-efficacy and better child outcome.

SOCIAL-COGNITIVE THEORIES

Bandura's social-cognitive theory (1989, 1997) emphasized the cognitive and information-processing capacities of an individual, such as a parent, that mediate social behavior. In particular, Bandura proposes that individuals' feelings of *self-efficacy,* or their beliefs about their ability to effect changes in the environment, constitute one of the keys to understanding human behavior (Grusec, 1992; Grusec & Ungerer, 2003). Many behaviorists have embraced his theory. The underlying assumption of this and other viable parenting programs is that processes direct the way parents think about child rearing and their role in affecting children, and parents' thinking combines with parent characteristics, child characteristics, and other environmental influences to affect a child's and a parent's ultimate growth. Few programs focus on parent or teacher self-efficacy although it is a very important factor in work with children, as has been demonstrated in recent studies (Eccles & Harold, 1996; Hoover-Dempsey & Sandler, 1997; Shumow & Lomax, 2002). Many theorists and practitioners have pointed out that a related focus on a person's need to feel competent (White, 1959) is very important.

The parent beliefs approach (Sigel & McGillicuddy-DeLisi, 2002; Sigel, McGillicuddy-DeLisi, & Goodnow, 1992) is also very important in our advancing understanding of parents' experiences and perspectives. Child rearing, in this approach, has multiple influences: parental values and beliefs, parents' previous experiences, information sources, and other people. This approach holds the promise of changing child-rearing behavior, if necessary, through *cognitive restructuring,* which means providing new information about children or child-rearing techniques and helping parents revise perceptions, correct erroneous attributions or expectations, train in problem-solving techniques, or any combination of these forms of assistance.

While it may sound like the "experts know best" approach, the parent beliefs approach is different because it takes parents' own beliefs as the starting point. The process of reflection on these beliefs may or may not result in change. The researchers who developed the parent beliefs approach focused on beliefs and values as an important ingredient in understanding the parent, the parenting role, and the parenting process. Consider the following example: If a parent in a particular culture believes that a teacher who asks for parental help must be incompetent, this belief will obviously impact that parent's relationship with the school. If newly immigrated parents participate with trusted parent peers in the community in a discussion about parent roles in the United States, the newly immigrated parents might reconsider the ways they can relate to the school. At least they will better understand school expectations. This topic will be discussed further in Chapter 5.

FAMILY SYSTEMS THEORIES

Satir (1988) and *Minuchin* (1974) added another dimension to understanding parent-child relationships and processes: *family systems theory* (see Bigner, 2006, and Christian, 2006). Everyone in a family may have different beliefs, goals, feelings, values, capacities, and so on. In family systems theory, the relationship among all members of the family must be investigated in order for family functioning to be fully understood. Researchers have found, for example, that fathers are more demanding of sons when wives are present than when wives are absent (Buhrmester, Camparo, Christensen, Gonzalez, & Hinshaw, 1992). Holden and Zambarano (1992) found that the stress of domestic violence results in more maternal aggression on children than if that stress were absent. Wekerle and Wolfe (1993) concluded that we need to optimize development of all family members and recognize the importance of empowering the whole parental subsystem to engage other subsystems adaptively. This attention on the whole family too must be part of parent education and support (Dunst & Trivette, 2006; Dunst, Trivette, & Deal, 1988).

Christian (2006) delineates six *characteristics of the family system* that are important for early childhood professionals to consider and that are relevant for teachers in all grades. They include boundaries, roles, rules, hierarchy, climate, and family equilibrium. These characteristics will be described in more detail when we consider culture in Chapter 5.

Often schools provide programs on parenting skills without spending much time thinking about how this new information or new parental behavior might be received by the whole family system. Parents need more than a new skill. They need to learn ways of discussing, relating to, and anticipating the reactions of different persons within the same family, some of whom may not be changing as much or as fast as the involved parent is.

SOCIAL RELATIONSHIPS THEORIES

Hinde (1989) explored parents' adaptations to changing children, changing family members, and changing environments over time. While adapting to changing children takes skills, it is more than merely the bag of skills usually taught in school parenting programs; parenting is a dynamic process (Holden, 1997; Kuczynski, 2003); hence, programs need to support this process. *Holden* and *Hawk* (2003) describe programs supporting *meta-parenting* that help parents think about their parenting. This skill involves anticipating, assessing, problem solving, and reflecting and will be demonstrated in practice in Part II of this book with a model by Heath (2006), cited by Holden and Hawk as exemplary.

Hinde's *social relationships theory* (1989) holds that ongoing human interactions forming interpersonal relationships represent the most important aspect of the environment for parenting. Dynamic interactions between parents and children are embedded in long-term relationships and are affected by both preceding interactions and expectations about future ones. Each relationship has its own uniqueness and history. Parent programs need to address these complex issues. Buckshot programs may not work because parents each look at their history (or lack thereof, in the case of a new stepparent) with a child. Wekerle and Wolfe (1993) define *parenting competence* as more than a set of skills; it also involves using them appropriately during interactions within an enduring and unique relationship.

As Holden (1997) and Kuczynski (2003) explain, the way parents adapt and adjust to a changing child, changes in themselves, or changing life situations is not captured by any static approach to parenting or by most parenting programs in schools. So how does one help parents plan how to integrate new ways of asserting themselves in a family or classroom where they have previously been seen as passive and compliant? Many calibrations and adjustments will be involved.

BIOECOLOGICAL SYSTEMS THEORY

■ **What Place Does Sociocultural Context Have in Developing Theories? How Do Current Ecological and Developmentally Based Theories Affect the Way Professionals Understand, View, and Engage Parents?**

Bronfenbrenner's bioecological systems theory (1979, 2005a) viewed child development as occurring within a nested series of contextual levels, from the immediate setting of the person's experience, typically parents and children interacting in the family (called the *microsystem*), to the next levels, such as home and school interacting about the child, and to other systems, such as a parent's work experience, which affects the child indirectly, or a society's view of the parent role, which affects the child as well. This theory adds more important information to what we know about how to understand and relate to parents.

In this approach, an appropriate question at the microsystem level might be, how might a parent's telling a child family stories affect the child? At the second level, the *mesosystem,* we might ask, how might a disagreement between a teacher and parent affect a child? At the third level of influence, the *exosystem,* which affects the child indirectly, we can ask questions such as, what is the effect of work on parents and how is it related to their child rearing? Bronfenbrenner's next level is the *macrosystem,* which is even more removed but still influential and has to do with the larger culture and institutions. Here we might ask, what do the current administration's funding priorities or tax policies tell us about how it values children and families? Finally, in the *chronosystem,* which looks at changes over time, we can ask such questions as, how will society's changing views of gender affect my child's experiences or options in high school and my new expectations of schools or society related to gender?

In sum, the ongoing parent-child-school-community environment in all these systems must be the focus of attention for those who support parents and teachers. We all need to keep trying to understand the impact of behaviors and events within multiple systems. For example, we could ask, how does globalization affect family values and families all over the world (a question adult parent-students from all socioeconomic backgrounds collaborate to understand and answer in a DePaul University course titled Family Values: Parenting in Cultural Context)? And we might also ask, how does poverty affect the families in our school, and what economic and societal changes are needed before these families can realize their full potential?

We need to look beyond the family to the systems affecting it and to the ways family situations affect other systems. Few parenting programs in schools provide a format for addressing these issues even though substantial research has demonstrated that these systems do in fact affect each other.

Belsky's perspective (Belsky, 1984; Belsky & Barends, 2002) focuses on both these *ecological systems* and his *parental competence* approach. His perspective is very similar to Erikson's. Belsky defines *parental competence* as sensitivity to the child's developing abilities and communications. It is influenced by such factors as *parental resources* (e.g., previous experience, psychological resources, education, and attitudes and expectations about child rearing), discussed earlier, the *child's characteristics* (e.g., temperament, health status, developmental level, size, gender), and the *family context* (e.g., quality of the marriage, social networks, support systems, cultural background).

Individual characteristics of the parent, the child, and the social context can mediate the impact of a process in each particular context. According to Belsky, a parent needs a buffer if one or more of these areas are weak. For example, if a parent is living in poverty but is motivated to do well, has supports, and has an easy child, the parent might be more effective than if all systems were weak. An example of the latter case would be a poorly educated, depressed teen parent with a difficult infant and little societal support. The outcome for parent and child is likely more negative in this case than for a teen parent with positive affectivity; a supportive boyfriend, extended family, school, and community; and a temperamentally easy child. Teachers can benefit from having a way to understand families in this systemic way.

Van der Pas (2003) rightly notes, though, that many of these theories do not really look at the parent-child process or the day-to-day "parental work" that goes on in average families. She suggests that in most models, the parent appears simply as a conduit to a child's outcome. Educators need to ask, what about the parent?

Demick (2002) talks about these systems and individual differences and specifies the parent component more than other theorists do. He proposes a *holistic, developmental, systems-oriented* approach to parent development that encourages one to consider (a) parents' biology, including age, physical health, stress, and so on; (b) parents' psychological-intrapersonal factors, such as how they think (cognitive style, decision making, meaning making, and planning), how they feel (motivation, personality, mental health, or stress), what values they hold (regarding family, career, leisure, etc.); (c) their interpersonal behavior, such as how they relate to children, teachers, coworkers, and others; and (d) the sociocultural context of a person's human activity (like religion, politics, work, socioeconomic status, community, media, educational institution, family and sociohistorical context, and so on (p. 403). Demick's focus on parental values and goals has been very important to educators (e.g., Hoffman & Hoffman, 1973) for decades. The model presented in Chapter 3 (Heath, 2006) attempts to integrate many of the variables highlighted by the theorists presented thus far, and Part II demonstrates how professionals can use this model to guide relationships and activities with parents. Rather than just studying the relationship of several variables out of the context of a particular parent with a particular child in a particular situation, this model puts the focus on the parent.

FAMILY SUPPORT AND EMPOWERMENT

Understanding families has moved over time from primarily seeing dysfunction to seeing *capacity, assets* (Benson, 1997), and *potential.* Just as the Search Institute (www.search-institute.org) has identified the "assets" children need to succeed, theorists reviewed in this text have demonstrated the "assets" parents need to succeed. From the Cornell *empowerment model* of *Cochran* (1993; Cochran & Walker, 2005), we can draw the following principles to guide our work with parents: help them feel hopeful, believe in themselves, be responsible, focus on strengths, and expect much of themselves and others. We need to bring out the good in people rather than see only their deficits. As a coach, an educator is a generalist and knows that parents are specialists, with an important body of knowledge about themselves, their children, and their situations (Weissbourd, 1994). Educators, too, have a body of knowledge and information to share.

We must try to enhance a family's capacity to support the growth and development of all family members. This means helping families and future parents see themselves as resources to all their members, to other families, to schools, and to

Photo by Debrah Clark.

A caregiver builds relationships and models feeding techniques with teen parents and their children.

communities. Any program intended to promote children's development must affirm and strengthen families' cultural, racial, and linguistic identities and enhance their ability to function in a multicultural society. Above all else, the goal is to empower future parents to be able to mobilize formal and informal resources to support family and child development.

SUMMARY

In speaking of empowerment and self-mastery, we have come full circle, back to Erikson. His emphasis on the active, coping, competent ego gives the educator a better reason for empowering parents than do models that emphasize the dysfunctional, incapable, and reactive parent. The ingredients that Erikson (1963, 1968) thought parents (and everyone) need to grow at all stages of the lifespan, or what he called "proven methods and a fund of traditional reassurance" (1968, p. 139), are clear. They involve guidance and support. The human communities of which teachers are a part need to provide parents and all professionals caring for children with both of these resources. Likewise, teachers, who are also active, coping adults, need guides and traditional reassurances as they collaborate with families to care for children.

Table 2.1 summarizes this chapter's review of parenting theories. Throughout this text, these theories will be revisited as they (a) relate to establishing a model of working with parents and families, (b) help in assessing how parents can and desire to be engaged in their children's lives at different times, and (c) help readers explore the goodness of fit between their current expectations of parents and families and the information gained from an understanding of the information in this chapter.

Table 2.1   Parenting Theory From a Historical Perspective

Recently, thanks to the increased focus on brain development we understand better that children are very complex, and there is much to learn in order to facilitate their development at every stage over the lifespan. In the past three decades, we have also learned a great deal about parent development over the lifespan. While early theories of parent and child development are inadequate to explain the complex social-contextual world of parents and children we serve today, we include them here to show the development of theories over time and to help educators better understand the theoretical foundations of the parent education programs and materials they use.

Theory Title	Person	Basic Tenets
Behaviorist	Watson	Children are what the environment (including parents) makes them.
Psychoanalytic	Freud	Parents are mainly responsible for a child's psychological development.
	Deutsch	Healthy women know instinctively how to parent, and this is natural.
	Benedek	Besides instincts, parenting behavior is also determined by how one was parented.
Individual psychology	Adler	Children are born individually unique; a social interest or a need to belong to the human community is innate; focus on a child's purposive goals and recognize the importance of society for the development of children.
Behavioral genetics	Gesell	The parent's role is to support the unfolding of a child's inner predispositions and provide an environment matched to a child's maturational readiness.
Transactional or interactionist	Lewin; Chess and Thomas	Behavior is a function of a person and the environment. Behavioral phenomena are the expression of a continuous organism-environment interaction from their very first manifestations in the life of the individual.
Psychosocial and lifespan development	Erikson	The inner biological and additional societal influences on child and adult psychosocial development over the lifespan are important.
Cognitive-developmental	Piaget	Parents need to understand how children think and reason at different ages in order to maximize the cognitive development of the child.
Social interaction	Vygotsky	Social interaction between an active, thinking child and a thinking caregiver is key to development.

(Continued)

Table 2.1 (Continued)

Theory Title	Person	Basic Tenets
Child effects approach	Bell	Children and parents regulate each other's behavior. Look at relationships.
Humanistic and reflective approach	Rogers; Maslow; Ginott	Parents use empathy to understand children's needs and feelings; parents then reflect back what the children are feeling in order to help the children grow in awareness and self-understanding.
Attachment theory	Ainsworth and Bowlby	If children trust that their caregivers will meet their needs, an attachment results that is necessary to facilitate social and cognitive competence and self-efficacy.
Traits approach	Schaefer; Baumrind	The focus is on a parent's personality styles or traits more than on the parent's adjustment to different children, individual differences, gender, ages, etc.
Social cognitive	Bandura	Individual beliefs about one's ability to effect change in the environment are the key ingredient. How parents think about child rearing is combined with the child characteristics and the environment to affect a child's ultimate growth and development.
Self-understanding, parental awareness and identity	Newberger; Shanook; McBride; Thomas; Belenky et al.	Recognition of parent needs and stages of parental awareness, identity, and understanding are prerequisites to effective parenting and good outcomes for parents and children.
Family systems	Satir; Minuchin	Relationships among all members of a family must be recognized for family functioning to be fully understood. Empower parent subsystems.
Social relationships	Hinde; Holden; Kuczynski	Parenting is dynamic and embedded within relationships affected by both preceding interactions and future expectations. Parent adaptation is key.
Bioecological systems	Bronfenbrenner; Lerner et al.	The parent and the environment influence the child, and vice versa. Development occurs within a nested series of contextual levels. There is a potential for individual change across the lifespan.
Empowerment and family strengths	Dunst and Trivette; Cochran	Caregivers have the capacity within themselves to support their own and family growth and development. Professionals help them recognize this.
Positive psychology	Seligman	Prevention and positive personality traits, not deficits, and constructive cognitions about the future, including optimism, hope, and faith, are key.

Theory Title	Person	Basic Tenets
Ecological systems and determinants of parental competence	Belsky	Parental competence, defined as sensitivity to a child's developing abilities and communications, is influenced by such factors as *parental resources* (previous experience, self-esteem, education, attitudes, expectations about child rearing, health, psychological resources), the *child's characteristics* (temperament, health, developmental level, birth order, size, gender, learning style, transient characteristics, etc.), and *social context* (quality of marriage, social networks, support systems, cultural values, work environment, sociocultural context, etc.).
Holistic, developmental, systems-oriented approach to parental development	Demick	The developmental changes in parents' experiences and actions are important. "Parents-in-environments," considering a wide range of variables including biological-physical, psychological-intrapersonal, sociocultural, environmental, and interpersonal, should be emphasized.

Some Activities and Questions for Investigation, Reflection, and Action

Think

1. Can you summarize for someone how the field has progressed in terms of understanding parents? How do the various theories on parenting relate to the way schools might have characterized parents and their roles in the past and how family support practitioners could think mindfully about them today?

2. Read an additional article on one theorist mentioned in this chapter. Then describe something you have learned from the article that might help you understand either the limitations of using one theory to explain parent-child relationships or the potential for one theory to do so.

Reflect

3. Reflect on this question in your journal: What resources do you draw on to be sensitive to a student's developing abilities and communications? In other words, what personal resources (see, for example, Belsky, Erikson, or Demick) do you bring to your work with children?

(Continued)

(Continued)

Plan

4. What kind of discussion would you like to have with a parent about something affecting you both, in terms of relationships with children, whether in your neighborhood, society, or the world?

5. Ask a parent you know to describe a concrete situation in which the parent had to adapt to his or her child as the child grew and developed. Did the parent have any support in doing this? What resources did that parent draw on?

6. With a classmate or friend, practice role-playing a discussion with someone at school who is planning a parent workshop on parental styles. On the basis of what you have read in this chapter, what kind of mindful questions might you ask this person, and what suggestions might you make?

Chapter 3

Understanding the Elements of Parenting and Caring

Theories and Research

No society can long sustain itself unless its members have learned the sensitivities, motivations, and skills involved in assisting and caring for other human beings.

—Urie Bronfenbrenner, 2005b, p. 14

Every human being has the capacity of knowing, of analyzing and reflecting about reality so that she becomes a true agent of action in her own life.

—Ada and Beutel (1991, p. 8, as cited in McCaleb, 1994, p. 57)

Some of the questions this chapter addresses:

- How does life experience prepare a person for parenthood?
- How does a person's "way of knowing" and thinking affect the way that person might relate to children and professionals in schools and other institutions?
- What other factors are related to effective caregiving of children and youth?

AUTHOR'S NOTE: All names of children and parents in this chapter and throughout this book are fictitious.

DEFINING PARENTS

In the last chapter, we saw how theorists and researchers have progressed in their understanding of the parent role and development within that role. Often we can substitute the word *teacher* for *parent* as we think about adults caring for children, but in many instances we can't. The National Parenting Education Network defines *parents* this way:

> Those who are so defined legally and those who have made a long term commitment to a child to assume responsibility for that child's well being and development. This responsibility includes providing for the child's physiological and emotional needs, forming a loving emotional relationship, guiding the child's understanding of the world and culture, and designing an appropriate environment. (National Parenting Education Network, www.ces.ncsu.edu/depts/fcs/npen/)

Parents in many countries have at least an 18-year commitment to the child. Van der Pas (2003) defines a parent as an adult who has an awareness of being responsible for a child. "This awareness, and its all-or-nothing quality—being unconditional and without a limit in time—distinguish a 'parent' from those persons with children who are not parents" (p. 40). (This awareness might even involve turning over custody to someone else while the parents get the help they need.) A tremendous amount of research has been done to determine what children need but not very much research on who parents are and what parents do on a daily basis to care for children. This chapter provides a theoretical framework for looking at parents in more depth. It describes the process of parenting and the characteristics and resources that have been found to be associated with successful parenting. The following case study illustrates what parents do and demonstrates that success for parents often depends on the context in which they attempt to do their "parental work." Then we will turn to Heath's theoretical framework (2006) focusing on the parenting process and parental competence and related research that can prepare professionals to understand and support parents as well as collaborate with them as caregivers of children.

A CASE STUDY ILLUSTRATING WHAT PARENTS DO

Here is a description of two mothers in a children's hospital in late March, when asthma attacks are often frequent. Mateo, Miguel, and Carlos have had severe asthma attacks at the same time. Mateo's mother got her neighbor to agree to watch Mateo's siblings and bring them to school, rushed Mateo to the hospital in her car, and called her husband, who took a cab from his work. Because she could do this so quickly, Mateo's lungs were in better shape than the other boys'. She got a colleague to teach her class and provided the staff with details regarding her son's status, as she had been taught by her doctor how to listen to his breath sounds with a stethoscope at home. The other mother, new to the neighborhood, had to wait until her husband returned from work to watch their four other children. She had to ride a total of three buses to bring Miguel and Carlos to the hospital. She was told there was room for only the toddler, so the infant had to go to another hospital. The staff did not talk to her much because she was not fluent in English. Mateo's mother heard a few people criticize Miguel and Carlos's mother for not being in the hospital all day. They must not have known she was going from one hospital to the other. Staff praised Mateo's father and parish priest for coming. They may not have known that before his shift, Miguel and Carlos's dad would come, bring Miguel homemade corn bread, change his sheets, and lovingly care for him. Mateo's mom was treated better and seen as a better parent by her hospital and church, and her son was in less medical stress because of her resources and financial situation and the support she got from various institutions, advantages the other loving family did not have.

Relationships between a parent and a child and then between them and societal systems are important in terms of understanding the parents with whom one works, because a parent can have good motivation and attitudes about parenting and even many skills but be seen by others (e.g., spouse, relatives, associates, teachers, doctors, nurses, social workers) as ineffective. Or one may be so preoccupied with basic needs that it is hard to do all that is needed for a child. In the situation described above, Miguel and Carlos's family lacked language, money, and community support. The two mothers were just as worried about their children's health and just as observant of their children's needs. They differed in the resources they could access at the time, the environments in which they lived, and the way others viewed them.

The model of describing parents presented in this chapter and used to frame and understand this case study is informed by the theories from the previous chapter and focuses on parents as persons in their own right. The model and the theory of the parenting process put forth by Heath (2006) are representative and integrative of the complexity of parenting suggested in the previous chapter and in this case study. There are many important questions to ask about parents. Here are some examples: Who are the people who walk into your classroom, office, or hospital? What are their thoughts and feelings? What is their cultural background? What body of information do they have about their child? What beliefs do they have about their role and about children? What resources do they have? What support from the community? What is it these parents do on a day-to-day basis? How can I support them? How can I learn from them? Heath uses Erikson's theory as the framework for analyzing the parenting process. She also draws on Bronfenbrenner's theory but adds more focus on the developing parent and child, something Bronfenbrenner (2005a) admitted got lost for a while in his important body of work on the environment. Heath and McDermott have been working collaboratively for two decades on using and refining this theory to inform theory building and practice.

THE PARENTING PROCESS: A THEORETICAL FRAMEWORK

Zigler has noted, "I have long believed that the development of a child does not begin the day he is born—or at age three—but much earlier, during the formative years of his parents" (1976, Foreword). From the day a child is born, the environment in which the child grows sets the stage for that child's own parenting potential, as Heath has demonstrated (see Figure 3.1).

■ How Does Life Experience Prepare a Person for Parenthood?

People will come to the threshold of parenting with different levels of energy and preparedness. They are influenced by those who care for them, usually parents, as demonstrated by the arrows on the figure. They may or may not be influenced by all the others shown in Figure 3.2, including extended family, friends, peers, school, church, medical institutions, work, the media, the community, or the socio-cultural context, in terms of whether they will possess the attitudes, information, and skills necessary to parent confidently and competently. Thus, arrows from these categories are not shown in Figure 3.2. This influence often depends on a person's age, health, resources, culture, and so on. For example, if someone is ill as a child, that person may have more contact with medical personnel than is typical of the child's peers. In many cultures, several people are very involved in rearing a child from the very beginning. In U.S. society, parents can often be quite isolated from others as they rear their children. The older a child gets, the more likely it is that media, schools, neighborhoods, and so forth will influence the child.

In some families, the church has a strong influence on children, while in others, it has little or no influence. Sikkink and Hernandez (2003) found that in many Latino families, church has provided an opportunity for parents who might feel alienated from schools to network with other parents of the same religion but higher socioeconomic status. This networking has often enhanced their social capital and their support for their children's educational success. While some had hypothesized that certain more fundamentalist religious affiliations might tend to isolate parents and children, the authors reported that in general, even Latino parents of these affiliations had higher educational aspirations for their children than did nonreligious parents. The authors also reported that connection to the church often meant that children had another source of support with schoolwork and a connection to civic and community activities, which allowed them to feel connected and efficacious. The researchers found that religious affiliation and involvement had the greatest positive impact on Latino teens in impoverished, as opposed to middle-class, neighborhoods.

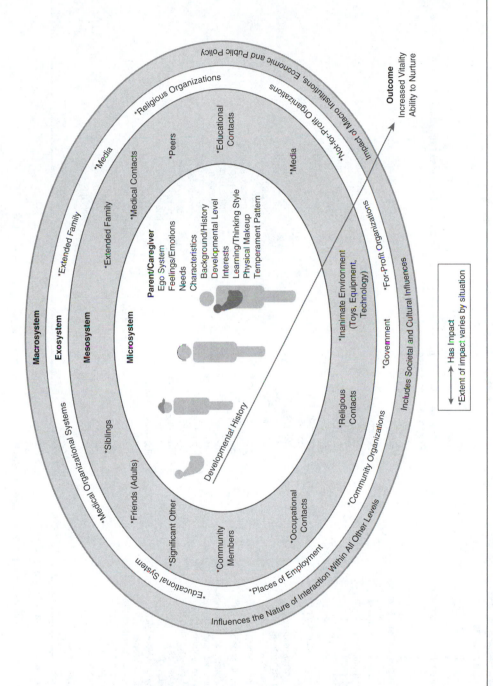

Figure 3.1   The Parenting Process: Developmental Determinants

SOURCE: Copyright © 1994, 1998, 2006 by Harriet E. Heath. Created in consultation with Dana McDermott.

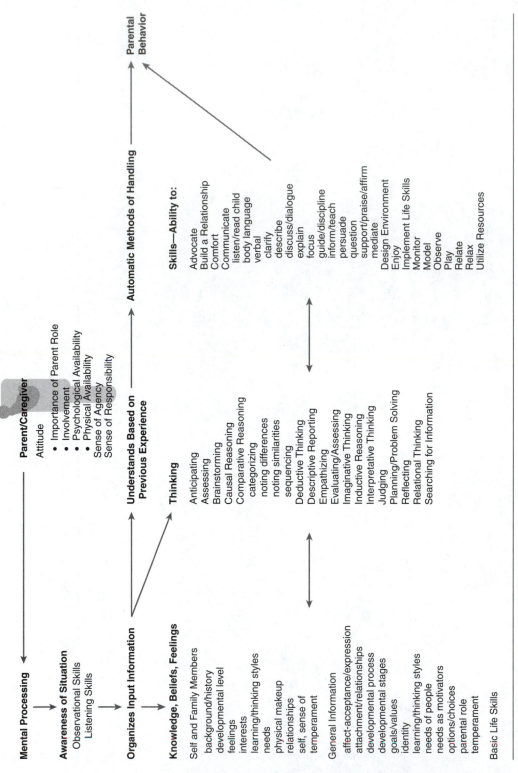

Figure 3.2   The Parenting Process: Ego Systems

In addition to the impact of some of these other environmental factors, people each come to parenting with their own unique psychological resources, physical and mental health, thinking style, beliefs, and so forth, all of which must be considered as well. Figure 3.2 describes the personal ego processes involved in parenting after the birth of one's first child. First, one needs to be motivated to parent and have the right attitude. This means appreciating the importance of the role and of being involved and psychologically available to one's child (Belsky, 1984; Fogel & Melson, 1986; Palacios, Gonzalez, & Marino, 1992; Van der Pas, 2003).

The right attitude is not the only requirement, however. Parents also need observation skills and an ability to describe situations clearly and accurately (Greenspan & Greenspan, 1985; Heath, 2000, 2006). They may or may not have developed these skills before parenting. Some parents and teachers just automatically respond once they have observed a child, and they do either what they saw their own parents do or what they might have observed elsewhere. This could be a mindless approach. Others go through a mindful process of filtering the observation through their own general and individual knowledge base, beliefs, feelings, and thinking, and then they act. Their final actions are effective based on the information and knowledge they possess (Goodnow & Collins, 1990; Sigel & McGillicuddy-DeLisi, 2002), the thinking ability and skills they have developed along the way (Holden & Hawk, 2003), and their own personal resources and situations (Belsky, 1984; Demick, 2002).

Practitioners also understand children in terms of accessing the sources of information under "Knowledge, Beliefs, and Feelings" in Figure 3.2. They first need to understand themselves, including their own background, needs, and so forth (Graue & Brown, 2003; Siegel, 2005). They need to understand child development, individual children, and their needs (prenatal, early care, physical, safety, emotional, social, and intellectual) and capacities (Brazelton & Greenspan, 2000). Simpson (2001) describes parents in the United States this way:

> Each parent unconsciously or consciously shapes his or her strategies to fit factors that often include his or her physical health, such as the presence of disabilities or chronic illness; mental health, such as the presence of depression; gender; temperament, such as ease with transitions and new situations; developmental level, such as capacity for perspective-taking; early experience, such as history of trauma and abuse; knowledge such as fluency in the English language and an understanding of the American educational system; beliefs and attitudes, such as religious and cultural beliefs about gender roles of mothers and fathers, daughters and sons; and skills, such as problem-solving and conflict-resolution skills. (p. 42)

Parenting educators, including many from the field of family and consumer sciences, have added to that list of needed skills *basic life skills* (e.g., planning, decision making, problem solving, time, household and financial management skills) and *relationship skills* (the ability to build and maintain positive and productive relationships as well as to communicate and resolve conflicts). So effective parenting is not based just on having the right attitude, although that is important. It is also about information, including knowledge about the self and others (Goodnow & Collins, 1990), beliefs (Sigel & McGillicuddy-DeLisi, 2002; Sigel, McGillicuddy-DeLisi, & Goodnow, 1992; Smetana, 1994), feelings (Belsky & Barends, 2002; Belsky, Crnic, & Woodworth, 1995), and thinking (Ehrensaft, 1987; Holden & Hawk, 2003; Kegan, 1994; Newberger, 1980), not to mention skills, but throughout it is also, as we saw in the previous chapter, about a dynamic and changing relationship that calls for mindfulness, or conscious attention to thoughts and feelings (Breslin, Zack, & McMain, 2002).

As Figures 3.3 and 3.4 illustrate, a parent and a child come to their relationship with their own developmental level, personality, learning style, needs, health, and other attributes. In addition to their interaction, other environmental factors may or may not affect the relationship. What actually affects the parent-child relationship often changes over the years between infancy and the teen years, with teenagers often being more influenced by factors outside the family, such as school and the media, than younger children are. Families with children of all ages, though, are influenced by their environment. Many educators strongly recommend that we should fix the environment in which families live, not just fix a child or a parent (Turnbull, Blue-Banning, Park, & Turbiville, 1999, p. 165). Doherty and Carlson (2002) have developed a model of citizenship or "community engaged" parenting education that empowers parents and professionals working with parents to focus on the larger environmental context (see Figures 3.3 and 3.4) and ways they together can improve their communities on behalf of children.

The Search Institute (www.search-institute.org/) also takes this systemic approach to supporting children. Project Cornerstone in California (www.project cornerstone.org/html/about/index.htm), using the Search Institute's developmental assets approach as a framework, has the goal of building a "web of support around every young person in our community." Founded in 1998, it now has more than 200 members, including schools, school districts, city and county agencies, businesses, corporations, foundations, community groups, and other organizations serving youth and families.

Heath's parental competence model encompasses both the differences in developmental level and the capacities or assets of each person involved, something not usually done in family systems theory. Her model of the parenting process is used as a reference, not only for understanding unique parents and children in social-cultural

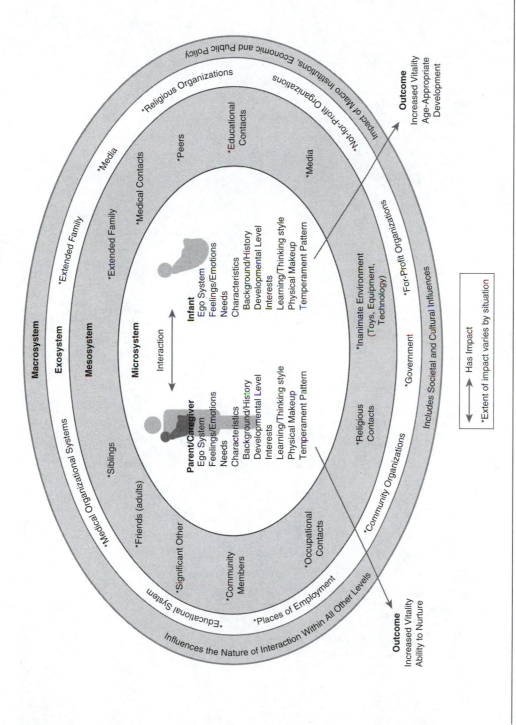

Figure 3.3 The Parenting Process: Context of Parent and Infant Interactions

SOURCE: Copyright © 1994, 1998, 2006 by Harriet E. Heath. Created in consultation with Dana McDermott.

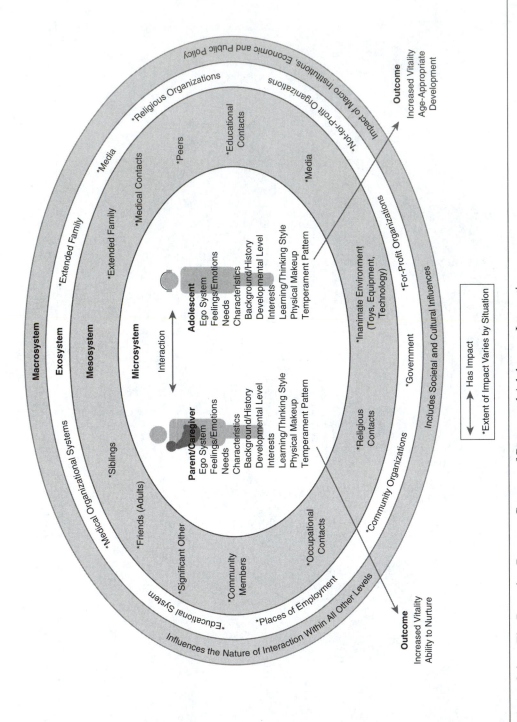

Figure 3.4   The Parenting Process: Context of Parent and Adolescent Interactions

SOURCE: Copyright © 1994, 1998, 2006 by Harriet E. Heath. Created in consultation with Dana McDermott.

context but also for developing school and community parenting programs that take all this information into consideration. Turnbull et al. (1999) say the role of the professional is shifting from focusing on just the child to enhancing a parent's ability to develop a strong support system and changing the environment of families so that their quality of life is enhanced.

RESEARCH DEMONSTRATES THE COMPLEXITY OF THE PARENTING PROCESS

A very important body of research by Chess and Thomas (1999) on goodness of fit further supports the usefulness of Heath's framework for understanding parents and families. Their findings, especially about environmental impact on temperament, are informative for teachers. They were concerned with theories of parenting that attribute any bad outcome to the parent. They found in their own work that some well-functioning parents had disturbed children and some disturbed parents had healthy children. They embarked on longitudinal research to look at the goodness-of-fit model. They were interested in the individual behavioral differences and styles of children and the environments in which those children lived.

Their original longitudinal study began in 1956 and identified a group of 131 children of middle-class, native-born parents. Chess and Thomas assessed temperament and collected other data, including parent-child interactions, parents' child-rearing attitudes, events in the families' lives, illnesses, and numerous clinical assessments of the children's behavior, and then followed the families over the years to measure the children's adjustment and development. Then in 1961, they identified a sample of 95 children of semiskilled and unskilled working-class Puerto Rican parents who lived in two housing projects in Spanish Harlem, in New York. The vast majority of children in both samples were in stable, intact families, and their parents were very committed to caring for them. The children in the second sample were followed through adolescence.

Chess and Thomas's findings were dramatic. Almost all the middle-class children attended good private schools with all the resources the children needed. If these children needed extra testing or tutoring, their parents got it for them. Children in the Puerto Rican sample almost all went to public schools that lacked many resources the middle-class children enjoyed. Chess and Thomas (1999, p. 112) found that the parents of the children in the second sample, lacking the education of the other sample's parents, had some trouble helping with homework and were less likely to critique or challenge the education their children were receiving. When the researchers looked at the school adjustment and academic achievement of all the children in their studies at 9 years of age, they found that almost half the

Puerto Rican children were assessed by teachers as excessive in motor activity and sometimes uncontrollable, whereas only one child in the other sample was assessed as uncontrollable. Chess and Thomas looked for the factors that explained this difference.

What they found was that many of the Puerto Rican children who might have started out with an activity level that was very active but within the normal range were often cooped up in small apartments and not able to play outside because of safety concerns. Their families often were large, so the home had little room for children, who furthermore did not have safe recreation areas, which the middle-class children did. Chess and Thomas (1984, p. 223, as reported in Chess & Thomas, 1999) found that one child assessed as uncontrollable was less so once the family moved to a home with a small yard in a safer neighborhood.

An even more disturbing finding was that by middle childhood, a large number of the Puerto Rican students had been placed in special education classes. This was surprising because when tested by Puerto Rican psychologists in good testing situations, the children had had normal IQs. As a result of this study, the children were tutored by the members of the project team, retested, found once again to score in "normal" categories, and mainstreamed into regular classrooms. Think about all the children who remained in special education classrooms because they did not have this help. Using a comprehensive theory to understand parenting is helpful in terms of deciphering the many sources of problems and the many parties who need to be involved in the solutions.

We can be more hopeful today because of the findings of Calabrese Barton, Drake, Perez, St. Louis, and George (2004) concerning a high-poverty urban environment where some parents are taking a more active role than in the past. The first parent described in this study, Miranda, though she had had bad experiences herself while in school, began to be engaged when one teacher cared about her son's well-being and saw him as having potential. Miranda was invited into the school, and the more she was in the school, the more she observed children and teachers. The more she was "present," the more confidence she had in challenging the teacher respectfully about a math concern. She had the advantage of being able to mediate on the spot. She created a place for herself, and when she could not tutor her son herself (as many cannot, beyond fifth-grade math), she made sure he got the help he needed so that he would not fall behind. What about all the other parents who were not made to feel comfortable in the school or who did not believe the teacher saw potential in their children? Here, if completing the diagram, one could not draw a positive arrow from school to parent and child on Figure 3.4.

Another parent in the study whose story is powerful and enlightening is Celia. This mother attended presentations on school reform and in particular about a special science education project in her school, and with the help of organizers who appreciated parents as adult learners, she became aware of how much she really "did science." She was helped to appreciate her knowledge of family health, plants and animals, and what she learned growing up within a community of farmers and fishermen. As she learned about the science education project planned for her school, she said, "I have known these things all my life but I never knew that was science" (Calabrese Barton et al., 2004, p. 10). Thus, again, if one were to fill in the diagram for this parent, an arrow from school to parent was positive.

Celia also became a "critical actor," not a reactor, in her school. She was helped in this by her child's teacher's fluency in Spanish. Another thing that helped was her experience as a cleaning lady for wealthy families. She saw that their children were learning more: "At the schools in rich neighborhoods children have more opportunities. They are different in every way. Even teachers are different in the schools in rich neighborhoods and they do not teach the same. At the schools in poor neighborhoods, they teach less" (Calabrese Barton et al., 2004, p. 9). She began to carve a space for herself in the school. Whether she was in a classroom or in nonacademic school activities, she got to know teachers, and as she gained awareness and confidence, she found herself raising questions to the teacher on behalf of her children. She was employing many of the thinking skills in Figure 3.2.

A poignant example of an African American mother who thought mindfully about the differences between her children's school experiences and those of white students in her neighborhood in the late 1930s was documented in *Maggie's American Dream* (Comer, 1988). It is essential reading for educators in order to see how parents without the educational and economic resources of wealthier parents in their environment have found ways to be strong advocates for their children and have a voice in educational institutions. And this mother's son, Dr. James Comer, honors his mother and families by designing schools that allow all children the opportunity to fulfill their potential in spite of environmental challenges.

Another wonderful example is Hurtig's work (2005) with urban Mexican mothers. Not only are they welcomed in their small bilingual and biliterate school, they take the lead in community building around activity and space issues that place children at risk. If the typically confining school classrooms are in neighborhoods that are unsafe, children may not even have outdoor recess. Parents are pushing for safer neighborhoods and more recreational spaces for their children, which demonstrates that parent engagement in all the systemic influences on children is legitimate, important, and vital parent engagement. If teachers would look at parenting through these systemic and developmental lenses, they might see parent engagement in community as just as important as engagement in schoolwork because all are necessary for children to grow and develop.

This research also highlights the importance of looking at the fit between parent and child as well as between child, school, and community systems. To review the findings above, a parent can have skills but have a child who does not respond as expected and in a rewarding way, as is sometimes the case with an autistic child. This absence of positive response may have an impact on the parents' sense of competence and their actions. What about a parent's own personality traits and resources? How does a parent's own temperament match the child's? Are the parents very intense but have a child who is shy? Do the parents have the necessary self-knowledge and general knowledge of temperament (see the column under "Knowledge, Beliefs, Feelings" in Figure 3.2) to understand this situation? Do they have the basic life skills, such as problem solving, to create an environment that helps minimize problems between children and parents who might not be a perfect "fit" with one another? Next, are they capable of thinking the way we teach children to think in school (see the column under "Thinking" in Figure 3.2)? If not, how do support systems help them in this regard? Finally, do they have the necessary skills to integrate all this knowledge and thinking (see the column under "Skills" in Figure 3.2)? Chapter 9 will describe a program in which children and youth are taught these skills and have opportunities to discuss the complexity and importance of the parenting role before they become parents (McDermott, 2003–2004, 2006).

THE PARENTING PROCESS AND PARENTAL THINKING

■ How Does a Person's "Way of Knowing" and Thinking Affect the Way That Person Might Relate to Children and Professionals in Schools and Other Institutions?

How do school parents in your communities think about their role? Most of us can recall a time when we wished others understood what we were thinking, experiencing, or feeling. We were frustrated when our gender, nationality, or role (child, student, parent, teacher, counselor, principal) was in the foreground and who we really are was in the distant background. Another case study illustrates this point. Margaret was at the sidelines of her daughter Lauren's championship basketball game. She could hear Lauren explaining to the coach that the other team had figured out Lauren's team's offense and so Lauren's team needed to go to another plan. The coach said, "Lauren, I am the coach, you are the child." He benched her for part of the game, and her team lost. Margaret shared her disappointment with other parents in the stands. Some characterized her as an overprotective mother, and some felt that as a woman, she knew less about the game than the coach did. The opposing coach, however, who saw Lauren not in a static role but as a team member who could adapt when necessary, asked Lauren to be on the all-star team.

Many people, especially those in positions of power, are rarely trained or rewarded for trying to understand the perspective of others with less power or status. Danielle had recently come to the United States from an eastern European country. Soon after her arrival, she learned her son had autism. Her husband could not handle this news, and Danielle suddenly found herself a single mother in a strange country. She was cooperative with teachers wanting the best for her son, but over time, she saw that the regular classroom situation was not well suited for her son's particular type of autism. He was regressing, and she tried to get the school to place him in a more appropriate setting, but the more she tried, the less she succeeded. Each meeting with school professionals felt to her as if the school decision makers were ganging up on her. She did not realize she could bring some-one with her to these meetings about her son's education. She went through years of frustration and of feeling she was perceived as hysterical, until she met another autistic child's parent, who happened to be a lawyer. That mom helped Danielle get a proper placement for her son. Now Danielle is pursuing a master's degree so that she can help parents in similar situations.

Sometimes we form expectations of parents or teachers on the basis of a particular role. If practitioners do not have time to know each parent as an individual, they might base their expectations on limited sources of information: the "typical" parent, as portrayed in the media, in teacher training materials, or by veteran teachers; their own parents and developmental history; the parent's behavior; or a limited view of parents' role (feed and clothe your child and help with homework). If parents deviate at all from these expectations, practitioners often don't know what to do. If you have dealt with parents who always seemed silent, trusting, and cooperative but who suddenly began to question your judgment about their child, you may feel they have become negative or regressive. In fact, these parents could be embarking on a different way of thinking and knowing. If we look at theories and research on the way adults think, we can better understand their diverse perspectives and behaviors, and this understanding is, of course, at the core of mindful learning.

PARENTAL "WAYS OF KNOWING"

Educators who draw from the theories and research of Belenky, Clinchy, Goldberger, and Tarule (1986/1997), Belenky, Bond, and Weinstock (1997), and Belenky and Stanton (2000) can hypothesize that parents like those described in the preceding paragraph may have proceeded from a stage of *silenced knowing,* in which they did not see themselves as capable of learning from instruction or words, through a stage of *received knowing,* in which they accepted everything said by authority figures, including school personnel, to a stage of *subjective knowing,* in which they may think they can trust only themselves and their own subjective experience.

Think about parents you have known who appeared uninvolved and isolated from the school and community and then one day, when asked a simple question by a child or a teacher, lashed out in a manner that you thought inappropriate. According to Belenky and her colleagues, at the stage of thinking and knowing called silenced knowing, a parent sees herself (think of this example as she or he, but *she* will be used because the research was done with mothers) as mindless and voiceless, and sometimes, when asked to do something she may not be able to do, she may use "words as weapons." She may have had parents or been in relationships with people who called her stupid and never really gave her credit for having good ideas. Recall from Chapter 2 that early theorists also did not care about or value parents' ideas. In terms of others, this parent may be distant and guarded, believing she cannot really learn from dialogue of any kind. She may fear that any talking or sharing she does will lead only to more betrayal. She may see her child as a similar threat, and even if the child simply asks her a question she cannot answer, she may hit the child. She may tend to use raw power (just as she may have experienced) to influence her child and may see no point in listening or explaining. Belenky's framework lets us see parents not in terms of deficits but simply in terms of where they are and where they may need to get eventually so as to be engaged with others in a mutually beneficial way.

Other parents may be described as received knowers (Belenky et al., 1986/1997; Belenky et al., 1997; Belenky & Stanton, 2000). They receive information from authorities and store it as is without adding their own thoughts or opinions. They tend to receive information from friends if it is similar to their own. They see their children as needing to listen to others and to take in information without questioning it. They expect their child to obey them and do what they do. They may also think the child will learn through rewards and punishments and by modeling adult behavior. These parents might be compared to Baumrind's description (1989) of the authoritarian parent. They may be seen as cooperative by school staff.

Belenky and her colleagues (1986/1997; 1997; 2000) found that parents who were subjective knowers had discovered their inner voice and believed truth comes from within more than from outside authorities. The subjective knower would value individuality and be able to tolerate friends' having beliefs different from hers. She can also see that her children have their own inner voice, and she is likely to let her children think for themselves. Even though this may be good for her children, it may cause trouble in the school, which may see this parent as non-cooperative or even hostile. Because these parents tend to trust their own concrete experience, instincts, feelings, and insights when it comes to rearing their children, they may not attend lectures. Sometimes these parents are seen as neglectful. While neither extreme—trusting all authority without question or trusting only the self—is ideal, for some parents, one or the other may be a step along the way to relating more effectively to self and to others.

Belenky et al. next describe parents who are *procedural knowers.* They are interested in examining thoughts and feelings of both the self and others and searching for systematic ways to do so. They do not mind being in a group in which others do the same. They will help their children use such procedures as gathering information and posing and evaluating alternatives to arrive at answers to their questions. In terms of child rearing, procedural knowing is more like Baumrind's authoritative parenting (1989), in which parents and children seek and provide reasons and background for their actions or decisions. Simply to gather information in an objective, logical way is called *separate knowing.* Others will seek understanding, not just proof. This is *connected knowing* and involves trying to understand the feelings, perspectives, and experiences of others, which requires drawing people out to better grasp their thoughts and beliefs and encouraging their confidence in their own abilities and strengths. This was the goal of Belenky and colleagues for the mothers in their studies and interventions and could clearly be a meaningful goal for teachers and parents as they relate to children, parents, and each other with openness to learning from everyone. This is the goal of the many new programs cited earlier in this chapter.

Finally, as a *constructive knower,* the parent not only gathers information but synthesizes it. As a mother in one of my parent groups said, "I was talking to myself more and to others. It made it easier to do this then with my child." Parents at this level would not want to get information from just their own concrete experience, intuition, feelings, and insights or from just the school but to combine ideas from all perspectives, come up with a joint solution that could be better than individual ideas, and then share that solution with school staff and others. The parent would hope the children would also listen not just to their own voice but to others'. Parents also hope children will not listen just to tear down someone else's argument, as is often the case in competitive societies, but will listen to "see the whole picture, understand, and build others and the self up in a creative and integrative process" (Belenky & Stanton, 2000, pp. 90–91).

This is easier in those school contexts in which cooperative learning and collaboration are a key mode of learning. If teachers are using this method, "doing collaboration" with parents could be a great learning opportunity as well. Parents then would see the need to draw their children out, share views, and come up with an action that is informed by different people and perspectives and takes all of them into consideration. The parents might also gather information about how past and present personal and social-cultural contexts figure into the situation. The Parent Education Initiative, the model development school described in Part II, makes time to facilitate this kind of exploration.

This research with women in rural Vermont and the documentation of other women's community building are very exciting and promising in terms of school reform and the facilitation of adult learning (Belenky & Stanton, 2000). It took time and great care to empower these women to move from silenced to connected and constructive knowing. As Belenky and Stanton noted: "The Silenced do not have the tools they need for participating in the kind of discourse community Mezirow describes. . . . To bring them into an ongoing dialogue requires the creation of an extremely safe and caring community where people draw each other out and listen to one another with the greatest of care. That experience can be profoundly transformative (see Belenky, Bond, & Weinstock, 1997)" (p. 83). The creation of such communities is also described in Hurtig's work (2005).

If parents are asked to be involved at school while they are in an early stage or way of knowing, they may give the impression that they are noncooperative, dysfunctional, or even abusive. Many parents who have been recipients of abuse or whose past experience prevented them from discovering their own voice may not be good candidates for PTA president right now; nevertheless, with the right support, they have the potential to be good partners in their children's school. How they think about themselves, their children, and school is not fixed. It can evolve to the point, as Kegan (1994) has described, where these same parents cocreate a better world for all with their children, their children's teachers, and fellow parents.

Belenky, Bond, and Weinstock's powerful book (1997), *A Tradition That Has No Name,* is about hope and potential. Now, what do a teacher and administrator do with this insight into ways of knowing? Are teachers expected to be a child's parent's teacher and social worker? No. It is an insight that helps us know ourselves and others better and understand that one-size-fits-all programs for parents will not work. You may not know where your students' parents are in terms of how they think and go about knowing themselves and their world. Parents at some of the levels Belenky identified may simply not come to your programs. But if you or your school offers only lectures dispensing expert advice for parents to accept without question or comment, then perhaps low involvement means many parents are at the stage at which they see a need for dialogue and process. On the other hand, as has been learned in programs with middle- and upper-class parents, some parents are capable of dialogue but do not want to take the time or cannot do so. Others, in all cultures and social classes, see dialogue as scary or inappropriate. When I taught in graduate school, students new to this country told me that no one ever asked them what they thought before. Some newly arrived students may have perceived a professor who did so as incompetent. The same thing happened when I worked with teachers and school psychologists in Russia a decade ago. They asked for my patience in letting them unlearn the received knowing they had used in school and elsewhere.

If parents are at the stage of silenced knowing and all you see is their abusive language around their children, your goal is to find a way to engage these parents rather than reject them. Belenky and colleagues (1986/1997; 1997; 2000) do this;

Shure (1992) has a very successful program for children called *I Can Problem Solve* and adult materials for parents (1988, 2004). She found in working with inner-city parents of 4-year-olds that if she could acknowledge their adult learning needs and get them discussing adult problems, discussing consequences, and talking about each other's feelings, they were much more likely to use the same tools to solve problems with their children.

Programs to empower parents have been developing with the help of the family support movement in the United States (see Cochran, 1988; Cochran & Walker, 2005; Dunst & Trivette, 2006). The state of Minnesota has been in the forefront, having decades ago mandated that all parents of children from birth through age 5 have access to parenting education and support (Cooke, 2006). Supporting parents may mean home visits like those from the "parent mobile" of the Fresno, California, Parent Engagement Center, outreach to homeless and hard-to-reach parents, or meetings on a parent's turf, such as a church or community agency or at work. The common bond for starting such an effort is that most parents and teachers want children to succeed.

RESEARCH ON PARENTAL THINKING

Other pertinent research has focused on parents' thinking and helps us understand the range of thinking in parents. In building on Piaget's model of children's stages of intellectual development, Sameroff and Feil (1985) posited parallel ways that parents and caregivers think about children. The interpretation of a child's behavior depended on how complex the thinking of the parent was. At the *symbiotic level,* parents often would not differentiate between themselves and their child and would see what they do for the child as key. Thus, it would be hard for parents at this level to reflect on how the child is developing separate from what they do for the child. If the child has an easy disposition, the family may not experience a problem, but if not, the relationship could be stressful, with the parent possibly rejecting the child.

At the *categorical level,* the parent sees the child's behavior as intrinsic to the child and separate from the parent. Parents at this level tend to place children into categories such as good or bad, based on their behavior. This may work well if children are seen as good, but if they are seen as difficult early on, they may be characterized that way even if they change. Parents in this stage also are limited to thinking in terms of only one cause for behavior: either internal dispositions of the child or the environment, but not a combination. In the *compensating stage,* parents can see children as separate from categories or labels. They can make exceptions and see that some behavior might simply be related to a child's age. Also, certain attributes might compensate for others. For example, a child who is not considered smart may nevertheless be considered hardworking and respectful.

Parents or teachers may not think in these either-or terms, but they may not be able to think through the relative contribution of a variety of factors, such as personality and living conditions, to a child's developmental outcome. Unfortunately, professionals sometimes assume that all teachers and parents can do this.

At the *perspectivistic level,* parents can think hypothetically and can see the child's behavior in context. So perhaps a child should be able to sit quietly in class, but because of the environment, the child does not. This is exemplified in Chess and Thomas's studies (1984) of children living in close quarters in dangerous neighborhoods. Some of the parents studied came to understand that if they had a larger house or safe places for children to play, the children might not be so "uncontrollable" in school. Of course, there are other issues at play. For example, many of the parents Chess and Thomas studied put a high value on obedience, which also might have colored their interpretation of rambunctiousness in their children.

What can we conclude from this research? As the authors wisely stated, one cannot look at parental thinking without looking at the characteristics of children and the environment and how all these factors interrelate. With an easy child, a parent's way of thinking may not be as significant as it may be with a more challenging child or in an environment that brings with it all kinds of additional problems. Furthermore, socioeconomic status and work role may relate to parental thinking. When we can benefit from a wealth of insight into the elements that affect parenting, it is remarkable that few studies of parents and children look at more than just two variables, such as parent style and child behavior, and how they might interact. It is helpful to think about parents' level of thinking as one of many factors involved in parent-child relationships. Parents and children have their own capacities and are embedded in other systems, including such things as school policies that limit physical exercise during the day, which might also affect outcomes.

Newberger (1980; Newberger & Cook, 1983) described the related construct of *parental awareness.* Newberger identified several levels of awareness based on parents' own experiences, needs, feelings, and cognitive abilities. For many, parental awareness is a growth process that progresses from self-centered, egoistic views, to conventionally oriented views reflecting cultural norms, to understanding that individuals are unique and different. The process culminates in an analytic, systems-oriented view of the parent and child in interdependent self-systems. Hence, it is similar in part to some of the other theories described in this chapter.

Newberger and Cook (1983) found that levels of awareness were significantly and positively related to age and experience as a parent but not to gender, race, or social class. Cook (1979) and Newberger (1980) found that abusive parents scored lower on parental awareness than nonabusive parents did. Sandy (1982) found significant increases in parental awareness in parents who received a parenting education intervention that included both child development information and time for discussion. This is an encouraging finding.

You may be dealing with parents at the *egoistic level of awareness.* They tend to see the child in terms of their own needs. An example is a parent who is tired and says the child is too tired to do homework or go out and play with peers even though the child is wide awake and wants to play or do homework. While it is important to acknowledge one's own needs and find ways to get them met, most parents know that children are very dependent on them, in the early years especially, and have needs that are very different from the parents' needs and that must be met by someone if the children are to survive.

At the second level of parental awareness, or *conventional thinking,* parents look to what is expected by society. They consult authorities and norms about child needs, including child-rearing books and other sources. A parent would not expect a child to be able to stay alone at age 6, but perhaps the child could do so by age 12, the age at which U.S. societal norms suggest children can baby-sit. In some societies, spanking is accepted, and in others, it is a crime. In many traditional schools, parents in the conventional stage are welcome. With so many families coming to the United States from other countries, it is very important for schools to understand the conventions of their students' country of origin. In some cultures, parents' never coming to school is the norm.

At the *individualistic level,* parents see their children as individuals. So while a very quiet and cooperative first child makes it easy for a parent to feel competent, the parent at this level would view a second, more outgoing, verbal child not as bad but as different and calling for a different kind of interaction. Finally, at the *analytic level,* parents see that they and their children are growing and changing within various systems within society and that, therefore, the way they relate can also change. These parents are able to reflect on ways systems impact each other, such as the ways government cutbacks or war or mandates like No Child Left Behind affect family and school life.

While research (Newberger, 1980; Newberger & Cook, 1983) has shown that parents move up the levels somewhat as their age and experience increase, one needs to consider that sometimes parents have the potential to act in a certain way but do not do so. So parents who know their child is unique and curious but want that child to succeed in a school that is authoritarian or traditional may encourage more-conventional behavior in their child at certain points. Other parents may decide to encourage their child to continue to question things even if the child is in an authoritarian school. These parents may assess how well their approach is working and help their child cope successfully with their choice.

Kegan (1994) is another educator who described parental cognition as thinking that is inseparable from feeling or social relations. He describes the "mental demands of modern life" as we organize how we think, feel, and relate to others. According to Kegan, we construct our sense of self in the relationship between our own point of view and others'. His *first order of consciousness* is childhood.

In Kegan's *second order of consciousness,* people focus their knowing or thinking on their own needs, and in the *third order of consciousness,* we focus on a moral-ethical code that comes from our group, family, culture, race, religion, or society. In the *fourth order of consciousness,* we respect differences in people's thinking and realize values are based more on situations and the way each person construes or views situations. At this level, one realizes one's view is just that, one view, which may differ from others' views, and so one can look objectively at how one sees the world. Kegan feels that in these times, parents cannot stay on the third level but need to move to the fourth level and understand how their thinking is viewed by their children and by others. Furthermore, parents need to be clear with children and others about where they stand.

There are some obvious similarities among these levels of thinking and aware-ness, Belenky and colleagues' ways of knowing, and Sameroff and Feil's parental concepts of development. For each, the thinking is more complex and deep at higher levels. It is important to be able to understand these constructs to better understand the parents with whom we work. While principles of adult learning need to be considered in work with parents, some parents may be better able to learn than others are. Dialogue, for example, is not always a choice even though it has been found helpful in adult learning. First, we would have to understand what dialogue means to the parents with whom we work. Some parents would need to reach several intervening levels before they are ready to dialogue. Talking to their children about their own lives or about migrant worker issues, for example, as a homework assignment would be much less threatening and more meaningful than talking to teachers about why they are not helping with home-work they cannot understand or do not feel is relevant.

EXEMPLARY PROGRAMS SUPPORT
PARENTS AS LIFELONG LEARNERS

McCaleb's unique project (1994), involving students' drawing out their parents' voices, is an example of how this can be done. This technique was also used in the Belenky research, with women telling their stories and having them written down. McCaleb was herself inspired by Ada and Beutel (1991), who stated that "every human being has the capacity of knowing, of analyzing and reflecting about reality so that she becomes a true agent of action in her own life (p. 8)" (as cited in McCaleb, 1994, p. 57). McCaleb goes on to describe the benefits of such a project:

> When family words and experiences are turned into the printed word the thoughts of the participants are validated. The new knowledge that emerges can subsequently or simultaneously be transformed into action. As families begin to

participate in this manner, their feelings of self-esteem increase. Parents begin to realize that their words and experiences merit a valuable place in the education of their children. (p. 58)

She delineates the benefits to parents and children of coauthorship of a book as a school project. Some parents might not even be ready for this without some preliminary work or support, as was the case with the silenced knowers encountered by Belenky and colleagues. In researching a family topic, students are involved with their parents in communication, dialogue, and sharing. McCaleb (1994) described her rationale and the benefits of this program in this way:

1. A child has a chance to ask their parents their opinions about things. Often a student interview of parents is a great process for inquiry.

2. Students and families can discover their voices are heard as opposed to reading some traditional text.

3. Everyone's history gets to emerge as worthy of study. Each person's experience is essential to complete the story.

4. Self-identity and self-esteem are strengthened. Students are positively affected when they see their parents have knowledge and are teachers in their own way.

5. As parents are asked to recall their childhood they often identify better with their children. Parents share joys, struggles and reveal successes and vulnerabilities.

6. When students write and talk important life themes emerge. The more we talk the more we identify what we value and we gain knowledge and understanding of self and others.

7. Students recognize all the knowledge in families and communities and hopefully have the schools validating this. Respect for family can translate to self-respect. When children show an interest in elders a new bonding and hope emerges.

8. By exploring what they know and do not know students become researchers and take family and community along with them.

9. Info from home and community helps teachers understand students better. Their lives come into the curriculum more and the teacher can be more effective.

10. This can lead to a culturally and linguistically relevant curriculum.

11. Studying their own lives can help students feel good about themselves and thus make them more motivated to learn. This helps students believe their home and school are not worlds apart. (p. 51)

Today this project of creating a book of students' families' lives is being done in many school and community settings, as are a variety of similar initiatives. The Caring School Community Program of the Developmental Studies Center (www.devstu.org) uses "homeside activities" to involve parents in their children's learning. Questions have to do with family beliefs, history, and values. The Tellin' Stories project (teachingforchange.org) involves parent-teacher workshops in which parents write and share their stories with their children and other parents. The program involves parents of various cultures and creates a place in the school where culture and traditions are highly valued. Parents in these schools feel they are playing a more meaningful role in their children's schools than they were before these kinds of interventions. Teachers get a much better view of their school families' realities. Teachers and parents also come together for workshops on topics of mutual interest, such as discipline.

Libros y familias is also an exciting family literacy and parent involvement project (www.ncpie.org/best_practices/LibrosyFamilias.doc). Parent-teacher-student book groups have been developed to further mutual understanding and to facilitate the school as a learning community model. Excellent Spanish literature (by such celebrated authors as Alma Flor Ada and F. Isabel Campoy) is used. Parents read books their children are reading. Bilingual and bicultural teachers facilitate the group discussions. The books are chosen so that when parents come to school once a month, they can discuss the materials in terms of their own experience. They then join together to enter their thoughts about the topic on a computer so that students can read their parents' writing in class. Parents are thus seen as having important experiences and wisdom to share with the school.

In California, another Project Cornerstone success story is the mothers of the "los dichos de la casa" program who come to school once a month to share cultural activities and read literature in Spanish to children. They share the proverbs and wisdom of their homes and culture. Teachers read the same book in English to the students. Thus, in addition to building dual language skills for themselves and the students, these parents who thought they would not be able to contribute at school are involved in a very important way, and in doing so, they build their child's "assets" (mentioned earlier; see search-institute.org/), such as "asset 6," involving parents in authentic and meaningful ways, and "asset 41," valuing the language, traditions, and culture of families. Schools were also shown how this activity aligned with standards in language arts, writing, listening, speaking, and visual arts.

Photo by Gerardo Santana.

A mother of the "los dichos de la casa" project in Santa Clara County reads students a book titled *The Woman Who Outshone the Sun,* by Rosalma Zubizarreta (original poem by Alejandro Cruz Martinez), and answers their questions.

In Chicago, Hurtig's Parents Write Their Worlds Project (2005) brings parents together to write their own stories, recording their rich life experiences, insights, and hopes for the future. This successful project produces excellent and professional literary magazines through the joint efforts of these women and their collaborations with Hurtig and the project team, who recognizes and nurtures their talent and who collaborate with a supportive principal to incorporate the stories into school curricula. This project allows children to learn about their culture not in a generic way but by reading their own parents' powerful stories about their traditions, knowledge, and experiences. Over time, the parents in this project see themselves not in the static, conventional roles that others often see but as school and community leaders.

The Study Circles project (studycircles.org) moves people beyond one school. People involved tell stories in groups to educate each other about issues of concern to all. The focus is on relationship building, networking, and action. Between 8 and 12 participants from a large geographical area meet in many diverse study circles and try to solve a problem shared by all. The key principle underlying these models is collaboration. They also respect adult learners who know there are many solutions to a problem. The assumptions are that everyone has something to contribute and that when people are inclusive, everyone benefits. When people

Photo by Janise Hurtig.

Parents in the Parents Write Their Worlds Project at Telpochcalli School.

collaborate in a face-to-face meeting, the result is often the kind of dialogue that leads to new and unexpected solutions. People try to find some areas of agreement (e.g., we all want this city to be less violent), and they try to find solutions together. If many people are part of the discussion, many more people will take ownership of the actual action plan.

These examples are just a few of the projects around the country that engage parents in a respectful and productive way. They may not be of interest to all parents, but they are an option for those who feel that school is safe and who are made to feel welcome. Some silent knowers may not think right away that they can profit from dialogue, especially about personal issues or parenting, but being part of a story or reacting to a story may feel safer and may pave the way for other discussions.

In reviewing ways of knowing, one might hypothesize that teachers are all at the highest level of thinking. Many are, but they may be working in conventional settings or school systems where there is little time, training, or reward for connected or constructive knowing with parents. Others may have been reared in a very conventional manner and may have foreclosed on that style. For them, the parent who wants to explore options might be seen as frustrating or difficult. So parents and teachers, in spite of their capacity for thinking, may for various historical, political, and personal reasons be at odds. It is important for future and current teachers and other family-serving practitioners to engage in anticipatory socialization to explore this area before and during their work with parents. Thus, they could avoid the hostility and defensiveness that may arise from making a judgment based on roles and stereotypes rather than on individuals.

CHARACTERISTICS OF COMPETENT AND CONFIDENT PARENTING AND CARING

Without knowing who parents are and what they bring to the process, we can't expect them to respond in a homogeneous manner to requests. But where do we begin? We need to consider much more than the environment and how parents think, though both are very important.

■ What Other Factors Are Related to Effective Caregiving of Children and Youth?

Table 3.1 is a chart designed to highlight research on some of the characteristics of effective and competent parenting and caring related either to parents' thinking or to other personal resources or situations in their lives. Much of the research cited in the table provides empirical evidence for the theories of parental competence described earlier. The job of the teacher is to understand that the role of parent, like that of teacher, is complex and that parents come with different resources. They are growing as they adapt to their children and work on their relationships. Their thinking skills vary. They were not all taught the attitudes, information, and skills of competent parenting before they had children.

Currently, a movement is under way to teach parenting to students so that when they become parents, they will be prepared to nurture children as children deserve to be nurtured. Most of the skills listed in Table 3.1 are taught in these programs. In the meantime, it is important for professionals to, first, assume parents want to support their children and, second, do what they can to help parents do so.

Many school reform programs, such as School of the 21st Century (Finn-Stevenson & Zigler, 1999), see the school's role as helping parents succeed in their role and helping them address the multitude of family needs they face today. Family life educators, parenting educators, and family support professionals are integrated into the school system. They provide the support necessary for parents to have some energy to spare to work on that important parent-child relationship. This is a family strengths model. In almost all cultures, communities rear children together. Today, families are often small, and they often move around the country and the world, so they often do not have the support they need to rear children

Table 3.1   Some Characteristics of Competent Parenting and Caregiving

Resources Needed for Effective Parenting	Supporting Research
Care for Self	
• Ability to care for self (physical, psychological, etc.)	Kohut, 1977; Florin & Dokecki, 1983; Smith et al., 1994; First & Way, 1995; Carlson, Healy, & Wellman, 1998
• An active coping style and sense of mastery	Crockenberg, 1988; Eisenberg & Valiente, 2004; Christophersen & Mortweet, 2004
• Self-efficacy—belief one can have influence and impact	Teti & Gelfand, 1991; Okagaki & Divecha, 1993; Coleman & Karraker, 1998; Shumow & Lomax, 2002; Sanders & Wooley, 2005
• Psychological integration, maturity, and ego strength	Brunnquell, Crichton, & Egeland, 1981; Hauser et al., 1991; Cowan & Cowan, 2000; Gerris et al., 1997; D. Heath, 2005
• Low anxiety and absence of depression or low depression levels	Cox, Owen, Lewis, & Henderson, 1989; Field, 1995; Heinicke, 2002
• Ability to function autonomously and have a capacity for mutuality as well	Heinicke, 2002; Jordan, Kaplan, Miller, Stiver, & Surrey, 1991; Sroufe, Egeland, Carlson, & Collins, 2005, chap. 9
• Ability to manage stress and tolerate daily frustrations	Belsky & Vondra, 1985; Smith, Cudaback, Goddard, & Myers-Wall, 1994; Brown, 2001; Crnic & Law, 2002
• Ability to make decisions alone or jointly	Clabby & Elias, 1987; Brown, Mounts, Lamborn, & Steinberg, 1993; Holden, 1983; Holden & Hawk, 2003
• Ability to make sense of parental experiences	Newberger, 1980; Vondra & Belsky, 1993; First & Way, 1995; Thomas, 1996
• Anticipatory socialization, ability to plan for parent role	Steffensmeier, 1982; Jaffe, Sudermann, Reitzel, & Killip, 1992; Heath, 2000
• Physical health, well-being, lack of fatigue	Tinsley, Markey, Ericksen, Kwasman, & Ortiz, 2002
• Absence of substance abuse	Mayes & Truman, 2002; Conners et al., 2004
• Employment—if desired and if child-care needs are met	Crouter & McHale, 2005; Fuller et al., 2002

Understand	
• Ability to read and understand children's physical, psychological, social, intellectual, and spiritual needs	Lamb & Easterbrooks, 1981; Martin, 1989; Brazelton & Greenspan, 2000; DeBecker, 1999; Dunlap, 2002
• Knowledge of own child and child development	Brazelton & Greenspan, 2000
• Ability to understand how experiences, social relations, and culture shape one's beliefs and feelings	O'Connor, 1990; Robertson, 1996; Thomas, 1996; Harkness & Super, 1996, 2002
Nurture	
• Ability to mirror child's emotions back to child and be empathic	Baker & Baker, 1987; Feshbach, 1987; Cicchetti, Toth, & Bush, 1988; Izard, 1991
• Ability to communicate openly and effectively	Black & Teti, 1997; Vangelisti, 2004; Galvin, Bylund, & Brommel, 2003
• Ability to be patient and tolerant	Belsky, 1984; Belsky & Vondra, 1985
• Willingness to be involved, commitment to role	Greenberger, Goldberg, Hamill, O'Neil, & Payne, 1989; Holden, 1997; Palsey, Futris, & Skinner, 2002
• Ability to display warmth, acceptance, appreciation	Whitbourne & Weinstock, 1979; Russell & Russell, 1989
• Ability to establish a trusting relationship, to bond	Ainsworth & Bowlby, 1991; Cassidy & Shaver, 1999; Cummings & Cummings, 2002
• Ability to maintain routines, high morale, traditions	Doherty, 1997; Furstenberg, Cook, Eccles, Elder, & Sameroff, 1999
Motivate	
• Ability to "scaffold" to facilitate learning in others	Kearn, 2000; Vandell & Wilson, 1987; Berkowitz & Grych, 1998; Abbeduto, Weissman, & Short-Myerson, 1999
• Ability to remember past events in order to better anticipate future actions (distancing)	Sigel, McGillicuddy-DeLisi, & Goodnow, 1992; Wang, Bernas, & Eberhard, 2005
Guide	
• Ability to plan, supervise, and monitor children	Ladd, Profilet, & Hart, 1992; Brown et al., 1993; White & Koffman, 1997; Crouter & Head, 2002; Capaldi, 2003; Brody, 2003

(Continued)

Table 3.1 (Continued)

• Ability to provide structure, guidance, and warmth	Baumrind, 1989; Steinberg & Levine, 1997; Pomerantz & Ruble, 1998; Gray & Steinberg, 1999; Pitzer, 2000; Chao, 1994; Chao & Tseng, 2002
• Ability to appraise situations or problems and resolve them; ability to address competing needs	Holden & Ritchie, 1988; Dix, 1992; Luster & Okagaki, 1993; Holden, 1997
• Ability to solve problems and brainstorm options	Spivack & Shure, 1974; Heath, 2000; Heinicke, 2002; Shure, 1988, 1992, 2004
• Ability to balance competing concerns and make behavioral adjustments in ongoing interactions	Dix, 1992; Grusec & Goodnow, 1994; Holden, 1997; Holden & Miller, 1999
Advocate	
• Ability to be a buffer and mediator for the child	Luster & Okagaki, 1993; Siddiqui & Ross, 2004
• Ability to talk about one's own experience	Belenky, Clinchy, Goldberger, & Tarule, 1986/1997; Belenky, Bond, & Weinstock, 1997; Taylor, 1997
• Ability to advocate for self and others in one's care and to locate resources and seek assistance	Smith et al., 1994; Wekerle & Wolfe, 1998; Dunst, Trivette, & Deal, 1988; Dunst & Trivette, 2006; Flaherty, 1999; Simpson, 2001
Factors Related to Competent Parenting	
• Marital satisfaction	Goldberg & Easterbrooks, 1985; Grych, 2002
• Absence of violence in home or neighborhood	Osofsky & Jackson, 1994; Gorman-Smith, Henry, & Tolan, 2004; Garbarino, Bradshaw, & Kostelny, 2005
• Social support from family, significant other, friends, community, and society	Cutrona, 1984; Cochran, 1993; Smith et al., 1994; Heath, 2004; Cochran & Walker, 2005
• Contact with others, absence of isolation	Tolan & McKay, 1996; Cochran & Walker, 2005; Sheldon, 2002
• Supportive work environment	Greenberger et al., 1989; Crouter & McHale, 2005
• Low income but has social support	Burchinal, Follmer, & Bryant, 1996; Webster-Stratton, 1997; Jack, 2000
• Emotional, instrumental, and informational support	Cutrona, 1984; Heath, 2004; Cochran & Walker, 2005

well. It is the job of the entire community to support parents and teachers in growing and learning along with the children in their care.

Many teachers could be more effective caregivers of children if they too possessed the attributes in Table 3.1, which go above and beyond knowledge of a school subject like math or one's college training. These characteristics and competencies echo the call for human development literacy by Brazelton and Greenspan (2000) and Comer (2001). How do people become more skilled in relating to other human beings? Surely professionals should be working on these attitudes and skills throughout their careers. Obviously, some of these attributes are more important in the very early years than others. Heath (1998) designed a tool to identify the skills and resources parents already possess, those they most need to develop, and the parenting programs they might choose to address their needs. DeBord, Heath, McDermott, and Wolfe (2000) did a similar project for the family support movement. This analytic approach makes more sense than thinking the parenting program du jour will serve all parents' needs. Unfortunately, the typical school program for parents tends to focus on just one variable, such as authoritative style, or just one topic, such as bullies.

As one can see from the discussion on cognitive style and the list of personal and contextual variables in Table 3.1, parenting is much more complex than the typical parenting programs would lead one to believe. Wadlington (1995) incorporated competency self-assessment as a tool for preschool teachers as adult learners working with children. In one scenario, teachers and parents could review the list of important parenting and caregiving competencies in the table, select those they can do well, and choose one or two they wish to work on during a school year or have the school's parent education and support program address. If, for example, a teacher and parent wanted to look at temperament and goodness of fit to better understand challenges with certain students, teachers, and parents, they could read something on the subject (e.g., Carey, 1997; Chess & Thomas, 1999; Shick, 1998) and do some exercises together (Wadlington, 1995). They could then document what they learned through the experience. If they chose empathy, for example, parents and teachers could assess themselves on empathy and then have a better understanding of how they understand and identify with what children are feeling and how feelings affect child behavior.

Of course, the list in Table 3.1 is not complete because the study of parenting is evolving rapidly. The supportive references are just a few of many examples to support each characteristic. The characteristics and very important early studies have stood the test of time, and it is hard to imagine that the attributes they have identified will not remain important over time. This is the work parents and adults who care for children need to be focusing on. In addition, contexts need to be supportive of this work. Thus, issues like work environments and opportunities, poverty, isolation, fatigue, and depression must be addressed by family support services, which can range from extended families and friends to schools and community or social service agencies.

A framework of critical parenting competencies and practices put forth by Smith, Cudaback, Goddard, and Myers-Wall (1994) has been used to structure the table. Smith and colleagues described the need for parents to care for themselves and work on their own competencies and confidence in their challenging role. They also described the additional parent tasks of understanding, nurturing, motivating, guiding, and advocating for their children. Simpson (2001) outlined a similar list of roles for parents of adolescents and provided a scholarly synthesis of research as a foundation for concrete parent actions. Many parent-teacher workshops and meetings sponsored at the Parent Education Initiative described in Part II addressed these tasks as a learning community.

The first critical parenting practice focuses on strengthening a parent's personal resources and caring for self in order to care for children. The tasks include managing resources, managing stress, and asking for help when needed. Asking for help is seen as a strength. Many of the abilities that Smith et al. (1994) include under caring for self were described in Chapter 2, in the section on personality and trait theories.

Understanding is the next category in Smith et al.'s list (1994) of resources for parents. Brown (2001) believes that "a parent needs the psychological resources to understand and consequently tolerate the daily demands and frustrations of an infant or young child. Needed are patience, sensitivity and responsiveness" (p. 5). Martin (1989) found effective parents are those who can read children's needs. The quality of *sensitivity* has been defined as "contingent, appropriate, and consistent responses to an infant's signals or needs" (Lamb & Easterbrooks, 1981, p. 127). We can help children develop these skills in the parenting classes mentioned earlier.

Some family centers serving school districts (such as the Clayton Family Center discussed in Chapter 8) provide places for new parents to come to sharpen these skills in a supportive environment. The Parents as Teachers program, now active in several states, provides this service through home visits. Some states, such as Minnesota, have funded mandates for decades so that all parents have access to quality education and support in the early years of parenting. Head Start and Early Head Start programs also fill this need. (Although some theorists see understanding as a skill needed to fulfill the more basic roles, such as nurturing and guiding, rather than as a role in itself, its importance is unquestioned.)

Nurturing is a very central focus in the kinds of programs just mentioned. Feshbach (1987) defined *empathic awareness,* a component of nurturing, as an ability to recognize the emotions experienced by a child and respond appropriately to these emotions. Baker and Baker (1987) defined *mirroring* as reflecting back to a child what the child is feeling. Russell and Russell (1989) defined *warmth* broadly as acceptance, appreciation, physical affection, approval for good behavior, joking, and sharing mutually rewarding activities.

Often a willingness to be involved with children affects one's nurturing. Holden (1997) defines *parental involvement* as a "commitment to a child's welfare and therefore motivation to meet the child's needs. At the most basic level, this involvement means providing for the physical needs of the child (e.g., food, clothing, shelter, and protection)" (p. 120). Understanding a child's needs is addressed in the parenting programs described later. As the child grows, affirming and maintaining family activities, rituals, and traditions (Doherty, 1997; Furstenberg, Cook, Eccles, Elder, & Sameroff, 1999) are also important ways of nurturing the child's sense of connection.

Empathy and affect awareness are skills even very young children learn in relationships at home and school. Learning to be empathic and to care is central to some new programs and caring school models, which are shared in Part II of this book. Often in the United States, the focus is on competition more than care; therefore, parents and teachers need to be deliberate about emphasizing the importance of caring in all they say and do with children.

Motivating is described by Smith et al. (1994) as teaching children about themselves, encouraging their natural curiosity and love of learning, and providing good conditions for learning. Many feel creating caring classroom environments facilitates this process. Educators (e.g. Kohn, 1999) contend that many schools focus more on extrinsic motivators such as rewards and praise, which often impede children's intrinsic motivation to learn. Many feel *motivate* may not be the correct term here, because one learns from observing infants that they are born intrinsically motivated to learn about the world.

Cognitive distancing is a skill described by Sigel et al. (1992) as asking children to remember past events and use their imaginations to anticipate future actions. It is a way to help children learn about themselves and the world and grow in self-confidence. It is not about giving them answers but about asking them questions that will allow them to find answers themselves. Scaffolding is also a parenting and teaching practice that motivates children to learn new things by challenging them but providing support for them to move forward in their development.

Guiding is a huge umbrella concept for much of the "work" parents and teachers do. Holden (1997) found that the core of effective parenting is in how the parent appraises the child and the situation and then helps resolve competing needs. Gray and Steinberg (1999) found that modeling (e.g., good life-style habits, choices, and behaviors) is linked to better skills in and child attitudes toward academic achievement, work, health habits, relationships, communication, coping, and conflict resolution. Parents' monitoring and supervising of peer interactions, as well as thinking through the steps of decision making with children, have been related to the quality of peer relations and to a child's ability to master the challenges of childhood and adolescence (Brown, Mounts, Lamborn, & Steinberg, 1993; Crouter & Head, 2002; Ladd, Profilet, & Hart, 1992). As one might guess, guiding is a key topic of parenting meetings at school and elsewhere. Many believe that it must begin much earlier than adolescence and that teaching a caring process of decision making to preschoolers builds a foundation for children to make good decisions in their teen years, when parents are not always with them.

Advocacy is a crucial topic for parents. Obviously, parents need to have a sense of self-awareness and understanding to advocate for themselves, and this helps them advocate for their children (Belenky et al., 1986/1997, 1997). Katz, Aidman, Reese, and Clark (1996) have discussed the advocacy role for parents of young children. Simpson (2001) and Steinberg and Levine (1997) detail what this means for parents of adolescents. The term *advocate* has been thought of as anyone acting on behalf of another person. The goal is the best interests of the child or person for whom one advocates. Often people have the idea that when one advocates for someone, it becomes a win-lose situation. This does not have to be the case. Adults frequently need the help of an advocate when they do not have the expertise, means, or energy to represent their perspective effectively to others.

Advocacy is important for parents and teachers to discuss even if the word makes people uncomfortable. It is more about seeking information, understanding and articulating multiple viewpoints and perspectives, understanding everyone's long-term goals and needs, and then doing what is in the best interest of the child. In some cultures, the concept is truly foreign to the usual way of doing things. People from these cultures deserve to know how advocacy works and whether they can engage someone to help them decide how to deal with this phenomenon from their cultural perspective. Involving the child in this process in an age-appropriate manner is also important and will be addressed in Part II.

Finally, the last section of Table 3.1 lists some of the contextual factors that also affect a parent's sense of competence and confidence at all levels, as described by Bronfenbrenner (1979, 2005a) and Heath (2006). These factors are considered in detail in the discussion of culture in Chapter 5 in order to provide a full view of the interactions of context and culture in parents' lives.

SUMMARY

The goal in this chapter was for the reader to understand the elements of the parent and adult caregiver role. This was demonstrated through learning about a theory of parental competence and supportive research and learning more about parents' thinking capacity and about what is needed for effectively fulfilling the caregiver role. Knowing all this no doubt informed Elias and Schwab's suggestion (2004) that schools allow parents to do their important work rather than pressure them to be teachers' assistants on homework.

Some Activities and Questions for Investigation, Reflection, and Action

Think

1. Think about the parents in all the case studies and stories described in this chapter (the parents of Mateo, Miguel and Carlos, Lauren, etc.). Make copies of Figure 3.3 and chart the kind of support these parents received by drawing lines connecting the parent to the source of support (schools, medical institutions, church, neighborhood, and so on). Place a plus or a minus sign on the lines to indicate whether the impact was positive or negative. Could you envision using this chart to think about the families with whom you work?

2. Go to the Web and read about these parental roles in more detail in either Simpson (2001), http://www.hsph.harvard.edu/chc/parenting/raising.html, or Smith et al. (1994), http://www.cyfernet.org/parenting_practices/preface.html. What did you learn about parents and children that will help you better understand their needs and responsibilities?

Reflect

3. Add this activity to your journaling: Examine Table 3.1 and identify 10 characteristics that will make you a good teacher or caregiver of children. Where and when did you or will you learn all these skills?

Plan

4. Show the chart to parents you know. Ask them which characteristics are or were most important in their parenting. For which would they have liked more information or skills?

5. Think about role-playing a discussion with a teacher who is criticizing parents who did not attend a meeting about how to help their children with math homework. What kind of "mindful" questions would help the teacher see the event in a new way?

Chapter 4

UNDERSTANDING PARENTS AND TEACHERS AS LIFELONG LEARNERS

As Sergiovanni writes, "A sense of belonging, of continuity, of being connected to others and to ideas and values that make ourselves meaningful and significant—these needs are shared by all of us" (1993). We, too, need the protective factors of caring and respectful relationships and opportunities to make decisions; without these, we cannot create them for youth.

—Benard, 1996, pp. 5–6

If parents are able to integrate knowledge into their own value and belief systems, they will overcome their "sense of powerless in the world."

—Pickarts and Fargo, 1971, p. 25

Some of the questions this chapter addresses:

- Have we focused on parents and teachers as lifelong learners?
- What do parents and teachers need to do in order to develop as adults and significantly affect children's development as well?
- How can knowledge of the ways adults learn enhance parent-teacher activities and relationships today?

AUTHOR'S NOTE: Names of parents have been changed in the stories in this chapter.

PARENTS AND TEACHERS ARE LIFELONG LEARNERS

Now that we understand the conditions that support effective parenting, we need to address the ideal methods of creating those conditions. This chapter connects theories of parenting over the lifespan within cultural context to a discussion of best practices for working with parents and caregivers of children. Kypros (1989a, 1989b) viewed best practices in educating and supporting parents through the lens of adult learning. Her research was based on the use of Heath's curriculum "Parents Planning" (revised in 2001 as "Planning"), which was created with adult development and learning in mind. Kypros was looking for an alternative to the expert approach to parents, which often does not take into consideration parent differences, such as learning abilities and needs; goals for children, values, beliefs, or sociocultural contexts. She wrote,

> Nor have they taken into consideration the parents' rich experiences in living or "their need to be treated as adults, their individual interests and needs, their ability to learn new things, their sensitivity to failure, and their need to have a variety of right answers for them to choose an approach that is useful and workable given their own situation and culture" (Landerholm, 1984). (1989a, p. 8)

Parents come with varied experiences, resources, and beliefs and cannot profit from predetermined, one-size-fits-all ideas about how to help them and their children. We can no longer assume a continuity model for parents, which would imply that parents can or will think and relate to their children similarly across time, situation, and child. We need to facilitate lifelong learning and development in parents, beginning when they become parents and continuing through their children's high school years and beyond (Simpson, 2001). As Holden and Hawk (2003) suggest, parents need opportunities to anticipate, assess, reflect, and solve problems as they adjust and modify their behavior to fit changing situations and changing relationships.

Comer, Ben-Avie, Haynes, and Joyner (1999) predicted what will happen to parents, teachers, and students if this issue is left unaddressed: "The best instructional methods, curricula, and equipment are not going to produce good outcomes in bad relationship environments, which are found most often where students, parents, and staff are all underdeveloped or unable to express their abilities and potential" (p. xiv). While parent involvement programs do not preclude learning and development, they tend to focus on capitalizing on parents to help their children in limited and unchallenged ways and sometimes with undemocratic methods of engagement. This is taking place at a time when student school success, as Comer and others (Calabrese Barton, Drake, Perez, St. Louis, & George, 2004; Coalition for Community Schools, 2003; Eisler, 2000, 2002) assert, is more about good relationships than anything else. When parents merely fill a scripted role, learning and development are often minimal (Langer, 1978; Lareau, 1989), since they require intentionality and reflection. Swick (1998) describes the parent-teacher relationship itself not as fixed but as emergent:

> Since teacher-parent partnerships are developmental in nature and best realized through a comprehensive approach, a framework for carrying out the process is essential. The following elements need close scrutiny: teacher and parent contexts, role understandings, and an appreciation of the partnership process itself. Further, a sensitivity to each other's needs, situations, and talents is a requisite basis for a viable program. (p. 2)

Bowman (1996) refers to parents as "diamonds in the rough" and says that "underneath even the most cautious guarded exterior is a person with talents, skills and dreams, looking for a place for the sparkle to emerge and be seen" (p. 27). Few preservice, faculty development, or parent involvement programs address this partnership process adequately, especially parent potential, the understanding of context, or an open discussion about roles. McDermott (1997) devised an exercise on roles and goals for parents and teachers to use before each school year to facilitate learning for both (see Table 4.1). The next question is, how, in the current school system, can we get time to use reflective exercises such as these? In some settings, such as the military schools cited at the end of Chapter 1 or preschools, time is made for such exercises without negative academic consequences for students. Often in the later grades, teachers and parents think that if they take time to reflect on what they are doing and planning to do, it is a loss to the student. The opposite is often true.

Please review the quotation from Benard at the beginning of this chapter. This is what many schools strive for. This kind of a community existed in the Fort Campbell, Kentucky, Military Base School featured on the *60 Minutes* broadcast mentioned in the summary of Chapter 1. It is not something that happens easily, especially when teachers and parents have different backgrounds and views about what children need or how to meet those needs and have not established the trust needed for good relationships.

Time to explore each other's ideas and values and to learn from them is difficult to find within the current construct of parent-school relationships and partnerships. As was seen at Fort Campbell, parents and teachers may never get to a point where everyone agrees on everything, but that is not what consensus is all about. At least these parents and teachers could understand each other's views and motivations rather than guess at what they might be, which often results in problems. They could then come to consensus, or, in other words, a solution everyone could accept even though it was not perfect for anyone.

Table 4.1   The Parent-Teacher Role Checklist

1. In the table below, please underline the ten most important roles that you feel a *parent* should assume in relationship to his or her child.
2. Please circle the ten most important roles that you feel a *teacher* should assume in relationship to the students.
3. Now, please put two checks to the left of the roles you feel *both parents and teachers* should assume.
4. Are there some roles you feel *only a parent* should assume? Please place a *P* to the left of these.
5. Are there some roles that you feel *only a teacher* should assume? Please place a *T* to the left of these.
6. Are there some roles where you feel there might be *parent-teacher conflict*? Please place a *C* to the left of these.
7. If you had to choose a role in which you feel children would profit most from *parent-teacher dialogue*, *clarification*, or *collaboration*, please put a ** to the left of this role.

Roles	
_____ 1. Meets child's physical needs	_____ 17. Observes the child
_____ 2. Meets child's safety needs	_____ 18. Facilitates child's social development
_____ 3. Meets child's emotional needs	_____ 19. Facilitates child's intellectual development
_____ 4. Plans for the child	
_____ 5. Provides a nurturing environment discipline policy	_____ 20. Makes decisions on classroom
	_____ 21. Makes decisions on curriculum
_____ 6. Sets limits	_____ 22. Makes decisions regarding hiring and firing of teachers
_____ 7. Provides disciplined	
_____ 8. Keeps busy	_____ 23. Provides child with first loving relationship
_____ 9. Is an advocate	
_____ 10. Keeps orderly	_____ 24. Provides continuity for the child
_____ 11. Encourages	_____ 25. Knowledgeable about child's uniqueness
_____ 12. Is a role model	_____ 26. Explores/investigates with child
_____ 13. Educates	_____ 27. Listens to the child
_____ 14. Transmits values	_____ 28. Is nutritionist for the child
_____ 15. Interprets the world	_____ 29. Learns from the child
_____ 16. Provides sex education	_____ 30. Facilitates the spiritual development of the child

SOURCE: From D. M. Murphy, "Parent and Teacher Plan for the Child," *Young Children, 52* (May 1997): 32–36. Reprinted with permission from the National Association for the Education of Young Children.

NOTE: This checklist can also be found on the Sage Web site for the book, www.sagepub.com/mcdermottappendices, as Appendix A1: The Parent-Teacher Role Checklist.

■ **Have We Focused on Parents and Teachers as Lifelong Learners?**

Rarely do people take the time to sit down and identify their ideas, values, and goals, as well as the meaning of certain family or school expectations, to all the parties involved. Taylor, Marienau, and Fiddler (2000) have reminded us that "unless people examine their own and others' ways of meaning-making and reaching consensus, they can be at the mercy of distorted perspectives that block communication" (p. 34). Distorted perceptions go hand in hand with mindless behavior. Often it is wrongly assumed that educators and parents either are or are not on the same page. School goals are often so general that parents do not question them or the methods for achieving them until they run into their own child's problems. Parents from some socioeconomic backgrounds would never question a school's goals even if they disagreed with them (Lareau, 1989).

CASE STUDIES EXAMINING PARENT AND TEACHER LEARNING NEEDS

Cara, an educator herself, learned this lesson personally years ago when a principal at a private school hit a boy and the boy's Vietnamese mother was very upset that Cara reported the incident. The mother feared her son would be sent to a public school, and she had never been taught to question authority. When Cara questioned the physical harm of a student, she was acting on the assumption that her school had the same ethical values she did. She assumed the school would never punish the child for her complaint. The school talked about a community of care. She learned on more than one occasion that she should rely more on asking questions up front than making assumptions without understanding the school's educational goals, philosophy, and methods. She also learned not to assume that all parents in the school shared her view of reality. We need to ask how our schools make time for teachers, parents, and administrators to discuss and understand each other's principles and assumptions about caring for children.

On a cold day in December at that same school, Terry asked her son's teacher to remind the first grader to wear his coat and face mask outside because cold air irritated his severe asthma, especially on the day of the first frost. Later Terry drove down the street, only to see her son running with his classmates to the gym in another building and wearing only shorts and a T-shirt. It was 22°F outside, not counting the wind chill! After three days in the hospital with her son and a chance to calm down, she returned to the school and asked the teacher why she had not seen to it that the boy was dressed properly. The teacher said she had to think of the good of the whole class and not delay their gym time because of Terry's son's needs. Terry suggested that if the teacher polled the other parents, she would find they saw taking the time to dress warmly as an important lesson in caring. After that interaction, the principal decided to protect her teacher from Terry and told Terry that if she did not like the school as it was, she could leave. Sarason (1995) would ask how trust and respect got lost at this particular school (p. 50). The principal saw the situation as a power and turf issue, with nothing but nonproductive struggle ahead (p. 51). We can better understand Terry's experience through reading Vincent's description (1996) of parents like her, "offered 'exit' but not 'voice'; that is, the chance to leave a school but not to participate in its development (Hirschman, 1970; Ball, 1987)" (p. 12). Terry had to find a more caring and safe school for her son and give up on trying to change what she saw as a closed system. Everyone has different ideas about how to meet children's needs. Some schools have strict rules about the minimum length of classes. If this was the case in Terry's situation, the teacher and principal did not communicate its importance effectively. Certainly, hearing everyone's ideas and values was not a priority.

Cushman (1998) reminds educators that while we enjoy an abundance of innovative methods for enhancing student involvement in learning, they are not being applied to parents or teachers in school reform efforts: "'The process is simple,' says Dan Rothstein. . . . it requires a shift from the habit of delivering information to parents towards facilitating inquiry.'. . . Simple it may be, yet educators' commitment to the habits of inquiry often stops at the schoolhouse door, notes Seymour Sarason in his book *Parental Involvement and the Political Principle* (Jossey-Bass, 1995)" (p. 2). These school reformers encourage parents and teachers to search for answers as they learn together, but traditional definitions of parent-teacher partnerships make this mutuality hard to accomplish. This kind of inquiry was seen in Terry's son's school and others like it as a threat to the power structure and as too time consuming.

Traditional ways to involve parents have in fact included learning, but the typical methods don't include approaches such as reflective inquiry (Sarason, 1995). Parent learning usually involves literacy training, how to help with homework, or how to be cooperative parents. There is little opportunity to inquire, or as Suchman (1972) describes inquiry, to gather and process data and test hypotheses, such as Terry's belief that parents would prefer children to care more about each other's health than about their minutes in gym class. Inquiry is also consistent with an adult learner's autonomy needs. *Autonomy* is related to being able to make choices. Kypros (1989b) adds, "The *inductive reasoning* used in this method of learning allows the learner to begin with his own particular life problem and situation and move outward seeking data and resources in order to assimilate the new experience or to accommodate conceptual structures so that the new experience fits in" (p. 208).

In addition, like children, adults learn well in climates that minimize anxiety and encourage experimentation (Daloz, 1986). Terry was not allowed to ask other parents how they felt about children's having time to put their winter clothes on before going outside. She wanted to think mindfully about the situation, whereas the teacher refused to consider a different solution. McCaleb's description (1994) of what often happens in schools is informative:

> Many of the existing family education programs follow a "transmission of school practices model" (Auerbach, 1990, p. 17) in which knowledge is transmitted from teachers to children and from the schools to parents to children. The following practices were noted as the most prevalent in these transmission model programs.
>
> 1. Giving parents guidelines, materials, and training to carry out school-like activities in the home.
> 2. Training parents in effective parenting.
> 3. Teaching parents about the culture of American schooling.
> 4. Developing parent language and literacy through skills, grammar, and behavioral approaches.
>
> Parents are taught to accommodate to the schools, but the schools are not expected to accommodate to the families' cultural diversity or lived reality. (pp. 7–8)

With all the challenges that required high-stakes testing presents, many ask, who can find the time to accommodate families?

Schools announce in letters, orientation meetings, and school handbooks that parents are expected to learn about school practices without filtering them through their own feelings, values, and goals. Graue (1998) notes that "the model is set out in terms of what parents can do to support the efforts of their children through agendas directed by the school. . . . As it stands now the schools get to decide who needs to be saved and the nature of the story line" (pp. 5–6, 12). Of course, when thinking of teachers and principals, one could add that departments of education get to write much of the script. Sarason (1995) adds that because of the way school systems are structured, teachers are often in the same position as parents relative to school administration: "outsiders who are looking and wanting in, while a 'superior' tells them what to do" (p. 32). How can things improve?

IMPROVING PARENT-SCHOOL ENGAGEMENT AND LEARNING

One needs to look not only at today's social context but at some theories of adult learning to better understand resistance to currently defined school involvement

expectations by parents and teachers and resistance from teachers to new government mandates. What do educators know about the way adults respond best to
information? Below are some basic principles underlying *andragogy,* or the art
and science of helping adults learn (Knowles, 1980). These principles are also
summarized nicely in Merriam and Caffarella (1999). It must be noted that not all
these principles have been tested in culturally diverse settings. Some clearly
appear to be more likely to fit within individualist societies than within more collectivist societies. Brookfield (1995) adds that it is not simply age but rather many
other variables, including social class, culture, ethnicity, personality, cognitive
thinking style, gender, and life experiences, that predict how one learns best.
Nevertheless, these principles contribute helpfully to the information we need if
we are to support parents and teachers as lifelong learners.

1. Adults learn more effectively through *experiential techniques of education
such as discussion and immediate problem solving* than from directives or lecturing (Florin & Dokecki, 1983; Knowles, 1980). Adults often wish to be able to
apply new learning or skills to their own immediate circumstances. Adults may
prefer to have these discussions within small, culturally homogeneous groups
rather than in large groups (DeBord & Reguero de Atiles, 1999).

2. Adults have *rich experience to draw on and integrate* to enhance learning for
themselves and those around them (Brookfield, 1987; Frieri, 1970; Kolb, 1999;
McCaleb, 1994).

3. If an adult is expected to learn something, the instructors must discern that
person's *readiness to learn* (Belenky, Clinchy, Goldberger, & Tarule, 1986/1997;
Knowles, 1980). Merriam and Caffarella (1999) would add that readiness to learn
is closely linked to the person's developmental tasks and social roles.

4. Adults learn best when a *listening-dialogue-(critical thinking)-action process*
is involved (Brookfield, 1987; First & Way, 1995; Frieri, 1970; Mezirow, 1990).
What does *critical thinking* involve? Brookfield (1987) describes critical thinkers as
follows: They engage actively with life, are creative, appreciate diversity, and see
many possibilities in life. Indeed, parental thinking has often been described as more
art than science (see Figure 4.1). Furthermore, critical thinkers continually question
assumptions and discard inappropriate assumptions. They consider context. Critical
thinking happens in positive or negative situations, and it may sometimes cause
inner discomfort and confusion. It is emotional as well as rational. It involves both
imagining and exploring options, as well as reflection leading to new understanding
of self and others (pp. 7–9). Hurtig (2005) demonstrated this process beautifully
with Mexican mothers in inner-city Chicago, as will be seen in Chapter 5.

Figure 4.1   Parenting Is an Art

SOURCE: Copyright © King Features Syndicate.

5. Adults' learning is enhanced when they have opportunities to *interact with peers* during the learning process (Brookfield, 1986; Brufee, 1993).

6. Many adults, though temporarily dependent on others for guidance, in many situations want to move toward *self-directedness* in their learning and actions (Knowles, 1980; Maslow, 1970; Merriam & Caffarella, 1999). This may be especially true for subjects about which adults feel very passionate, such as their child's well-being. Brookfield (1995) suggests that self-directedness may be more valued in individualistic societies and interdependence more valued in collectivist societies. He notes, for example, that "for the Hmong tribes people from the mountains of Laos who are used to working cooperatively and to looking to their teachers for direction and guidance, ways of working that emphasize self-directedness and that place the locus of control with the individual student will be experienced, initially at least, as dissonant and anxiety producing (Podeschi, 1990)" (p. 378). The meaning of self-directedness for the parents with whom one works must be understood first. It may be that what many adult parents desire in the long run is an ability to make some choices for themselves and their children in terms of what they are learning.

7. Adults often like to *plan their own learning experiences* (Belenky et al., 1986/1997; Brookfield, 1987; Kolb, 1984). All this applies to many teachers as well. For people from cultures in which planning one's own learning is not valued or relevant, this expectation may initially be stressful.

8. We also know from Bloom (1956) that the cognitive domains of learning involving *receiving, comprehending, applying, analyzing, synthesizing,* and *evaluating*

information rarely produce behavioral change unless learners can filter this information through the affective domains of their own beliefs, feelings, and value systems (see also Kypros, 1989a, 1989b).

The *affective domain* includes *attending to stimuli* (awareness, willingness to hear, selective attention), *responding to stimuli* (in terms of either compliance, willingness to respond, or a real satisfaction in responding, often referred to as motivation), *valuing* or *being committed to a phenomenon* (ranging from acceptance to real commitment and all that entails), *organizing a value system* (contrasting different values, resolving conflicting values, and creating one's own unique value system), and *being characterized by a specific value system* (internalizing a pervasive, consistent, and predictable value system unique to the adult learner) (Krathwohl, Bloom, & Masia, 1964). If the levels of the affective domain are not engaged, people will not go beyond the first level of learning, which is merely receiving basic information. This point is very important. Many parents and teachers are merely given information, and so they remain at the receiving stage. They do not have a chance to think about and discuss how the school's directives mesh with their own ideas and goals and what they believe children need. They end up consciously or unconsciously resisting what is asked of them.

Kypros (1989a, 1989b), using a parenting program that does justice to these complex learning functions, compared two groups: 23 first-time mothers enrolled in a 7-week program (based on Heath, 2001) that took a holistic approach to parent learning and development and included affective and cognitive skills training, and 19 control group mothers, who did not receive this training. After the training, mothers in the holistic program displayed significantly more "higher order thinking skills," such as application and analysis (specifically, the ability to set personal goals and identify values and then filter all educational information through this lens), than the control group did. The goal was to enhance their ability to be autonomous learners. In the chapters that follow, we will see how this same curriculum has been used with other parents of school-age children to achieve similar goals.

It is suggested that parents and teachers learn best if they have time to think about a school directive with school representatives or others, look at alternatives, make a commitment to the best one, and then personalize it. The degree of commitment to a behavior is often related to the degree to which a person has incorporated it into his or her value system (Beaver, 1983, as cited in Kypros, 1989a). Many parents and teachers do not value teaching with the sole goal of enabling children to pass a test, which accounts for many complaints about and low levels of commitment to the No Child Left Behind mandates. In fact, many school initiatives are unsuccessful because this complex process of parent engagement is bypassed.

9. Adult learning is enhanced when adults can effectively use the following learning strategies: *assess, collaborate, experiment, imagine, inquire, perform-simulate,* and *reflect* (Taylor et al., 2000). In Part II, we will see many examples of these activities put into practice within a model school. Think of these strategies in terms of the current formula for parent involvement and Terry's experience as a parent, described earlier. In her case, the teacher and principal were not prepared to partner with her on this type of journey, and she was so used to it, as an educator herself, that she was thrown back by their resistance. Where could one possibly begin to undo this situation? Wheatley (2002) has many suggestions in her book *Turning to One Another.* She describes adult conversations in which people listen to each other and feel heard. There is a way to imagine a better world for children, students, parents, and teachers and to share fears, hopes, and concerns.

These types of dialogues have taken place within schools of education and child and family studies programs. Courses on parenting have been developed for future teachers, school and pastoral counselors, psychologists, community psychologists, nurses, parent educators, and administrators. The courses are structured so that instructors and students can utilize all the learning strategies we have discussed, as well as mindful learning. The students could imagine what a caring school or community would look like. They could also reflect on what the obstacles to parent-professional partnerships are and what their own beliefs are in regard to child, teacher, and parent needs and roles. They could experiment, through internships and volunteer work, with different ways of relating. Rather than resignation to the status quo, the professionals taking these courses experienced a sense of an active action plan and optimism.

10. Finally, adults are more motivated to turn their learning into action if it is internalized and *comes from within rather than from external sources* (Brookfield, 1986; Merriam & Caffarella, 1999). The fields of parenting education and family support have advanced through this concept of *empowerment.* Bowman (1996) reminds everyone that empowerment is not something that can be given by those in authority but is something that must be taken. Often prep work is necessary before some parents can act on the resources they have within. Working with parents (as educators have discovered about working with students; Kohn, 1999) is not about directing, lecturing, rewarding, or punishing but about supporting learning. While some might be cynical of these new, often overused terms like *coaching* or *empowering,* many have found them very helpful.

Flaherty (1999) noted, "Coaching is a way of working with people that leaves them not dependent but more competent and fulfilled so they are able to contribute to their families, work and communities and find meaning in what they are doing" (p. 9). Many parents personally never find meaning in encouraging their children to do homework that seems to be busy work. They need an explanation of how it will help meet relevant goals for their child's learning. Then they will be more inclined to support teacher efforts.

Flaherty and many others have observed that it is not always just the events or communications from schools or governments that lead people to resist; often it is the interpretation or meaning people give to these things. This constructivist perspective has face validity for teachers. What meaning do parents and teachers see in another person's expecting them to do something that they are unable or unmotivated to do (such as math homework in the case of parents or student-parent counseling in the case of teachers)? How do they feel about these expectations? Teachers can help parents explore these dilemmas.

Christopher, Dunnagan, Duncan, and Paul (2001) found that parents (and I would add teachers, administrators, and other helping professionals) need an opportunity to *critically reassess current perspectives* and think about whether a current behavior is right for them. Robertson (1996) described this approach as learner centered, promoting autonomy, reflection, participation, and collaboration. He also found another important component of adult learning: a new understanding about the way social relations and culture have shaped one's beliefs and feelings. Therefore, rather than telling parents that homework is good for their children, educators could facilitate a dialogue on the meaning of homework to a teacher, a school, a child, and the child's family and community.

All these adult learning principles need to be considered as we evaluate parent education support and programming in schools. Is there room for parents to bring their own goals, values, and experiences into the learning or school activity? Is there room for parents and teachers to think critically? To imagine, inquire, and reflect? Is there room to interact with peers, apply learning, and share reflections and evaluations of the process? What is the parent's readiness to learn? It is suggested that schools use these principles to assess current parent activities and to plan future ones with, of course, the involvement of parents.

CONNECTING ADULT LEARNING AND ADULT DEVELOPMENT

As Merriam and Caffarella (1999) noted above, parents' readiness to learn is often related to their developmental tasks and roles.

■ What Do Parents and Teachers Need to Do in Order to Develop as Adults and Significantly Affect Children's Development as Well?

Certainly, we need to help parents link their own ideas, beliefs, and feelings about their roles and about children. The parent involvement literature speaks little about trying to help parents and teachers better understand how their beliefs, feelings, and past and current situations might relate to their experience of helping children. If the focus is on transmission of information alone, there is little chance the result will be changed behavior for adults or good outcomes for children. What is needed is a transformative learning experience for parents and teachers that can be beneficial both to their children and to them as growing adults, especially if we have *developmental intentions* for the adults we serve, which means focusing not only on learners' ideas but on their feelings, perceptions, and actions (Taylor et al., 2000, p. 23).

What if a teacher is asked to "parent" a child? What if she feels she does not even have time to parent her own children well? What if a mother is so beaten down by her boyfriend that she feels she has nothing to offer anyone at school? What if all she can think about is her child's safety and her own or getting some sleep? Few professionals are trained adequately to look at parent perceptions and situations even though it has been found that parental self-awareness, self-development, and learning are very important work for adults and often must precede helping their children (Belenky et al., 1997; Duncan, 1998; Holden, 1997; Newberger, 1980; Rogers, 1973; Weikart, 1980).

Researchers for the National Extension Parent Education Model (Smith, Cudaback, Goddard, & Myers-Wall, 1994) found,

> In many cases, these self-care concerns must be addressed before a parent can begin to concentrate on the child and the behaviors more directly related to parenthood. . . . Caring for oneself is not only a critical parenting skill, but also a skill for life. Critical care for self practices are: manage personal stress, manage family resources, offer support to other parents, ask for and accept support from others when needed, recognize one's own personal and parenting strengths, have a sense of purpose in setting child-rearing goals, and cooperate with one's child-rearing partners. (p. 20)

Imagine how overworked teachers would respond to parents who do not seem to be helping their children but who say they need more time to care for themselves. Teachers signed up to educate children and often are unprepared to face the fact that not all parents are ready, willing, or able to support their efforts. On top of that, teachers are asked to teach parents child rearing or to parent their children. Many think these tasks should not be expected of teachers. One model described in Part II involves having a credentialed parenting educator in each school (ideally a full-service school) or each local school district to support parents and school staff in the complex and difficult situations they face in caring for children as well as their own lifelong learning and developmental needs. If a parenting educator is not feasible, then staff should be trained and credentialed for that role. Furthermore, theories and methods of parent-teacher engagement and development should be a required course for all teachers and professionals working with parents, not just a preservice elective. The success of parenting educators or other professionals trained in this role depends on their collaborations with school staff open to new paradigms or ways of relating to families.

The goal of education and support in parenting and caring is *self-generation* for parents, teachers, and all who care for children: the ability to locate the resources within themselves and in relationships that would allow for continuous growth (Belsky, 1984; Flaherty, 1999; Rogers, 1973). A parenting and family life educator in a school or agency setting can provide information and support, help with the practice of new skills and language, help with reflection, provide opportunities to learn from others, and offer encouragement and respect for all efforts and viewpoints always. Many have applied this approach of reflective practice to mentoring youth, but few have applied it yet to working with parents who are also still developing and deserve this kind of support.

Many educators have been encouraged (see Florin & Dokecki, 1983) to change the initial focus of their work with parents from child centered to parent centered in order to enhance adult development, which is needed to facilitate a good child outcome. Changing focus is also a characteristic of mindful learning. The job of the parenting or family life educator as defined by Florin and Dokecki more than two decades ago was to be a resource to help families assess their needs and become active problem solvers engaged in their own development as well as the development of their children. Although the value of parenting education is well documented (see Erikson, 1968; Galinsky, 1987; McBride, 1973; Newman & Newman, 1988; Weikart, 1980), it is not even on the radar screen at most schools of education and federal or state educational institutions.

Preschool educators (Coleman & Churchill, 1997; Galinsky & David, 1988; Gestwicki, 1999, 2003; Kypros, 1989a, 1989b; Powell, 1998), who often focus on child development more than other educators do, seem to understand that parents have their own learning and developmental needs that must be appreciated, acknowledged, and met. With young dependent children, teachers are often very invested in engaging parents to help. Gestwicki (1999) told future teachers, "Personal development is a lifelong process. . . . Parents concerned with nurturing their children's development are also encountering growth in their own lives" (p. 41). She also points up the emotional dimension of parenting, the numerous roles parenting entails, and the problematic feelings of isolation, fatigue, guilt, and uncertainty that most parents (and I would add teachers) experience. The stresses parents face in modern living can pose obstacles to their growth.

Depressed parents and those with mental health problems or persistent worries about safety and daily living often have a hard time focusing on child needs (Lovejoy, Graczyk, O'Hare, & Neuman, 2000). Gestwicki (1999, 2003) and others

(Coleman & Churchill, 1997; McDermott, 1997) encourage early childhood educators to appreciate the perspective of parents and work to identify roles for parents and themselves that enhance both adult and student learning and growth. (Gestwicki addresses preschool teachers and focuses on early intervention.) Yet many other books for teachers still repeat the traditional complaints about parent overinvolvement, hostility, and indifference without exploring biological, psychological, and societal causes or contexts of these feelings and behaviors.

Garbarino and Bedard (2001), however, in *Parents Under Siege,* wrote, "Parents are afraid and confused, bombarded with contradictory advice from the Right and the Left, blamed if their children turn out screwed up, and swinging between hysterical overreaction and numbed resignation. Parents need compassion based on understanding" (p. 10). We can say the very same thing for teachers and other helping professionals.

IMPORTANCE OF PARENT AND TEACHER DEVELOPMENT

Nowadays we discuss human development concerns, including personal, social, emotional, and intellectual development, more than we used to, but most often as they relate to students. Haynes and Comer (1996) see healthy child development as the keystone to academic achievement and life success. The very successful Comer School Model, involving parents in planning and supporting child development in schools, addresses parent development, especially the self-confidence that comes from being part of a school-community effort for children, and parent opportunities for leadership and learning. Comer Schools, with their equitable, no-fault approach, help parent-teacher collaborations be a win-win situation. The Comer Home-School Coordinators build trust; involve parents, via breakfasts and other gatherings, to give input on school goals; and bring them and teachers to workshops at universities and other institutions so that both are learning together.

Understanding parents is an important component of this model school and the work of Heckman (1996), McCaleb (1994), and McEwan (1998). More educators need to perceive the different learning and growth needs of parents and teachers as normal and worthy of focus in their own right, because we are all lifelong learners, not finished products. Then we must convince policymakers that supporting parent-teacher learning and growth is not only necessary but also the quickest route to student success. This issue is addressed in Chapter 8.

Comer (2001) summarized his important insights in an article titled "Schools That Develop Children." This concept of development has carried educators beyond teaching and into focusing on the whole person. Some feel this expectation may be too much for schools (de Carvalho, 2001). Certainly the academic focus of No Child Left Behind has the potential of leaving no child whole (Meier, Kohn,

Darling-Hammond, Sizer, & Wood, 2004; Merrow, 2002). We need to transform schools and communities into places that develop teachers and parents by discovering how to focus on them as whole persons as well. Comer hopes adults will be able to understand child development and to facilitate it in children. Others believe teachers need to learn about adult development as well as child development in their training. Taylor et al. (2000) define *adult development* as "a process of qualitative change in attitudes, values and understandings that adults experience as a result of ongoing transactions with the social environment occurring over time but not strictly as a result of time" (p. 10). Without opportunity for inquiry, collaboration, reflection, and dialogue, it is hard to imagine this happening for any of the adults in children's lives.

For decades, some educators in graduate schools of education have been teaching courses on the development of parents over the lifespan and parenting in cultural context. In course assessments, students have rated these courses very highly in terms of transformational learning. The developmental tasks of identity and generativity for adults are specifically addressed in these courses. In my own interdisciplinary graduate course on parenting over the lifespan, students are amazed at the complexity of the parenting process. They also have an opportunity to think about their own ideas and beliefs about parent-child relations and how they may be at odds with the ideas and beliefs of the parents they will or do serve, as recommended by Graue and Brown (2003). Concrete examples of this process are provided in Chapter 5.

In *Child-Centered, Family Sensitive Schools: An Educator's Guide to Family Dynamics,* family therapist Garanzini (1995) described how a child's complex family context influences learning and development. He fills some of the void in teacher education with information about various adult situations and family structures that can function well but often do not. The book helps teachers understand dysfunctional families and the obstacles to parent and student growth. However, rather than the more typical focus on dysfunction in families, the family development and family strengths approach (Coleman & Churchill, 1997; Walsh, 2002) is much needed in schools struggling with rising violence and decreasing resources.

Comer et al. (1999) do support family strengths and work to facilitate good parent-teacher-student relationships. "The Family Interactive Center helps families to understand the society that they live in and to understand the practices that support their children's education" (p. 49). While child focused, this initiative suggests the need for reflective inquiry for parents and also includes a set of principles for teachers to consider:

- All children can learn
- Teachers make a difference
- Growth as a teacher requires inquiry and reflection

- Teachers are models of educated citizens
- Learning is a life-long responsibility
- There is power in collaboration (p. 281)

As we envision the next decade in education, we can see that these important principles for teachers also can apply to parents because they also can make a difference, are still learning, and need opportunities for reflection and inquiry if they are to grow. They also need societal support, as do teachers. Garbarino and Bedard (2001) assert,

> The essential point . . . is that the child development equation includes a constantly shifting and evolving interplay of the child's biology and the parents' actions, and both are influenced by other children and adults, culture, institutions, and history. The success or failure of parenting depends in large part upon the difficulties posed by the children and by the degree to which the social environment is toxic and hostile to children and parents, as opposed to healthy and supportive. (p. 26)

Schools can make an even more positive difference than they already do. In the spirit of the theory-to-practice theme of this book, a workshop for practitioners in schools and agencies and for parents, designed to help everyone grapple with the information shared in this chapter, is provided in Appendix B1: Parents as Adult Learners Workshop—Deconstructing Parent Involvement. It is available on the Sage Web site for this book (www.sagepub.com/mcdermottappendices). Think about using it in your classes or school settings. The appendix provides specific examples and includes the rationale for the methodology.

PARENT-TEACHER LEARNING AND DEVELOPMENT COLLABORATIONS

■ How Can Knowledge of the Ways Adults Learn Enhance Parent-Teacher Activities and Relationships Today?

Based on adult learning principles, parents are part of the process, not just passive recipients of lectures or school directives. The list below provides some examples of what has been happening in programs in Chicago and around the country and the world. (Feedback from teachers and parents about the meaning and effectiveness of many of these programs is provided in Chapter 8.)

- Instead of just going to a school open house at the beginning of the school year to find out what the teacher will be doing in the coming year, parents and teachers meet either at the end or prior to the beginning of a school year to plan ahead. Both discuss their hopes and concerns about individual children and the class as a whole. The teacher may have learned the children are having trouble with math concepts. A parent and the teacher may be concerned that bullying is on the rise in the class and affects a particular child. A parent might feel inadequate to help with the math but could do something with other parents about the bullying. The teacher and the parent make a plan for supporting each other. Then the first difficulties with math or bullying don't come as a surprise and may even be prevented. Communication and ownership of hopes, concerns, and solutions are shared from the beginning.

• In a model development school described in Part II, instead of teachers' deciding on speakers, each grade's parents and teachers were asked by parent leaders to list what they wanted to discuss or learn more about. Parents in one elementary school decided the issue of competition versus caring was very important. A few parents and teachers took the lead and, with the help of the parenting educator at the school, found and photocopied some good readings on the topic for all who wanted to read materials in advance and then had a meeting open to all parents to discuss the topic. Because some parents prefer listening and talking to reading, the articles were not a prerequisite for attending. One of the teachers in this school had already brought the topic to her 12th-grade psychology class, and these students made presentations to all the parents about their feelings about competition. The issue was then discussed in faculty meetings, the school chose a book on the topic for all faculty to read over the summer, and it also brought the author to the school to discuss the topic with parents and teachers. The parent educator discussed the same book with parents in small groups.

• In many schools, teachers give class assignments that involve students' interviewing their parents and families to make their experiences, customs, and traditions the subject matter in school. Even if parents cannot read, they can tell their stories and have them be valued and recorded by the school and the students. Children still learn skills, but they learn them in terms of meaningful content. Family culture would be seen as meaningful. As noted earlier, Hurtig (2005) has described the powerful impact of parent writing groups and the magazines created by parents at Telpochcalli ("house of youth") elementary school in Chicago. This bilingual, biliterate small school in Chicago celebrates the history, art, and culture of Mexico and encourages children to bring that experience in as a starting point for learning. The magazines are placed in every classroom library. In kindergarten and first grade, teachers often use the stories for literacy activities.

• Parents have also participated in family reading nights, in which the parents' stories are a focus of the night's activities. Some parents read their stories at school fund-raisers, at community functions, and throughout the city in educational forums and university-community partnership meetings. Teachers have encouraged students to engage with the parent writers for other projects. For instance, for a seventh-grade research project on immigrant communities, the group of students studying Mexican immigrants used the magazine stories as a resource and interviewed the parent writers.

- In Chapters 5 and 8, the ways these stories furthered the development of the mothers are described. Through the stories, the mothers became strong and influential leaders improving their schools and communities. They serve as a model for how schools and communities can support parents as lifelong learners and find a way for them to be involved in their children's schools and communities in ways that are consistent with their own goals and developmental tasks.

- In other schools, parents, teachers, and students all read the same book and have book discussions. This has been done in a high school with a book on globalization and global citizenship and in an elementary school with a book on gender issues, and both programs were very successful.

- In the Comer Schools, parents and teachers go to workshops together to learn about new technology, emotional intelligence, standards, and more. Some parents and teachers learn about such topics as temperament and then use that information to see how it might inform their goodness of fit or lack thereof with their children or students.

- In some schools, parents and teachers meet or complete a survey to identify their goals and values for children (see Chapters 5 and 6). Rather than just receive a student handbook, they reflect on their goals and see where they have consensus and where they differ, even in terms of what statements in a handbook mean. These activities are about more than receiving information. They are about analyzing it, synthesizing it, evaluating it, and filtering it through their beliefs and values.

- In many schools, teachers who are fathers meet with students' fathers to discuss the role of father in the 21st century. Other topics for all might be finding time for family rituals and traditions or transitioning during divorce, family illness, or a move.

- In some schools, parents, teachers, and students work with the community on a project in the neighborhood, such as working with the neighborhood church, the local university, and the park district of the city to build a garden in an inner-city neighborhood. People of all ages take on the roles of teacher and learner, and community building is powerful.

Photo by Dana McDermott.

Loyola University professor and Sophia Garden community advisory board member take their granddaughter to this city garden maintained by students, teachers, and community volunteers.

All these projects illustrate the idea that parent-teacher-student relationships are dynamic, not static. Everyone is embedded within a society and a time that often make it difficult for anyone to learn and grow. Often teachers and parents do not spend enough time together to really understand each other and learn from each other. It will be much easier to teach children about the important concepts of respect and relationship building if people can experience and model it themselves.

SUMMARY

In this chapter, some of the key principles for adult learning have been reviewed and linked to the less-often-discussed topic of adult development in homes, schools, and communities. The relationships between adult learning and development and the eventual success of children are also described. I hope this chapter gives us a glimpse of what schools as learning communities for everyone involved would look like in reality.

Photo by Hartwig Stein.

Children, teachers, and community volunteers plant vegetables and flowers and include their own artwork in this urban garden.

Some Activities and Questions for Investigation, Reflection, and Action

Think

1. Read more about the author(s) in this chapter whose theories or research you find most insightful or relevant to your own work. Describe the aspect of adult learning or development they address and how it might apply to your own work.

Reflect

2. Take time to record in your journal. Look at the list of ways to facilitate adult learning. Can you identify which you have been able to do in your own current adult educational experience and how that has affected your learning?

(Continued)

(Continued)

Plan

3. Complete the exercise on parent and teacher roles in Table 4.1 or in Appendix A1: The Parent-Teacher Role Checklist, and give it to another school parent and a teacher you know. What did you learn?

4. Share some or all the activities in the Parents as Adult Learners Workshop (Appendix B1) on the Sage Web site with a small group of parents, teachers, or school administrators. What did you learn, and how might it inform the theory put forth in this chapter?

5. Imagine that you have just been put on a planning committee for parent education activities for the year. What kind of "mindful" questions might you ask of the coplanner, who is a parent wanting to bring in two guest speakers for lectures during the year?

Chapter 5

UNDERSTANDING CULTURALLY DIVERSE PARENTS AND TEACHERS

Often our idea of cultural competence is understanding families so we can change them, so they are more like us, and that's not what cultural competence is all about. . . . We really need to be aware of our tendency to attribute our personal motivations to the behavior of others. . . . As a family support professional [cultural competence] is the ability to understand the effect of culture on child rearing and family relationships, and the ability to tailor my behavior accordingly. At the organizational level, it has to do with inclusion, responsiveness and equity. . . . This emphasis includes acknowledging the contribution of all people, the celebration of differences, the recognition of similarities, and a clear commitment to seeing differences as differences not deficits."

—Blanca Almonte (1995/1996, p. 5)

Some of the questions this chapter addresses:

- How do professionals working with families become culturally competent?

- What do professionals need to do personally before they can understand the diverse families they serve?

- What other factors, such as education, home or work environment, or social class, should professionals be aware of that might interact with a family's culture to predict parent behavior?

- How can schools learn more effectively from culturally diverse families?

Cultural issues are addressed throughout this book, not simply in this chapter. However, having put forth the theoretical and research findings on the parenting process and on the needs of parents as lifelong learners, such as the need to bring in their own experiences and engage in critical reflections, it is very important to extend the discussion to take into account different cultural contexts.

In this chapter, the dynamic nature of culture is discussed first. Suggestions are put forth as to how educators should learn about the diversity within and among the families with whom they work. We will discuss concepts such as the content and quality of parents' ideas about their own roles and about children. Then you will have an opportunity to ask yourselves a series of questions about your ideas and beliefs concerning parents, children, and families that all professionals working with families should ask themselves. Some of these questions may be especially helpful with particular parents. These include questions about parents' beliefs about children, children's needs, and child rearing. Other questions focus on parents' goals, preferred behavioral practices, and the impact of the environment on parents.

WHAT IS CULTURAL CONTEXT?

■ How Do Professionals Working With Families Become Culturally Competent?

Effective teaching and family support involve trying to understand a particular person's or audience's complex cultural background while at the same time not denying the uniqueness of that person or group. The goal is *cultural pluralism,* which is "the notion that groups should be allowed, even encouraged to hold onto what gives them their unique identities while maintaining their membership in the larger social framework" (Gonzalez-Mena, 1997, p. 9).

A Practitioner's Reflection

To address this challenge in my own work and to prepare to teach a graduate course titled Parenting in Cultural Context, I read about cultural competence (e.g., Bavolek, 1997; Lipson, Dibble, & Minarik, 1996; Greenfield & Suzuki, 1998; Lynch & Hanson, 1998, 2004; Family Resource Coalition, 1995–1996) and reread a wonderful book titled *Development According to Parents,* by Goodnow and Collins (1990). I now have more questions than before and few easy answers.

I also reflected on my own experience as a parent trying to integrate the beliefs from my Scottish, Irish, and Italian traditions with rearing my children in North America. I learned that one's culture should be seen as a resource for growth, not simply a static reference or historical fact. Culture is a dynamic, changing system. Just reading about history and traditions isn't enough. Those we serve continue to cocreate their cultures. We need to look for *meaning:* the meaning of people's behavior in terms of their cultural background as well as their developing cultural identity. We also must think about *diversity within diversity,* or the complexity of an evolving cultural identity affected by the immigration experience (is the parent a refugee or here in search of adventure, a better life, or something else?), socioeconomic status, rural versus urban experience, level of trauma, possible unresolved grief, spirituality, religious practices and traditions, and gender, to name just a few factors. We must not see parents as cultural stereotypes. We must look at history, but it will help us understand only a part of their cultural context.

As Cross (1995/1996, pp. 2–7) noted, we must think about the parents' cultural group's history with the current mainstream culture in which they live. For many, this history includes years of systematic oppression; for others it includes genocide and having children taken away from their families and placed in government boarding schools; for some it means wars, boundary changes, and changed status in one's own country of origin; for yet others it means exclusion laws and discrimination. In addition to considering the impact of these past experiences on a parent, we must honor the significant contributions made by each cultural group to the mainstream culture through the strength and courage of facing these hardships. We must learn history to inform present and future relationships, not to stereotype others. A parent at the Telpochcalli School described why she became part of a parent writing group:

> We write our stories so that our children—some of them born here—will know where they come from and what their roots are. We also write so that our children realize the effort and sacrifice we have to make as parents to make the decision to come to an unknown country, with a different language and lifestyle; and so that they understand everything we have to confront to survive and obtain a better quality of life than that which we had in our country. (Hurtig, 2005, p. 257)

To learn more about diverse parents, we educators and practitioners must spend time with strong, healthy people of their cultures as well as with parents who do not have the same personal resources. We cannot rely on the media, an occasional workshop, or our own perceptions or experiences of persons of a particular culture. Cultural guides willing to help people understand what they see should also be engaged. Literature (both nonfiction and fiction) by persons of different cultural backgrounds is another important element in this process, as are cultural events of the parents and families served. As Cross notes, seeing values and leadership in action in parents and families is essential. Finally, we must learn how to ask questions in sensitive ways. Those we ask would be considered experts in their own experience, not representatives of a whole group. The parents of a particular cultural group may be very different from one another in terms of their personalities, their urban or rural background, and their degree of *acculturation* (adjusting behavior according to the rules of a new culture without giving up the identity and customs of their culture of origin) or *assimilation* (taking on the identity and customs of the dominant culture). And I would hope that educators won't forget the history and legacy of North Americans like Jane Addams, who worked tirelessly to preserve the diverse cultural identities of immigrants like my own grandfathers, who came to Chicago decades ago and found people at Hull House to support them.

Many are uncomfortable with books about the way Latinos or African Americans tend to act or feel about things. It is much more helpful to learn about various cultural groups to broaden one's thinking and know the range of possible parent contexts, beliefs, and behaviors for every parent. Then we can avoid defaulting to our own beliefs regarding proper parenting. Building on Goodnow and Collins (1990; Goodnow, 2002) and other research cited in this book, I developed the questions in the next section to help parents think about aspects of their beliefs, roles, and relationships. I hope they can be a useful resource in the educator's ongoing search for cultural competence.

TERMS AND QUESTIONS THAT AID OUR UNDERSTANDING

Many find it helps to focus on the content and quality of parents' ideas. By ideas, Goodnow and Collins (1990) mean parents' thinking, but they do not exclude the actions and feelings associated with those ideas. They explain that *content* has to do with the substance of parents' ideas (in all cultures, we can look at parents' goals or standards for their children). For example, they found in one set of studies that the emphasis in child rearing for Japanese parents tended to be on "setting the child on a proper course." They found further that "Japanese writers thought educational intervention to be necessary to keep the autonomously developing child on the morally right course from the standpoint of adult society" (p. 22). They needed parental practices that guided the child in the right direction and encouraged self-regulation in the maintenance of that direction. On the basis of this research example, we can ask any parent, do you believe your child needs adult guidance in developing self-regulation? In addition, many cultures see children as being born independent and needing to become interdependent and socially responsible (Holden & Ritchie, 1988), which is different from the view of many Western societies that children need to become more independent over time.

Quality, according to Goodnow and Collins (1990), "refers to characteristics that may cut across content: characteristics such as the degree of certainty and openness to change, the degree of accuracy or elaboration, the degree of interweaving with other ideas, or the degree of consistency between verbal statements and other actions" (p. 9), and the degree of agreement between a child's parents. This takes on special significance if people are in a new environment. My Italian immigrant grandfather Donato often spoke of being the "boss." In Italy, his family relations were quite hierarchical, and children had to fit into the adults' activities (see, e.g., New, 1988). In fact, in his own actions (more than his words), he deferred to my grandmother and his Americanized children and grandchildren to make many family decisions and was open to being influenced by them. Changed behavior can precede verbalized ideology or follow it. For example, in my work in Chicago with fathers in the 1980s and 1990s, upper-class fathers talked about changed family roles more than they actually took on new roles, whereas poor fathers did not "talk the talk," but because of their wives' need to work while the children were home, these men were actually redefining their own fathering in their actions.

Ideas Regarding Directions of Child Development. These questions cover parents' goals, expectations, and timetable of change in terms of stages or phases of a child's development. Goodnow and Collins (1990) propose we ask the following questions:

> Is childhood seen as a time to be endured until one reaches the pleasures of adulthood . . . ? Or is it a time to be enjoyed, a period of relative license before one takes up the inevitable hardships of adulthood? "Let them play while they can," in effect or, in the words of a Lebanese born mother in Australia, commenting on whether her 10-year old daughter had any specific household tasks: "Why should she? She'll get lumbered with them soon enough." (p. 26)

Think about the usual school advice that giving children chores is a good thing. What is the meaning of chores for the parents in your school? It has been found (Goodnow & Collins, 1990, p. 27) that some parents in some contexts believe that their children will just know or learn what to do (*role theory point of view*), and others feel the need to teach skills such as household tasks early on so that children will be prepared and have the right attitude when they assume various roles (*trait theory point of view*).

Ideas in Terms of Parenting Conditions. Goodnow and Collins (1990) suggest that the following questions might be asked: What do parents think about the impact of heredity versus environment, effort versus luck, the potential for parents to influence others, the responsibilities of parents, and the range and effect of methods parents should use to accomplish their goals? If parents think the outcome of parenting is mostly about luck, they might not try to have an impact.

Heath's description of rural black families in the United States (as cited in Goodnow & Collins, 1990, p. 41) is very informative in terms of their perceived parental responsibilities and strategies to maintain their unique and valued family identity. Parents consciously sought "to fix and stabilize the identity of individuals as members of their own group and as outsiders to others' cultural groups" (Heath, 1990, p. 499). They read newspapers together and retold stories, with children sharing in the narrative, not just passively listening to an adult. It was a communal, not hierarchical, experience. This is an action that demonstrates goals and perceived needs of children. Professionals can now ask, for all parents with whom they work, what is the importance, use, and function of storytelling in their families? Those working with Native American parents know that in answer to a student's questions or in response to a child's behavior, parents and grandparents often tell a story (Philips, 1983, pp. 112–115). Educators can help students and future practitioners understand and appreciate this approach to socialization, communication, and connection.

THE ROLE OF STORIES IN CULTURAL IDENTITY

The importance of stories is articulated in the research of Samara and Wilson (1999):

> Some of the greatest and accessible assets families have are their stories that root children's cultural identities. The transmission of cultural values through the oral tradition has been an essential component of African American families' lives and has served to build a sense of continuity, belonging, ethnicity, confirmation of self-worth, and documentation of their faith and resiliency. (p. 502)

Hurtig (2005) demonstrated the impact that not only telling but writing their own stories had on Mexican American mothers. They better understood the value of their own personal experience, and they helped their children and their children's schoolmates and teachers not only understand their family history but also better understand their important role in parenting and in effecting social change for the betterment of all in their community. Hurtig summarizes one mother's story, "La fuente" (The Fountain), in which the mother beautifully describes a neighborhood fountain and park where families can find pleasure and no doubt thinks of her own childhood in Mexico, where she enjoyed such beauty with her family. The mother then makes the point that these kinds of safe and beautiful places are rare in her current neighborhood. In reading her story, we can imagine that it could be followed by social activism to push for places "where our children are safer, places where they can practice their sports and recreate" (Hurtig, 2005, p. 270). Another mother's story pointed to the way "one could find happiness as a child in Mexico without material things," where children could use nature as their playground without safety concerns (Hurtig, 2005, p. 255). Many other mothers in the writing group also questioned the materialism of their present society, lamented the lack of safety, and were empowered by those stories to hold on to their values and, as caring mothers, to transform their new communities rather than assimilate materialism or allow their neighborhoods to continue to lack safe places for children.

Goodnow and Collins (1990) described Anglo-Saxon families as seeing "the family as a 'launching pad,' a base preparing children to move into a world of peers who will, in time, become more important than family" (p. 41). In contrast, parent-child ties in many cultures are often expected to deepen over time (although some parents whose children have not returned home since age 18 may view parents in those cultures as "too involved").

A Practitioner's Reflection

During my experience as a parent educator, I devised a program to use the value of enduring parent-child relations over the lifespan to help parents. In 2000, I organized a gathering for international parents in a school where I worked. One Italian family was struggling with criticism from American parents because the Italian parents wanted their daughter to attend Northwestern University rather than leave Chicago for an Ivy League school to which she had been accepted. The parents and I were able to help the family figure out a way to turn this issue into a win-win situation for all the family members and a victory for their bicultural identity. They did not have to abandon their values in this case. The student chose to stay nearby in student housing, attend this academically comparable school in the Midwest, which she had preferred despite her peers' surprise, and visit home more easily when she chose to do so than if she had been hundreds of miles away. She told her peers that many diverse students would be at Northwestern and she felt her transition to adulthood would be easier if family were nearby. She valued autonomy along with closeness and interdependence.

Many professionals have worked with students or were themselves students who, as the first generation in an ethnic family to go to college, did not have as easy a time as this young woman did. Their families felt that their young adult children should stay home while in college and, when at home, should act as if family, not homework, was the priority. Clearly, seeking to understand the values a family holds in areas like autonomy, dependency, and interdependency is very important.

Another case study reveals another insight often not considered in terms of cultural identity: Lena is a young woman whose parents had been in North America for her entire childhood. When they returned to their country of origin, they realized that they had reared their daughters in a much more traditional way than parents of their own generation back in their native country had reared theirs. For Lena's parents, traditions had stood still, and maintaining them was important for acculturation in North America. For their cousins back in Europe, cultural identity had been changing over the same period.

SOME QUESTIONS ENHANCE OUR UNDERSTANDING OF PARENTS

Figure 5.1 contains questions developed on the basis of the work of Goodnow and Collins (1990) and other researchers. They are intended for use by those working with parents of diverse cultural contexts. Which questions one asks depends on what service or intervention is provided. Teachers, for example, might find half a dozen questions in the table that will help them relate effectively to particular school families, but the full list is provided to show how many things may make each family unique. Figure 5.1 also shows how these questions, or a selection thereof, might be presented to parents in a questionnaire format.

■ **What Do Professionals Need to Do Personally Before They Can Understand the Diverse Families They Serve?**

Teachers and other family-serving professionals should answer all the questions in Boxes 5.1 through 5.5 themselves in terms of their own children, if they are parents, or in terms of hypothetical children they might care for. Graue and Brown (2003) said it is very important for future and current teachers to answer relevant questions in anticipation of their work with families.

As you answer these questions from your own perspective, you may be wondering what is behind them. Is there a certain bias or socially desirable answer, such as "Negotiation is better than parental dictates"? In fact, many themes and research findings are embedded in these questions. It is hoped that the questions will demonstrate the need to find the meaning of certain behaviors within cultural context. Some of these questions echo the parents' ways of knowing or thinking styles discussed in Chapter 3.

Some of the areas the questions in Figure 5.1 and Boxes 5.1–5.5 tap into are the collective or interdependent versus the individualistic or independent approach to

Dear Parents,

As all of us plan for the coming school year, we would like to connect with you on an individual basis and learn more about your family and your goals for your children. Too often, parents and teachers assume they agree on goals and how to reach them, only to learn, when a problem arises, that they might not be in agreement after all. We ask you to share a little about your beliefs about your children's needs and your role in supporting them. This information, supplemented, we hope, by excellent family-school communications throughout the school year, will benefit our students and all the adults who care for them.

About Your Beliefs

1. What does your child (children) need from you to become a good and successful person? Be as specific as you can.

2. What do you look to the school to provide your child (children) to help her or him become a good and successful person?

3. Is it important to you and your child (children) to have time to play? To have unstructured time?

4. How have you found that your child (children) learns best? Give examples.

5. Do you think your child (children) needs homework? If so, why? If not, why not?

About Your Goals

6. What characteristics or attributes do you want your child (children) to have at age 18?

7. Do you have family traditions and rituals you hope your child (children) will continue? If so, please describe them.

About Parent-Child Relationships

8. How do you and everyone in your family who cares for your child (children) view your child's (children's) questioning of rules or asking for explanations of them?

9. How often do you think or worry about the environments your child (children) inhabits? Please answer: 3 (very often), 2 (often), or 1 (not often)

_____ Home

_____ School

_____ Peers

_____ Neighborhood

_____ Society

Please add anything you would like to share about your child (children), her or his educational needs, or your family that you think would help us better collaborate in the coming year. Please use the reverse side if you need more space to answer these questions.

Figure 5.1   Getting to Know Our Parents

NOTE: This questionnaire can also be found on the Sage Web site for this book, www.sagepub.com/mcdermottappendices, as Appendix A2: Getting to Know Our Parents.

life, intimacy and communication with children, self-efficacy in parents, goals for children, beliefs about authority and control, and the support parents seek, in addition to other situations in a parent's life that interact with culture to predict parent behavior.

PARENTS' BELIEFS ABOUT CHILDREN'S NEEDS: COLLECTIVE VERSUS INDIVIDUAL FOCUS

Much has been written about *collective* (*interdependent*) versus *individualistic* (*independent*) assumptions about rearing children (see, e.g., Greenfield & Suzuki, 1998; Lynch & Hanson, 1998). Many children in the world are reared to be interdependent, meaning parents hope they will grow to be socially responsible. In contrast, other cultures believe that while children are born dependent, they need to grow to be independent. What are the consequences and correlates of these differing views? In collectivist cultures, children are reared to read parents' and others' needs nonverbally. The focus is on empathy; keen observation of others; group participation; sharing; duties and obligations to the family and group; and harmony, respect, and obedience.

If the parents also believed in Confucian ethics (Ho, 1994), they would emphasize obligation and filial piety to others rather than individual rights. In collectivist cultures, it would be acceptable for parents to give their children directives. Children would also know that parents would feel morally obligated to help them all their lives and remain connected to them over their lifespan. Emotional dependence would be expected. Children would expect to see their parents' love in their physical closeness and actions more than in explicit words such as "I love you." Likewise, children's obligation to listen to parents and support them would be lifelong. Chen and Uttal (1988) noted that in expecting family interdependency, Chinese parents would not neglect a child's individual intellectual pursuits. Intellectual performance is considered important to improve the self, and thus high expectations in this area are important in many collectivist cultures.

From the view of individualistic societies, the goal is not interdependence but independence, self-reliance, and self-fulfillment. The parents' goal is to help their child become autonomous, and often this means much verbal interaction, questions, and negotiation. An article titled "Safeguarding Wordless Voice in a World of Words" (Ohye, 1998) describes its author's reflections as a third-generation Japanese American mother reared with a collectivist family philosophy but rearing her own daughter in an individualistic society. While this subject has elicited a rich literature from many collectivist societies, Ohye gives us a particularly powerful demonstration of a dilemma many parents face today.

Ohye asks, "Will my children hear my 'voice' if I do not speak?" (p. 135). In the context of a U.S. society where more value is placed on the spoken word than on reading nonverbal communications, such as a person's expressions, touch, or actions, it is understandable that parents might fear their children will not "hear" them or will interpret their lack of talking as lack of interest. Yet why should they have to give up their ways?

In the parenting classes described in Chapter 9, children as young as 3 and 4 are taught both how to read the nonverbal communications of others and to reflect on how others might understand their own nonverbal behavior. They are asked to consider what an infant or parent they are observing might be communicating in how they are looking at each other or touching each other or in what the adult is doing for the infant. The children are learning the meaning of varied communication modes that are important for human development literacy.

It is clear from Ohye's reflection below that the foundation for a strong parent-child attachment is, as discussed in Chapter 2, very likely to occur with this philosophy of parenting, which values attentiveness to another's needs:

> I wish to suggest the possibility that a mother's "voice" can be heard without speech, that knowing another can occur in a context that does not emphasize speaking, and that my children will come to discern much about their mother and her heritage through silence. This silence is not that of a drowned or silenced voice, but rather is silence that is eloquent and resonant, embedded

Photo by Alfred B. Rasho.

With this parent's guidance, students learn to read nonverbal cues from an infant and other students.

within a universe that steadily and powerfully directs one's attention away from the "self" to the "other." (p. 135)

This universe holds the ideal of knowing another through quiet observation and of being known by another without speaking. It is a universe of abiding trust in the other's capacity to satisfy one's wishes. (p. 135)

Finally, Ohye explores motivations for parent-child behaviors and the possible meaning of them today. One can see her own bicultural identity as she critically assesses what her children need to succeed, but she does not throw out all her own beliefs and values. She talks of assertion with respect. She critically assesses prior values (e.g., choosing a behavior to please the mother). She commits to becoming a guide for her children to negotiate their own changing world, but she does not relinquish all her values in the process. Ohye also shares that her daughter has come to feel entitled to explanations, to make reasonable demands, and to have her parents respect her personal autonomy. Ohye may feel frustrated by these expectations from her daughter, and this frustration is heard frequently from adult college students who are parents reared with more collectivist family values. It is also heard from parents reared in individualistic societies. Parents feel their children really do not understand how parents struggle with these expectations of them.

I did not relate to my mother's requests as something separate from her, as something that could be evaluated for logic and degree of mutuality. My mother's requests were my mother, and thus my actions were a direct statement about my feelings for her. (p. 144)

Think about how many times educators encourage parents to tell their child, "I love you, I just do not like your behavior." This is very difficult for young children to understand, and their cultural norms may make this advice quite strange to many parents also. A child's arguing with a parent's ideas is viewed as a potential rejection of the parent. Ohye also felt frustrated when her daughter and a friend were having a disagreement and Ohye asked her daughter how the friend might be feeling. (This important parenting practice of *inductive discipline* [Berkowitz & Grych, 1998; Hoffman & Saltzstein, 1967] is supported by educators concerned about moral development in children.) Ohye described her frustration as follows:

I felt trapped. I could exert my influence as her mother and answer in the way that felt congruent with my own upbringing and its emphasis upon maintaining harmony within relationships to others at all costs, and the attendant idea that pursuing harmony demonstrates maturity, tolerance and self-control. But it was quite obvious that answering would incur the loss of my daughter's confidence.

. . . Alternatively, I could . . . let her know that she had my permission to "take care of herself." . . . I could sense that this was what she wanted to hear. (p. 145)

Ohye found it difficult to endorse an option that denied the needs of the other. Many educators (e.g. Eisler, 2000; Kohn, 1999; McDermott, 2003–2004, 2006; Noddings, 1984) have acknowledged with sadness that what the U.S. culture could learn from other cultures in terms of a more caring approach to living is being lost in a competitive system that seems too entrenched to change quickly enough for many. Yet caring is one of the skills that are needed in a global society.

Ohye provides another example: A teacher says, "Your child is so full of life," and the parent wonders whether the child is drawing too much attention to himself or herself, because fitting in harmoniously is much more valued within the parent's own cultural upbringing. While the teacher thinks the comment is a compliment, it is a stressful thing for many parents to hear. The following case study will elaborate. Maureen's son Brendan and his friend Jay, who was a third-generation Japanese American child, told their parents about their dilemma in class.

Both got straight A's in subjects, but Jay got a check for not speaking and Brendan got a check for speaking too much. Brendan knew his friend so well that he would speak Jay's thoughts to the teacher. The boys thought they had a great system going that was built on their own comfort levels. Maureen had spent a lot of time encouraging her son to understand the feelings of his peers. The teacher felt Jay needed to speak more, so she penalized him for not doing so and penalized Brendan for speaking for him. Jay was just not comfortable speaking up. He did not want to put a spotlight on himself.

Ohye also shares her thinking about her changing parenting practices. How difficult it must be to support one's children in an individualist society while regretting that they may lose sight of the communal values at the heart of their own parents' upbringing and identity. As earlier chapters have shown, many educators today (Eisler, 2000; Kohn, 1999) believe Ohye's values are of more worth than the values promoted in individualist cultures. It would be very helpful if discussions on these value dilemmas faced by parents could take place in schools and communities.

A Practitioner's Reflection

In my own practice, I have spoken with Chinese American high school students in the United States who have experienced their parents' support in terms of hard work to pay for a good school. While they knew in their heart that their parents cared for them, they could not help but feel sad when their parents were among the few who did not attend awards ceremonies or praise them for their

(Continued)

> (Continued)
>
> accomplishments. The students understood the situation intellectually, but emotionally they needed their parents to respond to their successes differently, and yet they couldn't articulate their need to their parents out of respect for their parents' own upbringing and the value it placed on not drawing attention to oneself. My challenge was to help students come up with a way of resolving this situation that took everyone's needs, feelings, and beliefs into consideration. (We succeeded, by means of the caring process of relating discussed in Chapter 6.)

Ohye's experience ended positively and hopefully when a teacher informed her that her daughter, while self-confident and accomplished, was also sensitive to others' needs and rejoiced in their accomplishments. Ohye's reflective narrative clearly describes what goals she has for her children. It is very easy for teachers to assume that family goals are consistent with the goals of the dominant school culture. This is often not the case, however, and in fact the differences may be causing a good deal of sadness and concern for parents and students. Differences within culture are also ignored in the case of parents in the dominant culture who do not value grades, awards, and other activities that affect a child's intrinsic motivation negatively. These parents feel a similar sadness and concern when their values are ignored.

The questions in Box 5.1 are related to parental ideas and to cultural beliefs such as collectivism versus individualism. It is suggested that professionals ask themselves these questions and then think about posing some of them directly to parents to better understand their personal and cultural perspective.

BOX 5.1   Parents' Beliefs

- To what extent does the family believe it needs to place the collective interests of the family above the interests of the individual?
- Do the parents believe the family should be characterized primarily by intimacy or by a certain degree of emotional distance?
- Do the parents believe it is important to work toward family consensus, or do they believe parental commands or directives are more appropriate for solving family problems?
- How much responsibility do the parents believe they have to influence a child's choice of friends, activities at school or after school, or other situations and so on?
- Does the family have beliefs about how conflict should be resolved?

- Do the parents believe in reciprocity?
- Which beliefs do the parents hold most dearly and yield most reluctantly?
- Have the parents you work with had an opportunity or a forum or place to think about their beliefs about children? About parents? About teachers?
- Are the parents able or willing to change beliefs or expectations of the child on the basis of new information they might receive?
- Are the parents' beliefs about parenting and children shared by others around them?
- Are the beliefs of parenting partners about their roles and children's needs similar to or vastly different from each other's?
- Do the parents believe it is acceptable to openly express caring by hugging and kissing children, or is there a different way to show love and caring within their family and culture?
- Do the parents believe they will have different amounts of influence on their children at different ages and stages?
- Do the parents have fairly rigid beliefs about divisions of labor in the family? On what are these views based?
- Do the parents believe it is disrespectful for a child to look adults in the eyes directly?

PARENTAL GOALS

Rarely in elementary and high schools are parents asked about either their short- or long-term goals for their children. Early Headstart and Headstart programs (Gadsen-Dupree, 2006) and early childhood education programs more often intentionally ask parents about goals. They do so for a reason. One needs to know what the goals of parents from other cultures are and how they feel about discussing their goals. Much has been written on goals (Dix & Branca, 2003), and Gross's study (1996) from a nursing perspective deals well with general themes about goals. In an insightful article titled "What Is a 'Good' Parent?" Gross recommended that in a pluralistic society, one must look for a model of good parenting that is based on understanding diverse social contexts and parental goals. She begins with the obvious: "Constructs and models developed for a European American, middle class majority culture may not transfer well to other groups" (p. 178). In reviewing the literature on *parental goals,* she found some similarities, which can be a starting point for a discussion: "Parents across cultures share three primary goals: (1) to provide for their children's physical survival and health, (2) to provide children with the competencies necessary for economic survival in adulthood, and (3) to transmit the values of their culture (LeVine, 1988)" (p. 178). If a goal such as survival is threatened, the others, such as the transmission of values, will be of less immediacy. Thus, some of the questions below about a child's autonomy, questioning of authority, and trustfulness may not be primary to a family living in a dangerous neighborhood or situation. Not challenging authority and having a little mistrust might be necessary for survival. Gross describes a mother who ties her children to herself at night with a rope. When we learn that she is in a homeless shelter, we better understand her goals of knowing her children are nearby and safe.

Gross (1996) also noted that regardless of context, researchers (Taylor et al., 1994) have found that most North American parents want their children to "receive a good education, to be respected, to respect themselves, and to feel loved" (Gross, 1996, p. 179). But some parents want their children to be respected by teachers even if the children are not independent or self-promoting all the time, as was seen in the reflections by Ohye (1998) and in parents with whom many teachers have worked. Many parents have the goal of rearing children to be interdependent and deferent to authority. Children who are not competitive might end up being seen as less motivated by teachers. Thus, it is very important to ask questions about goals before school begins and in preservice education so that agreement on some goals is not wrongfully assumed.

Gross (1996) found some consistency related to parental goals. She concluded that in all situations, certain common factors should be present for all good parenting across cultures:

- The parenting goals are clear to the parents and children, and the goals support the children's survival and well-being.
- The strategies are consistent with their parenting goals.
- The parents possess the knowledge and ability to adjust their child-rearing strategies to be consistent with changes in the child-rearing context and the parenting goals.
- The parents have the resources to apply those adjustments. (p. 180)

(One reason researchers do not always find positive and significant connections between parents' goals and their behaviors is that parents may lack the knowledge and skills to achieve their hopes and dreams for their children [Okagaki, Frensch, & Gordon, 1995; Price & Witchterman, 2003]. Some parents are not even aware of all their own personal resources to help children reach their goals. The family support principles essential to Head Start and other parent programs help parents develop those personal resources.)

These factors are consistent with the description of parental resources and social support in Chapter 3. The assumption underlying these factors is that parents have thought about their goals. Gross (1996) noted something that confirms the experiences of many educators: "Some parents cannot articulate their goals because they have not thought about their children in those terms, or the stress of daily life has made it difficult for them to focus on goals. However, many parents have never been asked" (p. 181). She cites Taylor et al.'s study (1994), in which parents of preschoolers were asked to think about what they would like their children to be like in 15 years. The parents were caught off guard. Gross added, "No one had ever asked them this question before. Some became tearful, but all were able to describe their hopes for their children's future" (p. 181). A similar experience occurs in my work with culturally diverse adult college students and parents in my classes on Parenting in Cultural Context. Parents wondered why educators and other professionals had never asked them about their goals before.

The caveat of the four principles of good parenting is that some goals may not enhance a child's well-being or safety. Some goals may not be compatible in new situations or environments. The kind of autonomy or responsibility given a child in a small village or in a rural area may not make sense in a big city. Professionals and other peer parents or community leaders may help parents evaluate goals in light of new contexts and times and see if their strategies for reaching them make sense. To illustrate, Shirley, a school counselor, was working in a school where a goal of newly arrived Mexican families was to have a family meal together daily. She described a family in which the father worked a late shift, so the children stayed up late for the family meal, woke up late, and came to the school as they had in their tiny town in Mexico: when they woke up. The school's goal was teaching reading to all students at 9:00 a.m., and the students who slept late were missing their reading lessons. Without denying the value of either goal, Shirley had to help the parents discuss this issue with the teacher.

Goals and to whom they "make sense" is another point worth considering. It might make sense to a parent new to this country and a teacher that spanking is no longer considered the best way to help a child learn to make good choices, but the idea may be unfamiliar to the family. The school may encourage the mother to try alternatives to spanking, but it must also prepare her to bring this new strategy home to her own parents, parenting partner, or in-laws living in her home, who may have strong religious and cultural beliefs in spanking children and who often have decision-making power regarding the child in the family. Are we being hypocritical when we say, "We respect your culture, but don't do that"? What should we do in this case?

What professionals in education want children to do in school may be quite different from what their parents think the children need to do in other settings, such as at home or in the community, and the professionals need to think more about this dilemma. Gross (1996) cited an example reported decades ago by Comer and Schraft (1980) of low-income North American parents who socialized their children to behave one way in school (thoughtful, reflective, and goal oriented) and in a different way when in a dangerous neighborhood (quick, impulsive, and action oriented). Do parents have different goals for children in different contexts today? Are teachers judgmental of or impatient with young children who cannot make the switch from neighborhood-community behavior to desired school behavior quickly enough? Most would also concur that we should rethink what skills are most needed on the street as well as in school, including a need to anticipate dangerous situations and think about goals and needs. Lareau's book (2003) about her time spent in homes with parents as they faced daily struggles like these is a must-read for helping professionals.

The model introduced in Part II of this book is consistent with Gross as well. In a caring model of decision making, parents clarify their goals and filter the information they might receive from leaders through their own goals, values, beliefs, and life situations. Gross suggests that parents' talking about goals "increases their confidence in their own ideas" (p. 182). She would likely be in agreement with findings of Belenky and her colleagues (1986/1997; 1997; 2000) and other researchers that some parents are just too stressed financially or mentally and physically to parent effectively or have these kinds of discussions immediately.

Photo by Katie Montell.

Parents meet in the beginning of the school year to discuss parent and school goals related to diversity.

Gross (1996), like Belenky and her colleagues (1986/1997; 1997; 2000), found that focusing on what parents already do with their children that is effective, and building on that, is the best route to parental self-efficacy. Often parents need to feel efficacious before they can even think about goals. Gross concludes her report by citing Berrera's wise advice (1994): "Come to recognize and respect a family's subjective world as it affects the behavior and development of a particular child— rather than to fit that world into what the assessor's professional community identifies as 'objective' and 'valid' reality" (as cited in Gross, 1996, p. 182). The questions in Box 5.2 can help educators understand the goals of their students' parents.

BOX 5.2   Parents' Goals

- Why did the parents wish to have children?
- What do they want their children to be like?
- How important is it that their children be obedient, loyal, independent, happy, healthy, and able to support themselves, observant of the family religion, not too different from most other boys and girls, not too similar, and so on?
- What do the parents want from their children?
- What do the parents want for their children?
- What qualities do the parents want to see their children develop?
- Do the parents have a preference for child compliance at all times, parent-child negotiation, or both at different times?
- Do the parents want parent-child relations to deepen or diminish over time?
- How would you assess the parents in terms of their willingness to grant rights and self-direction to their children?
- Do the parents have primarily realistic or unrealistic expectations for their children?
- Do the parents have past or current traditions and rituals that they wish to pass on to their children? What might they be? Are they ones with which you are comfortable? Can they be integrated into the curriculum?
- Have you asked these parents to describe their long-term goals for their child(ren) by listing the attributes they would like their children to possess when they are 18? (See Chapter 6.)
- Do they and can you distinguish between parent-centered goals, child-centered goals, and socialization-centered goals?
- Do they think about values and their relevance in making choices for their children?

PARENTS' THINKING AND BEHAVIORS TOWARD THE CHILD AND OTHERS

In addition to goals, practitioners need to consider parents' thinking about their children and about the role of other adults in their and their children's lives. Some of these questions are related to family systems theory, introduced earlier. Christian (2006) describes six *family systems characteristics,* boundaries, roles, rules, hierarchy, climate, and equilibrium, that are important for teachers and family-serving professionals to understand. These family systems topics are discussed in detail in Appendix C3: Communication Newsletter—Enhancing Effective Communication in Home, School, and Community, found on the Sage Web site for this book (www.sagepub.com/mcdermottappendices). *Boundaries* refers to whether families are open to influence by others outside the family. Some families may be closed and choose to focus on family togetherness. Closed boundaries may involve choosing or controlling children's friends and activities. Special education is an area in which closing boundaries is often functional. Snell and Rosen (1997) describe the actions of the family of a special needs child, Shelley, as follows:

> When extended family members chose to have a minimal contribution during crisis or their input was challenging or critical, they were emotionally and/or physically excluded from the activities of the family unit, were considered covertly or overtly, "out" and not sought for advice or support. This type of boundary defining can sometimes be a very painful experience. In fact the Donahues experienced the realization that there would be little support from either of their extended families as "more damaging" than Shelley's disability. In response to this lack of support, they circled the wagons tighter around the nuclear family unit. (p. 434)

Family systems theory often refers to *roles* different parents and children may have in families. For example, the oldest or female child might have the helper role. Some schools may see this role as being at odds with the student's needs to achieve personally. Usually roles are discussed in somewhat negative terms; for example, if one person in the family is the peacemaker, decision maker, placater, or problem solver, others may not learn these skills. On the other hand, decision-making, gender-related, and helper roles may be supported by centuries of cultural tradition and need to be explored very carefully.

In some settings, parents have experimented with different roles with much success. Getting parents to learn something new along with their children is a way to break down certain rigid definitions of authority many parents bring with them from their culture of origin.

> **A Practitioner's Reflection**
>
> In my work in Russia, I met a psychologist, Dr. Viktor Semenov, of the Center for Diagnostic Consulting, who brought parents and their children to the Tretyakov Art Gallery, where they learned a new project together in music, art, sculpting, or some other medium. In this experience, parents were connecting with children in nonhierarchical ways and feeling they were affecting their children positively in a society where they usually felt they had little impact.

Rules are also often culturally based. Parents may disagree with schools on rules regarding children's not hitting children who hit them or rules about which parent or extended family member gets approached to solve problems or make decisions or gets invited to parent-teacher meetings. The related term *hierarchy* refers to who makes decisions in a family. As Christian (2006, p. 17) noted, many decisions are based on gender, age, culture, religion, or economics. She suggests that questionnaires sent to parents early in the school year include questions such as "How and with whom would you like information about your child shared?" (p. 18).

Climate refers to the environment of the family system. While physical environment figures in, the emotional quality of a family is also important to its climate and does not depend on economics. Climate often relates to beliefs about children and their needs, mentioned earlier. A child could be wealthy but feel "unsafe" and receive little emotional support from parents.

Equilibrium refers to a sense of consistency, even when change occurs. It relates to the importance of rituals, routines, and traditions in families (Doherty, 1997; Furstenberg, Cook, Eccles, Elder, & Sameroff, 1999). Many believe that schools need places for parents and teachers to meet to better understand change in their lives and, through support and collaboration, maintain balance and consistency for their children in spite of change. Questions for practitioners to consider regarding parents' thinking and behavior are listed in Box 5.3.

BOX 5.3   Parents' General Thinking and Behavior Toward the Child and Others

---

- Do the parents go to their family for all or certain advice? Do they go to experts, books, and other sources outside the family for all or certain advice?
- Is it traditional in their culture for family members besides the father and mother to make decisions about the children?

(Continued)

BOX 5.3 (Continued)

- Are the parents willing or capable of seeing a behavior as having several potential causes?
- Can the parents thus frame a problem in different ways?
- Have there been instances when changes in the parents' thinking have occurred, irrespective of personal or cultural norms?
- Do the parents prefer actions and nonverbal communication to words or reflections about behavior? Do the children need to hear what their parents think, or can they draw conclusions from the parents' actions?
- What do the parents do when they become aware of views regarding children or parenting that differ from their own?
- Is there a shared understanding of events or issues between parents, parents and children, other family members who have decision-making power over children, teachers, counselors, and other parents?
- How do the parents think about their family?
- What are some of the family's themes and rules?
- Does the family have some rules, too many rules, or too few rules?
- Do the parents have customs, traditions, and rituals they wish to preserve?
- Do the parents see their children as accurate and trustworthy sources of information?
- Do the parents look for and read nonverbal cues from their children or others?
- Where do the parents get their information regarding what children need?
- Do the parents seem aware of current formal theory and research (e.g., negative effects of spanking, positive effects of negotiation and discussion)? If so, do they accept it, evade its application, or challenge its validity?
- What do the parents do when there are discrepancies between what they expect children to do and what actually happens?
- Do the parents seek information primarily in anticipation of a problem or regardless of whether there is a problem?
- How does this family view the "outside world"? Does it establish rigid or permeable boundaries?
- Do the parents feel the need to justify their child-rearing decisions to others (e.g., their own parents, peers, siblings)?
- How do the parents think about, discuss, and define emotions for children?
- Do the parents take responsibility for assigning their children to various "niches," such as play, sports, ethnic groups, schools, work?

- Do the parents think or worry about the impact of various environmental settings on their children? If so, which ones? Home? School? Community?

- If these parents attempt to exercise authority with their children, what justification if any do they articulate to the children (e.g., appeals to reason, fairness, politeness, authority, or responsibility)?

- To what degree do the children's ideas match their parents'? If they don't match, where is the disagreement?

- Do the parents see themselves as advocates for their children?

- Do the parents see themselves as capable of meeting their children's needs?

- Do the parents see themselves more as observers or as actors in their children's life?

PARENTS' IDEAS ABOUT THE NATURE OF CHILDREN

Often parents and teachers hold conflicting ideas about children. Thinking about why there might be disagreements or misunderstandings between parents and teachers is time well spent. As mentioned earlier, some parents believe that if children are safe and fed, they will develop naturally, without much parental intervention (an approach some teachers may view as neglect). This view is found more often in families of lower socioeconomic status (Lareau, 2003). Middle-class parents and many middle- and upper-class families of diverse cultural backgrounds believe their role is "conscious cultivation" to help their children achieve as much as possible.

Ironically, as Lareau (2003) notes, middle-class parents of many cultural backgrounds may so overstructure their children's lives that there is little time for spontaneous play, which poorer children and children in many other cultures tend to experience often. This is ironic because of the increasing appreciation of the importance of play and discovery in children's lives. As schools become more competitive and more focused on academic excellence, there may also be fewer opportunities for the inquiry-based learning that characterizes the preschool years and occurs in many cultures naturally. Rather than focus on impressing on poor parents the need to provide children with extracurricular activities, Lareau suggests that middle-class children may indeed be at a disadvantage because they are deprived of the time to interact with family and people of all ages that poorer and culturally diverse children often experience.

The following reflection makes another point about play that many teachers will find familiar.

A Practitioner's Reflection

When teaching a parenting class to students in Grades 5 through 7 in an inner-city public school, I invited a parent new to the community to come monthly with her infant to visit this bilingual class so that she could become integrated into the school in a meaningful way that focused on family relationships, which was more comfortable and of more interest to her than a lesson in early American history. The class is described in more detail in Chapter 9. Each month when the mother visited, students put a book in the infant's hands and then various toys. At first the baby learned about the object with his mouth. Infants relate to objects differently as they grow older, focusing more on the images and words of parents as they read stories to children. The mother admitted that until she came to North America, her infant had never touched a book or toy. The children were all sitting on the classroom floor around a blanket. In a culturally insensitive class, this mother would have been seen as deficient, but instead, these students learned that in her village in the Dominican Republic, children could contract parasites by putting a toy from the dirt floor into their mouth. The students were able to see how different contexts meant different parent behaviors. Over time, the mother became more confident that her child would not be in such danger here, and she ended up with more books from all the students than she could ever use. She also grew in her view of herself as a parent who cared about her infant's safety and was open to new information as well. The students learned that children could learn about the world simply by exploring their natural surroundings without store-bought toys. Dialogue on this topic is needed.

Box 5.4 is a list of questions to help us understand parents' ideas about children.

BOX 5.4 Parents' Ideas About Their Child and the Nature of Children

- Do the parents see value in play and discovery activities for children?
- Do the parents view their child as competent?
- Do they see their child as a problem?
- Do the parents feel the child gains knowledge more via formal direct instruction or more from personal discovery?
- Do the parents believe child behaviors should be built in as early as possible?
- Do the parents believe behaviors and skills can wait until the child is ready to learn them or take on a new role?

- Do the parents think children of a particular age or gender are basically all alike?
- Do the parents believe that as long as children are safe and healthy, they will develop on their own?
- Do the parents think children need to be externally controlled or more self-directive? Does this vary for different children in the same family?
- How do the parents think about human nature? For example, are humans basically good or bad?

PARENTS' OWN STATUS AND CONTEXT

■ What Other Factors, Such as Education, Home or Work Environment, or Social Class, Should Professionals Be Aware of That Might Interact With a Family's Culture to Predict Parent Behavior?

A discussion of the contextual factors that might influence parent behavior certainly fits within a discussion of cultural context. However, conclusions based on just the variable of culture can miss many artifactual variables, such as dangerous neighborhoods, that better explain some parent behavior than does culture by itself.

It is important for teachers to know what life is like for their diverse school parents. It is not always like the life of the teachers or like the lives of the teachers' parents when the teachers were schoolchildren. Factors in addition to culture are often at work in their lives. For example, research demonstrates that a parent's work situation may affect how a parent from any culture interacts with children at home. Kohn (1977) and Ogbu (1981), for example, found that a job helped parents decipher which skills their children would need in order to succeed, and these skills would then become part of their goals for their children in their new environment.

Crouter and McHale (2005) found that if parents had to defer to supervisors and never or rarely had an opportunity to share ideas or be self-directed, they tended to relate to their children in similar manners. Of course, parents would have their own thinking capacity, cultural experiences, and beliefs that preceded these jobs, and the interaction of prior beliefs, motivation, personal resources, and current work role should all be considered. Undemocratic work environments might be consistent with a new immigrant's views on parental authority, so one cannot look at either a parent's culture or work situation alone. Research in child abuse has shown that parents' motivation to provide a home environment for their children that is different from what they themselves experienced may moderate the impact of their hierarchical work setting or previous home environment.

Parents in entrepreneurial jobs, despite their own collectivist socialization, might emphasize achievement more than interdependence, and parents in bureaucracies might emphasize cooperation more than independence. Parcel and Menaghan (1994) found that even when they controlled for a mother's age, education, mental ability, income, and other factors, mothers with more job complexity created more-stimulating home environments for their children (p. 14). It is important for teachers to understand that many factors in addition to cultural background might contribute to how parents interact with their children.

In terms of stress at work, Repetti (1989) found that air traffic controllers who had had stressful days at work were more withdrawn and less emotional with their children than when their workday was unstressful. Many new immigrants, as well as other parents, are faced with long and often stressful work situations. Thus, it might be difficult for very stressed parents to always do what schools expect them to do in the evening. Repetti and Wood (1997) found the situation was even more complicated than work-related stress alone might suggest. Work stress interacts with personality type, so that temperamentally intense parents with work stress had a harder time refraining from negativity toward children at home than did less intense parents. Overall, though, mothers were better able to keep work stress from children than fathers were.

In terms of peer support at work, Greenberger, Goldberg, Hamill, O'Neil, and Payne (1989) found that despite the type of work, having supportive coworkers seems to reduce role strain for many parents. Lerner and Galambos (1986) found that if mothers were satisfied with work, their satisfaction had a positive impact on their relationship with their children when home. If they were not satisfied, they were able to keep those feelings from affecting their parenting negatively more often than men were. Therefore, social networks at work could also provide support and affect parenting positively.

What about other aspects of parental status? We must also look at parent support from others in their lives, including others at work. Recent research reviews in the United States (Fincham & Hall, 2005) reported that mothers who feel supported by their husbands often have more-positive attitudes toward parenting than do mothers who do not feel supported (Bronfenbrenner, 1986, as reported in Fincham & Hall, 2005). In some cultures, however, there is little expectation that husbands will support child rearing but higher expectations of support from one's own parents, siblings, family, or friends.

For both parents, marital problems are often associated with negative parent-child relationships and little parental involvement in children's lives (Buehler & Gerard, 2002; DeVito & Hopkins, 2001). Alternatively, marital satisfaction and adjustment correlate with parenting that is sensitive, responsive, warm, and accepting (Goldberg & Easterbrooks, 1985; Grych, 2002). Cummings and Davies' work

(2002) has been very informative. Frequent but never-resolved arguments between parents have a negative impact on children and can affect how children respond to stress in the future, including at school. These children seem less able to regulate their emotions during stress. Grych and Fincham (1992) also found that what had the most negative impact on children was parents' arguing in front of them without resolving conflicts and arguing about the children.

Little research in this area has been done in culturally diverse groups of parents. We need to understand more about children whose parents often communicate nonverbally and, for the sake of harmony, do not argue in front of children. Does nonverbal parental discord affect children's development? How does one assess the impact of marital problems on these children?

Homework assignments go home to parents under all kinds of stress, much of which might affect their capacity for parental involvement as it is narrowly defined. The best parent involvement in these cases might be to not argue in front of the children, to work on the marital relationship if possible, and to get support from others to help with family needs. Researchers and counselors suggest that after divorce, the best intervention would be to help parents coparent more effectively rather than to pressure them to volunteer in school.

Feinberg (2002) strongly recommends that separated and divorced parents get support, if needed, to improve communication between them so that they can focus on being sensitive, warm, and consistent with their children in spite of their feelings toward each other. This would be parent involvement enough for many educators at such a difficult time in a family's life.

But is focusing on the couple enough? No. One must also look at the environment that affects their situation. Parents may need help finding jobs and getting the education and resources they need to be less stressed and less hostile toward each other. Fincham and Hall (2005) suggest that "the ecological niche of the couple—their life events, family constellation, socioeconomic standing, and stressful circumstances—can no longer be ignored" (p. 225). They cite a study by Conger, Rueter, and Elder (1999) that points to economic pressure as the predictor of marital problems in the predominantly rural parents they studied.

As was mentioned in Chapters 2 and 3, parents need to be understood in sociocultural context, and one must not attribute all their failings solely to individual inadequacies or their cultural roots. Our society needs to help them get the support they need to better meet all family members' needs, and we also need to understand how different cultures view help with marital or family problems. It is wise to speak with practitioners who have experience working with parents of a particular cultural background to learn how to convey offers of help so that they will be well received.

In terms of support outside of the home, Burchinal, Follmer, and Bryant (1996) studied 62 mothers of low socioeconomic status and found that mothers with large social networks of people to rely on had more developmentally supportive homes through their children's preschool years and were warmer, more involved, and less directive with their toddlers than were mothers without large social networks.

What is *social support*? It consists of help from others that is emotional, instrumental, and informational. Cochran and Walker (2005) add the following details:

> With respect to families, emotional support refers to expressions of empathy and encouragement that convey to parents that they are understood and capable of working through difficulties in order to do a good job in that role. Instrumental support refers to concrete help that reduces the number of tasks or responsibilities a parent must perform, typically household and child care tasks. Informational support refers to advice or information concerning child care or parenting. (p. 141)

That kind of support was seen in Hurtig's mothers' writing group (2005):

> Recognizing the personal strength they gain from the group, some writers have described the workshop as therapeutic, while others have said it has helped them become "leaders" or "teachers." One mother told the group that writing and sharing her stories gave her the strength to carry on. (p. 256)

But is all support effective? Voight, Hans, and Bernstein (1996) found that "when support is provided by someone who is also a source of stress, the combination of support and conflict may be related to poor maternal adjustment" (p. 70). This finding has very important implications in schools. If families fear school personnel, support from the school may in fact be stressful. As Snell and Rosen (1997) assert in discussing parents of children with special needs, the practitioner needs to be seen as "a resource rather than an intruder who saps precious energy from an already burdened system" (p. 438). This has been found to be especially true in cases of emotional and informational support.

There are often cultural and socioeconomic differences in terms of the amount of control that parents have over who is in their support network. Cochran and Walker (2005) note that poor parents are at a disadvantage:

> Recent studies indicate, for instance, that in the United States an unemployed, poor, African American, single mother has far less control over who is included in her personal network than does a European-American, married, middle-income mother working outside the home. (p. 241)

They also cited findings of Fischer (1982) that educational level affects social networks:

Other things being equal, the more educational credentials respondents had, the more socially active they were, the larger their networks, the more companionship they reported, the more intimate their relations, and the wider the geographic range of their ties. In general, education by itself meant broader, deeper, and richer networks. (as cited in Cochran & Walker, 2005, p. 243)

This is why projects like Hurtig's writing program (2005) for Mexican immigrant mothers are so important. It has been shown (Jack, 2000; Webster-Stratton, 1997) that low-income parents with many supports have been more nurturing and positive with their children than parents without supports. Thus, often the best support for students is to help their parents extend their networks of support with people they choose. Sheldon (2002) found that expanding social networks at school (number of parents at the same school with whom a parent interacts) to even only two people helped in terms of parent involvement at school, and expanding social networks in one's community (relatives, educators, parents with children at other schools) to three people could expand involvement with children at home. So if a parent's initial beliefs regarding parental involvement minimized their role, experience with even a few other people in their network could clarify norms of involvement and could be moderated by people in the networks and how they viewed the school and a parent's role.

Samara and Wilson (1999) also found that the family school project they designed helped parents expand their social networks of school parents. McDonald (1999) reported that one of the many positive outcomes of the Families and Schools Together program was that inner-city, isolated, at-risk parents who came to this multifamily parent involvement program reported 2 to 4 years later that they continued to see friends they had made at the program.

SELF-EFFICACY, SOCIOECONOMIC STATUS, AND CULTURAL CONTEXT

Teachers, having studied self-efficacy for their work with children (Bandura, 1989), should not find it hard to understand that parents who think they can do something effectively are more likely to try to do it than are parents who do not believe they can actually make something happen. It is also not hard to understand that parents new to this country, in spite of their experience in another place, may not feel self-efficacious here. And even if they may feel efficacious in their homes, they may not feel the same in their children's school. Wilson (1987), as well as Bandura, noted that the environment can indeed have an impact on a parent's sense of self-efficacy. Many researchers are studying parental self-efficacy and cultural differences, but often these factors are combined with social class differences because many newly immigrated families have a low socioeconomic status due to the challenges of learning a new language and finding good jobs that pay a fair wage.

Research with native-born, middle-class elementary school children (Hoover-Dempsey, Bassler, & Brissie, 1992; Hoover-Dempsey & Sandler, 1997) has found a positive relationship between parental self-efficacy and child development. With middle-class parents of both elementary and middle school children, self-efficacy predicted increasing numbers of educational activities with children, higher amounts of volunteer time at school, and fewer phone calls to the teacher. Hoover-Dempsey et al. did, however, find that some parents with low income and with limited educational experience also had a sense of self-efficacy. Hurtig (2005) found that the mothers she studied believed clearly that one could indeed be a good and successful parent without being fluent in writing and speaking English.

Eccles and Harold (1996) also studied middle-class parents of elementary school and preadolescent children and suggested that a relationship exists between a lack of energy, time, and resources and less self-efficacy, as well as a relationship between parental self-confidence and parental involvement in helping a child with homework. Brody, Flor, and Gibson (1999, as cited in Luster & Okagaki, 2005) found a relationship between African American mothers' perceptions of adequate family finances and their parental efficacy and developmental goals for their children. When finances were adequate, mothers had more parental self-efficacy and held higher expectations for their children. They talked more about goals, which were identified earlier in this text as a helpful topic for parents and teachers to discuss. This research clearly supports the view that family-serving professionals must work to improve the conditions in which parents do their parenting "work" before placing generic, one-size-fits-all involvement expectations on parents.

Shumow and Lomax (2002) filled a research gap by looking at self-efficacy, socioeconomic status, and neighborhood quality in a culturally diverse, national, stratified random sample of parents of high school students in the United States. Of the 929 parents, 387 were European American, 259 African American, and 283 Latin American.

They found that some environmental factors did predict efficacy. Age was a factor: Parents of older teens felt they had less impact than did parents of younger teens. However, even within children's age groups, some differences emerged. Latin American parents who valued interdependency, respect for authority, and close family relationships over the lifespan (see also MacPhee, Fritz, & Miller-Heyl, 1996) did not think their impact would be lessened as their child became older. Thus, cultural background moderated (made less powerful) the impact of children's age on parental self-efficacy.

For African American parents, poor neighborhoods and low socioeconomic status did not always predict low parental self-efficacy. Shumow and Lomax (2002) found that these parents' experiences with extended-family members and the strength of their religious beliefs or community organizations also affected parental self-efficacy positively. Shumow and Lomax concluded that because they had found a link between parental efficacy, parenting behaviors, and adolescent outcomes, it made eminent sense to offer programs to enhance parental self-efficacy (p. 127). Of course, more good jobs, educational opportunities, and other advantages are also needed.

Samara and Wilson (1999) also focused on parental self-efficacy. Their project indicated that sensitivity to the richness of culture and a strengths-based approach with diverse parent groups paid off in enhancing the self-efficacy of students and parents. The four specific goals of the program were (1) to promote families' advocacy for their children's learning and their own through dialogue, writing, reading, and technology; (2) to facilitate the documentation of families' oral histories; (3) to provide opportunities for children to show their families what they were doing in school with computers; and (4) to explore how to connect preservice teachers with families so that the future teachers could hear about the environmental forces that have shaped families' lives, school experiences, and dreams of their children's education. Samara and Wilson's program, called First Teachers, brought parents into the school to write stories about their families with their children, using the school computers. The researchers asked the students to show their parents their computer skills and teach their families about technology. This activity alone built children's sense of efficacy and self-confidence.

After the program, families felt more aware of how their own family struggles and strong relationships were a good model for their children's motivation to persist and succeed in school. The extra benefit of such an intervention is that isolated parents came into contact with other parents and built community, thus enhancing their sense of efficacy as well. The principal told the parents how their own caring as a community of parents made the school a more caring place for all (Samara & Wilson, 1999, p. 520). The authors summarized the result of their excellent project as *reciprocal enculturation,* citing the definition by Winters (1993, p. 3): "a process whereby new cultural patterns are acquired by both systems, family and school, as they develop and mature, and each can be endowed with new energy that changes its configuration" (Samara & Wilson, 1999, p. 524). Many initiatives to enhance parents' use of technology may be found on the Family Involvement Network of Educators Web site (www.gse.harvard.edu/hfrp/projects/fine.html). Questions to help us think about parents' self-efficacy in relation to socioeconomic status and social and cultural context are found in Box 5.5.

BOX 5.5   Parents' Own Status and Context

- What is the work environment of the parent: Is it restrictive? Allowing for autonomy? Supportive? Entrepreneurial?
- Do the parents experience high or low degrees of role strain?
- Do the parents feel supported by each other, family, friends, community, and school?
- Do the parents have an opportunity to observe other parents or caregivers interacting with their children?
- Are you as a professional taking into consideration parental factors such as family and other social supports?
- What about the number and perception of stressful life events in the family?
- Do the parents feel the neighborhood, state, and government have responsibility to help the child or family? What do the parents do when this support does not materialize?
- How are the parents' neighborhoods affecting their parenting?
- How are marital relations or relations with a partner affecting their parenting?
- Are enough mental and physical health resources available for the parents?
- Do the parents have a sense of self-efficacy in their various roles?

A RATIONALE FOR USING QUESTIONS TO UNDERSTAND PARENTS

The lists in this chapter have been generated both to demonstrate the breadth of information we should know about parents that may be related in some way to their cultural roots and to suggest that the answers are often related to many other factors, including how parents think and make meaning in their world as well as their life situations. It is a practitioner's responsibility to ask these kinds of questions rather than to place parents into categories. Even providing parents with a list of questions selected from all those above can be an intervention in itself. If they have not thought about some of them, a few questions might spur their thinking. Parents themselves can decide which questions they might want to explore in more depth with others. Some parents may have foreclosed on their own parents' cultural beliefs. Others may be, as many are, "in transition," and others, as James Marcia (1980) found with youth, become "identity achieved" and may use these questions to critically evaluate their beliefs and choose the ones that best fit their own experience and social context.

■ How Can Schools Learn More Effectively From Culturally Diverse Families?

Practically speaking, many educators have used these questions to inform their practice with students, helping professionals, and parents. You can use them in your own educational discovery process as a lifelong learner. You can use some of them before you begin a parent program or school year and decide which questions will work for your parent-teacher population. Which will help you better understand everyone's view on critical questions? These kinds of questions can be asked of teachers and parents in school to see where there is convergence and divergence with school beliefs, values, assumptions, and practices. Heath's parent program (2001), "Planning," is designed to give parents opportunities to answer many of these questions as they decide how to parent confidently and effectively. Heath noted, however, that some questions, such as those dealing with personal adult relationships and views of authority, may be sensitive and lead parents to be defensive. When Heath and McDermott were in Russia in 1993, authority was a touchy subject for parents and one we thought better of as a discussion opener. If we had started with sensitive questions rather than ones with more face validity and that simply asked about family traditions or family needs, we might have shut down conversation (Heath, 2002).

There is no doubt that issues will arise that need to be addressed even if parent and professional beliefs collide. Beliefs, as one knows from experience, run very deep. When reading the list of questions in Box 5.5, for instance, you can probably think of many ways parents might disagree with a teacher's strongly held beliefs. These differences cannot be ignored. As Gonzalez-Mena (1997) reminds teachers, "When cultures collide, we can't just 'make nice' and hope the differences will resolve by themselves. We have to first notice them, and then we must address them" (p. 1). How does one address them? She suggests a manner very consistent with adult learning principles: dialogue. She differentiates dialogue from what people in Western societies are most familiar with, which is arguing or debate, with clear winners and losers. Dialogue is different from arguing in these important ways, according to Gonzalez-Mena:

> In dialoging, rather than trying to convince someone of their own viewpoint, people try to understand the other perspective. The idea is not to win but to find the best solution for all people involved in the conflict. Here are some of the differences between an argument and a dialogue:
> - The object of an argument is to win; the object of a dialogue is to gather information.
> - The arguer tells; the dialoguer asks.
> - The arguer tries to persuade; the dialoguer tries to learn.

- The arguer tries to convince; the dialoguer tries to discover.
- The arguer sees two opposing views and considers hers the valid or best one; the dialoguer is willing to understand multiple viewpoints. (pp. 3–4)

Dialoging is one aspect of what Gonzalez-Mena (1997) describes as an ideal multiethnic view, which also involves transformative education and culturally competent care for children. By *transformative education,* she means that "when we acknowledge that our experiences with one another are important, when we stretch to understand different points of view, we become transformed by each other's life experiences to a different level of knowledge and sensitive multiethnic care. That's good for children" (p. 15). Her definition of *cultural competence* is also helpful: "Caregivers and parents understand how program and family values may differ and work together toward blending differing value systems" (p. 15).

SUMMARY

In this chapter, you have seen that one needs to consider the cultural background of a parent and family as just one piece of information to add to an assessment of the whole world in which the parent exists. One must consider the interaction between culture and social class and also understand the goals of parents, which may differ from the stereotypes of their cultural group. Schools need to work with family support agencies to help parents gain the personal resources (such as self-efficacy) and external resources (financial support, jobs, good neighborhoods and community services, good child care and elder care, and so on) they must have if they are to be involved as they might like to be. Everyone must also learn what parent involvement means in different cultures, because in some, active work in schools with teachers is not expected of parents. The next chapter presents a caring school model that takes much of this chapter's information into consideration.

Some Activities and Questions for Investigation, Reflection, and Action

Think

1. Identify 10 questions about parents listed in this chapter and the ideal answers to these questions based on the theories and research you read in Chapters 2 and 3. Cite the theories or research that supports your choices.

2. From all the questions in the chapter, identify the 10 you would most want to ask your students' parents as you begin a school year.

3. Look at the research relating to social contextual variables and culture. Try through an outline, table, diagram, or mind map to organize the data to help you better understand and visualize how these factors are related to a parent's behavior and to each other.

Reflect

4. Take time to journal. Think about your own answers to the questions chosen in the second activity above. How many of your answers are similar to your own family of origin's views and how many are different? If different, why do you think this is so?

Plan

5. Plan a workshop for new teachers. Outline the key themes you would emphasize in terms of cultural competence.

6. Interview a parent, teacher, or classmate who is of a different cultural background from yours. Ask the person a select number of questions from the chapter. Discuss which answers are similar to those of the person's family of origin and which are different. Ask what influenced the person's similar or changed goals or beliefs.

7. Role-play a situation in which a school staff person describes some parents who never volunteer in the school as uninvolved in their children's lives or uninvolved in helping the school. What kind of mindful questions might you ask this person to broaden his or her understanding of what involvement could look like for various people?

Part II

FROM THEORY TO PRACTICE

Fostering Caring and Culturally Sensitive Parent-Child-School-Community Relationships

As an educator and applied psychologist, I was fortunate to have the opportunity to immerse myself for 5 years in a preK–12 school to better understand the perspectives of teachers, administrators, parents, and students through my own experiential learning. The results are shared in the following chapters to demonstrate that designing a parent program in a school, building on the complex theory from Part I of this book, is not only possible but beneficial and exciting.

We will begin with a very practical tool (the caring process) for working with parents and teachers in schools. It is aligned with the principles of adult learning and cultural competence elaborated in Part I. Understanding them is essential because the caring process implies being open to others' experiences. After carefully listening to parents, teachers, students, and staff during this model project, I identified not only many concerns but also many creative ideas. Then, after meeting with and listening to parenting educators around the country and the world, I distilled several themes.

The reflections of parents and teachers that I recorded make the case for focusing on the growth and development of parents and teachers, even in this era of No Child Left Behind. As Simon & Lambert (1990) noted in their work on generativity: If the river is to nurture the land, it must receive inflow or it will dry up and nurture nothing. Because of the complexity of the parenting and caregiving roles on the one hand and the richness of parents' experience on the other, I strongly recommend that this role not be left to chance but that parenting be a subject in school from the earliest years. Our society must be open to a new way of looking at education and the role of home, school, and community in that process.

Chapter 6

FOSTERING CARING WAYS OF RELATING

Since teacher-parent partnerships are developmental in nature and best real-ized through a comprehensive approach, a framework for carrying out the process is essential. The following elements need close scrutiny: teacher and parent contexts, role understandings, and an appreciation of the partnership process itself. Further, a sensitivity to each other's needs, situations and tal-ents is a requisite basis for a viable program.

—Swick, 1998

We, too, need the protective factors of caring and respectful relationships and opportunities to make decisions; without these, we cannot create them for youth.

—Benard, 1996, p. 6

Some of the questions this chapter addresses:

- Is it possible to find a caring way for parents and teachers to relate that would also be a model for students to emulate?
- What would the components of such a caring model be?
- How does the model reflect principles and best practices of adult learning?
- What would this model look like in schools?

AUTHOR'S NOTES: Special thanks to Dr. Beth Kypros, whose dissertation work focused in part on connecting Heath's curriculum to Bloom's cognitive and affective domains of learning. Some of what is shared in this chapter is from McDermott, D. (2006). "The Complex Dimensions of Caring in Parent, Teacher, and Student Relationships." *International Forum on Teaching and Studies, 1*(2), 30–37. Used with permission. More information on the use of Heath's adult parent curriculum is available in Heath (2000, 2001).

In spite of all the evidence in Part I of this book that parenting is complex (Holden, 1997; Holden & Hawk, 2003; Kegan, 1994; Kuczynski, 2003) and that parents have the potential to learn and grow as they adapt to their growing child(ren) (Erikson, 1968; Galinsky, 1987), few schools have developed parent programs that take all this information into account. "Sage on the stage" presentations for parents, take-home parent-student academic activities, occasional newsletters, and brief parent-teacher meetings at the start of school and report card time remain the norm. Content of parent programs often focuses on skills related to producing a smarter and better-behaved child but less often a more confident, competent, and developing parent, child, and teacher. This neglect is occurring at a time when experts (Brazelton & Greenspan, 2000; Comer, 2001; Kessler, 2000) see human development literacy as an essential focus in schools and when both teachers and parents are often in Erikson's developmental stage of *generativity* (1963, 1968), in which their major task in life is to care for the next generation. The theories and research presented in Part I of this book and Swick's recommendations (1998) in the quotation opening of this chapter must be considered in developing effective parent-teacher partnerships in schools. Swick suggests parents and teachers need to understand their roles, including, it is to be hoped, their developmental role to care for their children, students, each other, and the world.

■ Is It Possible to Find a Caring Way for Parents and Teachers to Relate That Would Also Be a Model for Students to Emulate?

Any group of parents and teachers, with the right preparation, motivation, and support, can use a "planful," caring decision-making process (Heath, 2001) that is culturally sensitive and allows all involved to bring their own feelings, needs, goals, beliefs, and experiences into the process (McDermott, 2006). Such a process provides a way for parents and teachers to develop and change their behavior because it considers both their cognitive and their affective capacities (Krathwohl, Bloom, & Masia, 1964) in a way that is culturally sensitive.

ADULT LEARNING PRINCIPLES FRAME THE MODEL

The ideal way of working with parents is not a lecture but a plan-do-reflect process in which caregivers identify concrete experiences in their lives about which they have strong feelings; reflect on them; become informed about what educators know about the developmental capacities of children and adults; and then actively experiment with some new strategies inspired by their learning, reflection, and sharing in the group. This often transformational learning opportunity will be explained first as it relates to parents and later to teachers. It is informed by Kolb's model of experiential learning in adults (1984, 1999) and extends Chapter 4's discussion of adult learning processes.

Kolb (1999) defined learning as "the process whereby knowledge is created through the transformation of experience. Knowledge results from the combination of grasping and transforming experience" (p. 41). In describing adult styles of learning, he differentiates between those who grasp experience or new information through their senses and concrete reality and others who do so more abstractly and through thinking or analyzing. Some adults learn by watching others and reflecting on what they observe while others learn by doing. Kolb's Learning Style Inventory (1985) (see Figure 6.1) is a tool that informs adults about their preferred learning style, which he suggested was based on their biological predispositions, their past life experiences, and the demands of their present environment.

He describes *four stages of the learning cycle:* In the stage of *concrete experience,* one learns from feeling (from specific experiences, relating to people, and being sensitive to both feelings and people). In the *reflective observation* stage, one learns from watching and listening (carefully observing before making judgments, seeing issues from many perspectives, and looking for the meaning of things). The reflective observation stage reflects the goals of mindful learning. In *abstract conceptualization,* one learns by thinking (logically analyzing ideas and systematically planning and acting on one's intellectual understanding of a situation). Finally, in *active experimentation,* one learns by doing (getting things done, taking risks, and influencing others through action). It has been suggested that work with parents should provide opportunities for all four styles of learning.

As one might guess, a single learning style might describe a parent's preferred style of learning but not all the ways the parent learns in the course of daily activities. Rather, adults tend to combine these four learning styles. In Heath's "Planning" curriculum (2001), parents have an opportunity to go through the cycle and learn in all ways, as will be demonstrated shortly. While Kolb's model is very useful in planning for diverse teaching and learning experiences with parents, educators must add to it the information about parents' various cultural experiences and beliefs (discussed in Chapter 5), their preferred communication modes (see Chapter 7), and their different thinking capacities. We also need to connect all these factors to an important area of research on parental thinking called meta-parenting.

META-PARENTING IS ANOTHER HELPFUL CONSTRUCT

Holden and Hawk (2003) have defined *meta-parenting* as "a class of evaluative parental thought concerning the child-rearing domain that typically occurs before

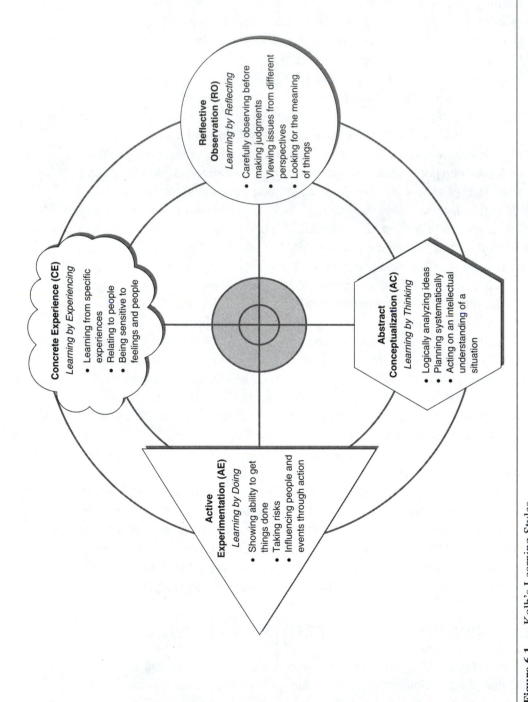

Figure 6.1 Kolb's Learning Styles

SOURCE: Copyright © David Kolb, Experience Based Learning Systems, Inc.

or after parent-child interactions" (p. 191). It involves the four cognitive activities of anticipating, assessing, problem solving, and reflecting, which help parents learn about their children and think through how to care for them effectively.

Heath's approach (2001) to parent learning and development allows for all Kolb's learning styles while also reflecting Holden and Hawk's construct (2003) of meta-parenting. Holden and Hawk suggest that parents (and teachers) should always be adjusting their behavior and modifying it to fit different situations and contexts and that they need support and places for doing so (p. 189). The researchers believe parents need the time to think about parent-child interactions outside the actual event. Parents cannot learn about their children just by actively experimenting. Holden and Hawk cited Caspi and Roberts' research (2001), which looked at the way parents' internal cognitive processes effected changes in parent-child interactions. This internal process corresponds closely to mindful learning and also echoes Palmer's strong advice (1998) that teachers who desire more success with students should focus on their own internal thoughts and emotions about their role before and after they interact with students.

Meta-parenting, then, is related to parents' internal cognitive processes of (a) observing themselves, (b) observing others (including their child), and (c) listening to others (Holden & Hawk, 2003, p. 190). The components of meta-parenting are very relevant to what working and learning with parents should be about:

Anticipation has to do with thinking about what might happen before it happens; for example, what will happen if my child does not have enough sleep on a school night? *Assessing* involves parental awareness and evaluation, which were explained in detail in Chapters 2 and 3. Parents can and should monitor behavior, and do it intentionally. For example, they could ask, why did my child bully that boy? or what effect did my rush to judgment have on my teen? or how is the war on terror affecting our family daily?

With *problem solving,* parents assess and evaluate various parenting issues, identify problems and their source, identify various solutions and anticipate outcomes of each solution, test the solutions, and evaluate their success. With *reflection,* parents reassess their behavior. This step takes a longer view than assessing one situation. In this phase, parents look back to look forward.

So meta-parenting, like mindful learning, is deliberative. Holden and Hawk (2003) believe it should promote social effectiveness in children. The rationale is that if parents modeled thoughtful, reasoned action, they would have children who are more anticipatory, *agentic* (i.e., action oriented rather than passive), and thoughtful as well (p. 196). Can parents overdo meta-parenting? Holden and Hawk would say yes; parents could either be inhibited from taking action or become overcontrolling, overprotective, or intrusive.

Conditions that facilitate appropriate meta-parenting, according to Holden and Hawk (2003), include parents' willingness to be involved with their child and a sense of self-efficacy, that is, a sense that they can control outcomes and make things happen.

Besides a willingness to be involved and a sense of self-efficacy, parents need certain "necessary conditions" (Holden & Hawk, 2003, pp. 197–198), such as time and energy for anticipating, assessing, problem solving, and reflecting. Also, certain illnesses, such as depression, can impede the process. As mentioned by Belsky and Barends (2002) and several of the social cognitive theorists mentioned in Chapter 2, parents also need to be mature and capable of abstract thinking.

Finally, as suggested by bidirectional theorists, "easy" children might not seem to require as much meta-parenting as children who are perceived as more "difficult." But as families' lives become more and more complex, it is suggested that professionals help all parents think mindfully about their children and situations. Langer's work on mindful learning (2000) also supports meta-parenting (rather than mindless, automatic, and unthinking parenting). Holden and Hawk have singled out Heath's approach as a reflective model that supports meta-parenting (Holden & Hawk, 2003, p. 198). Heath refers to her model as a "caring process," and Palmer (1998) refers to a similar process for teachers as "caring activity." Now we need to ask what caring involves.

A CARING MODEL OF PARENTING AND RELATING

What do we mean by caring, and how is it related to the parenting role, adult learning, and meta-parenting? In my own studies of caring and the development of a caring model of decision making in homes, schools, and communities (McDermott, 2006; Murphy, D'Anna, D'Anna, Heath, & Towey, 1994), Mayeroff's definition (1971) of *caring* as "having another person's growth and development in mind" (p. 1) has been very influential. Using this definition, one might conclude that parents who want their children to feel and be competent and confident when they reach adulthood will not do their homework for them out of consideration of their children's long-term developmental needs. Caring students will think not only of their own immediate needs but will step outside themselves and do meta-thinking by assessing how a decision to exclude a classmate, for example, affects that person's self-worth and well-being in both the present and the future. Thus, caring would involve several different learning styles (concrete experience, reflective observation, abstract conceptualization, and active experimentation) and several different components of meta-parenting.

Noddings (1984) has said that caring "involves stepping out of one's own personal frame of reference into the other's" (p. 24). She goes on to say that "When we care, we consider the other's point of view, his/her objective needs, and what he/she expects of us. . . . There is a dimension of competence in caring . . . (the need to) acquire skills in caretaking" (p. 24). She believes that the main aim of education in schools should be to produce competent, caring, loving, and lovable people. She also believes that we should help children choose prosocial behavior, not to avoid punishment, but because others deserve care. This definition certainly applies to parent-teacher relationships as well.

A personal experience helped confirm my own thinking in this regard.

A Practitioner's Reflection

When in Russia in 1993, working with parents, teachers, and school psychologists to help create caring schools, I was taken to the Tretyakov Art Gallery in Moscow. I was shown many icons of a mother and child, often referred to as the "Vladimir Godmother of Tenderness." One Moscow University school psychology graduate student who accompanied me and who felt Russian schools had nurtured her mind and body but not her spirit cried in front of these icons. At the same time, she said she felt hopeful. She explained that the angry look on this particular Godmother icon was directed at the hostile and violent society of the time. We felt that the Godmother looked connected to her child, committed, protective, loving, sad, and determined, like many parents before and after her, to help her child survive and thrive. She had the right attitude.

Was that enough? Was that caring? It's not enough just to want to care. The Godmother and the student needed not only a willingness to be involved in creating a more caring world but also information, skills, and a society that places a high value on children and caring. Some say that if children have good self-esteem, they will be caring. What if they are not motivated to care? What if they have little opportunity to learn how to care? What if they dwell in families, schools, and communities that reward aggression more than care? They may not be able to promote the growth and development of others.

A cab driver in Russia asked me about my work on caring. He reminisced that when he was a student, schools focused on the communal self and the good of the state, the society, or the group, with little focus on self-care, personal development, and self-identity (often thought of as U.S. values). The concept of the individual self was foreign to him. He felt that his teachers knew his answers before he spoke because everyone had the same expected answer. He had little practice in anticipating, assessing, problem solving, or decision making about whom and what to care for and about, and he had little personal impact on outcomes in school or elsewhere. He now felt the same way as a parent. He was asked by teachers to limit his caring to providing food, clothes, and shelter and to making

(Continued)

(Continued)

sure his children did 4 to 5 hours of homework daily. He felt that teachers did not have time or interest in knowing his views or allowing him to help plan to create a safe and caring school and community for his children (or what would be called *anticipation* in meta-parenting). He did not feel cared for, and his ability to effectively care for his family and community had been impaired and undeveloped. Bronfenbrenner (1985) believes that schools' and families' success in caring for children depends on how each supports the other's efforts (p. 7).

In talking with Russian school psychologists and teachers, I found they also wanted schools to be more caring for all—including parents. They wanted children to develop good academic skills and a unique self-identity (room to care for the self) but not at the expense of losing their communal self. By the end of our workshops, they decided their students would feel more cared for if the school fostered more-nurturing parent-teacher relationships and increased opportunities for parents and students to have a say in planning and decision making about learning and caring. These goals are reinforced by Kohn (1999, 2005) in *The Schools Our Children Deserve* and *Unconditional Parenting*.

My Russian hosts were very caring to me in terms of another definition of caring, by Thayer-Bacon (1993): their "openness to my new ideas and their respect for some of my different views" (p. 323). They were being mindful. We felt that we really had similar goals, that is, to develop caring and cared-for children who are confident and socially and academically competent and also have an ability to make good decisions.

THE PARENTING-CARING CONNECTION

One of the best ways to understand caring is to watch what many parents and teachers do when they decide what is best for children. In her research on parenting, Heath (2006) observed that when parents and teachers care effectively for children, they display the following knowledge, abilities, and skills, all of which can be learned:

They show a willingness to be involved. They have and seek information about the child and children in general. They have knowledge of their own beliefs, values, and goals. They display an awareness of situations around them and an ability to describe events objectively without simply attributing motives to others. They are able to "do meta-parenting"—anticipate events, plan, problem solve, listen, empathize, brainstorm options, assess consequences of choices, and act and reflect on their own actions. They also have well-developed observation and communication skills, as well as the ability to implement plans and utilize resources. Caring takes work. It is not all about feelings. How and when do children acquire the skills involved in caring, which will make them good parents one day? According to a familiar Chinese proverb, they learn by observing and listening and then most effectively by doing.

■ What Would the Components of Such a Caring Model Be?

Figure 6.2 demonstrates what the parenting-caring process involves.

The following questions will help parents decide how to deal with a situation.

A. Planning

1. What is the *situation*?

2. What are the *options*?

3. Make a plan.

Use the following guides when deciding which options to implement:

    a. Which of your *goals* and *values* are related to this situation?

    b. Which of your *beliefs*?

    c. What are the *needs* of the people involved?

    d. What are the *feelings* of those involved?

    e. What are the specific *characteristics* of the people involved that should be considered?
       Their physical makeup
       Their temperament
       Their developmental level
       Their learning styles
       Their backgrounds/previous experiences
       Their interests

    f. What are the family rituals, routines, and ways of interacting that impact the situation?

    g. What are the conditions in which the parenting is occurring that influence the choices?
       Amount of energy
       Available time
       Financial security
       Other

B. Doing/Implementing

C. Reflecting: Assessing Your Progress

Figure 6.2   The Parenting Process

SOURCE: Copyright © Harriet E. Heath, 1999

For parents deciding about how to care for their child, we would ask, what is the *situation* you are concerned about or the one for which you are planning? We often ask students to identify a situation in which fellow students have been uncaring. We pose questions to get specific details, not false inferences.

What are all the possible *options* for resolving this situation? Here we "brainstorm" every possible solution without judging its appropriateness. We free up the mind to think of alternative solutions. What are the *guides* for deciding which options to choose? We need to gather a lot of information to lead us to the best and most caring decision for all involved. Our guides include the following:

Goals. What do I want my child or this student to be like at 18? or for the students, is it important for me to stay friends with this person? If this is so, I need to find a different way of acting and relating. As Mayeroff (1971) suggested, we focus on developmental intentions.

Beliefs. What are my beliefs involved in this particular situation? For example, what is a valid parent or teacher role here and what do I believe children need? An example for students would be, what do I believe makes me a caring friend?

Needs. What are the needs of everyone involved? These could be physiological, safety, social, self-esteem, curiosity-competency, artistic, self-actualization, self-transcendent, or idiosyncratic needs. This discussion is very well received by students and parents and gives them a new language with which to communicate their perspectives.

Feelings. What are the feelings of everyone involved, and how can and should they be handled? The feelings in question are not simply happy, sad, angry, and mad but a much broader range of affect. Fortunately, affect awareness can be taught not only in affective education but in most school subjects. Feelings of parents and teachers also matter.

Characteristics. How do the person's age, developmental level, temperament, learning style, physical characteristics, past and present experiences, interests, family patterns, living conditions, available time, and energy all figure into this situation and what options we ultimately choose?

Doing. With all the information above, we can now decide on the best option for all involved and try it.

Reflecting. Did it work? If not, we try another option and repeat the plan-do-reflect process.

PARENTING-CARING AND ADULT LEARNING

■ How Does the Model Reflect Principles and Best Practices of Adult Learning?

Let us walk through the components of the caring process of decision making in more detail to demonstrate how this unique model supports adult learning principles and cognitive and affective development of children and all the adults in children's lives.

1. *Describe the situation about which you are concerned.* This activity is based on helping parents develop observation skills. It is comparable to Bloom's first cognitive domain (1956), basic knowledge, which has to do with describing, recalling, listing, recognizing, and data collecting. Bloom's taxonomy of cognitive and affective domains (Bloom, 1956; Krathwohl et al., 1964; see Chapter 4 for domain definitions) is used because it is very much a part of my own and my students' education. Although other taxonomies are emerging and researchers debate the sequencing of levels and stages, Bloom's taxonomy suffices to demonstrate that the caring model for working with parents acknowledges their complex thinking and feeling.

Rather than just attribute motives to a child, as in "She is just trying to punish me" or "He is in a power play here," we encourage parents to become aware of the situation using nonjudgmental awareness techniques of mindfulness (Johnson, Heath, & McDermott, 2006). As parents become tuned in to a situation, they become able to list a sequence of events objectively. This is similar to what students learn as the scientific method. They become able to reflect objectively on such questions as, what happened first? Then what happened? What time of the day does this happen? Does it always happen this way or just when he is tired?

The goal is to get parents and teachers (and future teachers) to pause and try to think about a situation in a new way. As they start to process this information and see relationships (e.g., child seems to be more resistive when tired or when the class assignment is written out but not explained verbally by the teacher), they move into Bloom's second level, comprehension. At this level, they gain insight into some of the correlates of the child's behavior. At Bloom's next level, application, parents and teachers use their descriptive information in creative ways, such as changing the time of day when they ask the child to do certain things or changing the way they ask (e.g., in the classroom, by means of both written and verbal formats). They are open to looking for a range of possible causes and using these possibilities to begin crafting solutions.

2. *Brainstorm.* Here, we ask parents, teachers, or students using this process to think of all the possible ways to deal with the problem. We make lists of every

single thing we could do, whether it is good, bad, or in between. Each member of the group is asked to come up with 10 different ways to deal with the situation of concern. This is a very important step because it demonstrates that there is more than one way to deal with a situation. Often people get into serious problems when they think they have only one option. Several of the most successful problem-solving programs (Heath, 2000, 2001; Shure, 1988, 2004) involve the formulation of alternative solutions, which taps into the same creativity present in mindful learning. Next we need guides for deciding which option to choose.

3. *Identify goals.* Our goals are key when we choose among options. When teaching parents of diverse socioeconomic status a college-level course titled Family Values: Parenting in Cultural Context, I often use Heath's book (2000) *Using Your Values to Raise Your Child to Be an Adult You Admire,* which delineates the model. Box 6.1 contains the instructions I give to my students at this point in the process.

BOX 6.1   Identifying Goals

As parents help children develop good decision-making skills, they need to think about *goals*—both short- and long-term goals. What are the goals involved in the situations where children are making decisions? What do we and our children want to happen in a particular situation? Before we guide our child regarding the right option to choose in a particular situation, we need to think about how this decision might affect our child's long-term capacity to make good decisions. Your children and other family members can also do this exercise. If you want your daughter and son to "say no" to unwanted advances or pressure to take drugs, you cannot expect them to always do what you say without telling you how they feel when you tell them to "kiss Uncle John whether you want to or not." Try to always use your identified goals as your guides when making decisions.

Please circle the 10 attributes you would most like your children to possess by age 18. Afterward, we will have a chance to explore how we can help them attain these attributes.

active, adaptable, affectionate, aggressive, ambitious, argumentative, assertive, autonomous, aware, can make decisions, can say no, caring, clear thinking, compassionate, competitive, confident, conforming, considerate, cooperative, creative, determined, emotional, empathic, family oriented, feels for others, gentle, happy, humorous, independent, industrious, integrated, intellectual, involved, nurturing, other centered, patient, peaceful, plans ahead, reflective, religious, responsible, self-centered, self-confident, self-controlled, self-reliant, sensitive, skillful, stable, strong, takes initiative, trusting, warm

Do parents agree on goals? What about parents and students, or parents and teachers? Parents and others (e.g., partners, teachers, children) need to have a place to discuss conflicting values and come to consensus, which implies a decision they can live with even though they do not totally agree.

This focus on long-term socialization goals is often missing in parent and teacher planning or discussions about a child. Parents and teachers tend to focus instead on immediate relief, such as getting the child to behave or do what is asked. However, the selection of goals, using the exercise in Box 6.1 or something similar, shifts us to long-range thinking. Furthermore, the list of positive attributes in Box 6.1 also engages our affective domain (Krathwohl et al., 1964), deepening our involvement in the process. Parents and teachers can keep their list of long-term goals for the child and refer to it each week as they gather information and decide on options.

Then the parents are asked to think specifically about their goal for the particular situation in light of their list. This request strengthens the engagement of the parent's affective domain because it requires a commitment to one or more of the goals. With a specific goal or goals in mind, parents revisit their brainstorming list and omit the options that are inconsistent with their values and goals (which corresponds to Bloom's fifth level of cognition, synthesis). If the parents' goal for their child in a particular situation is to be kind to the teacher and classmates, for example, certain brainstormed options like hit the classmate or embarrass the teacher can be rejected.

4. *Consider needs.* Box 6.2 provides an abbreviated introduction to the topic of needs for practitioners using Heath's model but not her whole book (2000).

BOX 6.2   Thinking About Needs

We draw on the psychologists Abraham Maslow (1969, 1970), Erik Erikson (1963, 1968), Robert White (1959), and Harriet Heath (2000) for this list of human needs. Students find the language enlightening. It helps them understand that in spite of their strong social needs, for example, they must think about basic safety needs they might be jeopardizing.

(Continued)

BOX 6.2 (Continued)

- *The Physiological Needs.* These include the need for food, warmth, sleep, elimination, and reproduction. These are basic needs relating to life, death, and species survival.

- *The Safety, or Protection, Needs.* Infants cannot be dropped; children shouldn't be left alone. A toddler cannot be allowed to run into the street; a young adult cannot take toxic amounts of drugs if life is to be sustained. People sometimes jeopardize their safety needs because of social needs.

- *The Social Needs.* These include the need to be loved and to love; the need to be cared for and to care; the need to belong and the need to include. Life will not cease if these needs aren't met, but we know from studies in orphanages that children who are fed and safe but not stimulated and cared for socially do not thrive. Having the social needs met forms the basis of trust and acceptance, from which a child meets other needs, such as self-esteem, curiosity, and competency needs.

- *The Self-Esteem Needs.* We need to feel good about ourselves—to feel that we are adequate. These needs are satisfied by others' thinking well of us and by our own satisfaction in who we are and what we can do.

- *The Curiosity and Competency Needs.* These include the need to understand, comprehend, cope, and deal effectively with life. Curiosity is seen in animals, in space missions, in explorers, and in the classroom. From early childhood, children take pride in feeling competent by declaring, "I did it myself!"

- *The Artistic Needs.* These include the need to enjoy and to create beauty.

- *The Self-Actualization Needs.* One's personal potential often is fulfilled when other basic needs are met. Self-actualization needs have to do with being everything that one is capable of becoming.

- *The Self-Transcendent Needs.* Maslow described this area as furthering causes beyond the self. This may involve putting aside one's own needs to focus on "service to others, devotion to an ideal (e.g. truth, art) or a cause (e.g. social justice, environmentalism, the pursuit of science, a religious faith), and/or a desire to be united with what is perceived as transcendent or divine" (Koltko-Rivera, 2003, p. 43).

- *The Idiosyncratic Needs.* Heath describes additional needs that vary greatly but do not fit into the categories above; for example, some need privacy, neatness, or order. Many of these needs vary by culture. People in the United States may "need" more privacy and space than the Japanese do, for instance.

The first two needs are absolute. Only when these are satisfied will we have time for intellectual and aesthetic pursuits. Social needs are vital for healthy development, and the remaining needs are necessary, according to Maslow, for life to be full and meaningful. It is important to acknowledge your children's needs and your own as well (e.g., "I need to know you are safe").

Looking at the needs of everyone involved in a situation—child, parent, teacher, other children, other family, and sometimes the community, country, and beyond—is very important and very therapeutic for all involved. These needs are identified via Bloom's third level, application, in which we use knowledge gained and then take action based on that knowledge. Information about all persons' needs enters into the caring process of decision making. This information on the needs of all involved is then thought of in terms of options brainstormed and filtered through their values and goals (Krathwohl et al.'s third and fourth levels, [1964]).

5. *Think about feelings.* Box 6.3 provides a way to guide parents and practitioners to think about feelings.

BOX 6.3   Thinking About Feelings

The list of feelings below is much more detailed than most children will understand. It includes many negative feelings because adults find them difficult to hear from their children. It can be part of a school's and family's vocabulary to enhance affect awareness between male and female students. We should also try very hard to be very specific about modeling affect awareness ourselves. This list has been expanded over the years from Heath's list of feelings (2000, pp. 21–23).

abandoned, afraid, aggravated, agitated, ambivalent, annoyed, anxious, ashamed, astounded, awkward, baffled, belittled, betrayed, bold, burdened, capable, cheated, condemned, connected, controlled, defeated, devastated, discouraged, distracted, dominated, doubtful, eager, embarrassed, empty, envious, exasperated, flustered, foolish, frantic, frazzled, frustrated, furious, generous, gratified, grief stricken, guilty, hassled, homesick, hopeful, hopeless, humiliated, hurt, ignored, impatient, inadequate, inert, intimidated, invalidated, isolated, jealous, judged, kindhearted, lacking, leery, let down, liberated, limited, lost, melancholy, mesmerized, misled, motivated, needy, neglected, numb, obstinate, odd, offended, optimistic, overwhelmed, panicked, passionate, perplexed,

(Continued)

> **BOX 6.3** (Continued)
>
> persistent, pessimistic, petrified, pressured, protective, provoked, radiant, rambunctious, rattled, regretful, reliable, separate, shameful, sorrowful, stifled, stressed, susceptible, sympathetic, tempted, tense, trapped, unsettled, useful, useless, valued, vulnerable, weird, wilted, wired, yielding, zany, zealous

Looking at feelings involves Bloom's first four levels of cognition (1956) and Krathwohl et al.'s third level of the affective domain (1964). From a cognitive perspective, parents and teachers are listing feelings, gaining insights, and considering a wider range of feelings than is typically discussed. They start to see how feelings might affect the situation. From an affective perspective, they acknowledge and identify how the feelings of everyone involved relate to their values and goals. If they want their son to be a nurturing husband and parent one day, they may begin to ponder why they become upset when he is sensitive rather than aggressive in school. This process is related to important recent work on emotional intelligence and emotionally intelligent parenting (Goleman, 1995; Gottman, 1998; Elias, Tobias, & Friedlander, 1999).

6. *Recognize individual characteristics.* Box 6.4 provides information about an important dimension often omitted from problem-solving models for parents. Heath (2000) is another source of information on individual characteristics.

> **BOX 6.4** Individual Characteristics and Situations
>
> We encourage adults to identify how a child's gender, size, health, temperament, learning style, interests, beliefs, and so on figure in as they search for solutions to problems. Books like Steinberg and Levine's *You and Your Adolescent* are helpful. Parents have also found Schick's *Understanding Temperament* and Carey's *Understanding Your Child's Temperament* very helpful. Materials on helping children with homework often have sections on learning style, and teachers may have handouts on the topic. We also ask parents to consider their own individual characteristics, as well as their beliefs, time, energy, and resources, as they brainstorm and evaluate options.

This area, too, involves Bloom's fourth level and Krathwohl et al.'s third level. Parents and teachers identify and describe developmental differences and other individual characteristics in people and extrapolate those characteristics to the situation of concern. Is the child's resistance related to temperament? Is a parent's resistance to a lecture related to the parent's preferred learning style, which is not auditory? Is the child's gender a factor in parent and teacher expectations? Information on developmental factors and other individual characteristics leads to understanding. Note how this process involves Belenky and colleagues' ways of knowing (1986/1997) described in Chapter 3 and takes parents beyond just receiving lectures to bringing in their own experience, instincts, and feelings and then using them to analyze different options and different points of view. From there, they can engage in connected knowing or trying to understand the perspectives of everyone in the situation and then construct options that are based on all the information they have gathered from their own thinking and the thinking of others.

The next step is for parents to take action, which corresponds to Bloom's last level, evaluation. They compare options, justify which one is best and most consistent with their goals and values, implement it, and appraise the results. They can decide if it works for that situation or whether they need to do something different. Our hope is that parents will internalize this caring model of making decisions. It would benefit children greatly to know where their parents stand and what values guide their decision making.

CASE STUDIES EXEMPLIFY THE CARING PROCESS

Heath and McDermott have been using the caring process in schools for several years. McDermott (2006) worked with a class of sixth graders at a culturally diverse parochial school outside Chicago. This school taught parenting classes for children from kindergarten through Grade 8. Students had been learning that one of the best ways to learn parenting was to watch what parents do when they care for children (i.e., employ the caring process of relating experientially through observation and discussion). The parenting educator then sat down with each of the sixth-grade students one-on-one and asked them to describe a situation of concern to them in which classmates did not behave in a caring way. In other words, the educator was asking them to do what Kolb would call "reflective observation." All 22 students described the exact same situation! They described boys being mean to the shortest boy in the class, Jimmy. The only ways Jimmy differed from his tormentors were that he was short, had allergies, and was escorted to school by his mother. After the parenting educator reviewed the whole caring process with each student individually and had the students list what they thought everyone's goals, needs, feelings, and options were, they all decided on a more caring alternative. But this did not happen immediately. First they thought mindlessly about the situation. They noted they had to be mean because Johnny, their leader for the school year, told them to be. They were asked to think about the situation more creatively and mindfully by brainstorming three other ways they could relate to the boy. This step freed them and helped them gain control of something that was burdening many of them. For the remainder of the school year, the students each did "active experimentation": They all answered the same set of printed questions, which reflected the caring process, anytime they got into a conflict. By the end of the school year, most of the children did not need to go through the whole process on paper. They just knew the caring way to act. They had internalized it. The teacher, principal, and parenting educator were very encouraged. The principal then asked these students to help younger students learn the same process. She also described the project to school families and made the same model available to school parents in an 8-week parents planning program.

The same caring process was used with a group of culturally diverse parents in Chicago public schools in the late 1990s. All their children, who were seventh and eighth graders, had been selected for an enrichment program from a private school to help these students gain entrance into the best high schools in the area. The parent educator began the meeting by asking the parents about their concerns for their children, beginning with worries and feelings. The parents expressed concern about the following issues: when to push their children to achieve, how to teach them to speak positively and appropriately in different settings, how to remind them of the importance of academic work, how to get them to resist peer pressure, how to get them to make good choices, whether to be honest about their own past when the children inquired, how to keep communication lines open, and how to deal with ethnic and social issues.

Goals of Parents. They were then asked, "What do you want your children to be like when they are 18; what attributes would you like them to possess as adults?" After reviewing a large list of attributes, the parents made their own lists and then reached consensus about the following attributes: assertive, trusting, adaptable, clear thinking, ambitious, conforming, making decisions easily, humorous, compassionate, feeling for others, involved, peaceful, taking initiative, creative, caring, independent, intelligent, happy, active, responsible, confident, self-confident, cooperative, integrated, and strong.

Application to Parenting. After asking the parents about their own concerns and goals for their children, the model of the caring process of decision making was described. Parents were asked to describe a specific situation about which they were concerned. One mother described getting her 14-year-old daughter to come home right after school rather than stop with friends to eat and hang out. Then the mother described a specific instance of the problem. She told her daughter to come straight home after school, but when the mother called at 3:00 p.m., her daughter wasn't home. She had stopped at a restaurant with friends, as she did three or four times a week. The daughter came home at 4:30 p.m. and called her mom, who yelled at her.

The parents in the group were asked to brainstorm all the possible actions they could take, and they generated the following list:

- Take away other privileges.
- Give her the benefit of the doubt.
- Find out why she's not coming home right away.
- Enroll her in an afterschool program.
- Make her feel guilty.
- Make her come to her mother's office after school.
- Make her call her mom from wherever she is (restaurant).
- Make her go straight home and do homework.
- Get someone to pick her up and bring her home after school.

The parents were then told they must decide what to do, on the basis of understanding everyone's *needs, feelings, age, learning style, developmental level and personal characteristics, energy, beliefs,* and so on. They began by looking at *needs.* The parents listed the following needs from a list provided: The child had safety needs, social needs, curiosity needs, competency needs, and self-esteem needs. In addition, the mother had a need to feel effective and competent to provide for her daughter's needs. They then looked at how everyone might be *feeling.* They guessed the daughter might be feeling hungry, angry, confused, and wanting to please both her parents and her friends. The parent might be feeling betrayed, angry, frustrated, incompetent, helpless, and worried. When they looked at the *developmental characteristics* of 14-year-olds, they acknowledged the child had a strong need for peer acceptance, might not be inclined to focus on consequences, might be more concerned with social issues than with academic progress, might be inclined to challenge family rules, and might need help in decision making and understanding parents' reasons behind rules. The mother had the time and *energy* to deal with the problem. She believed children should listen to their parents, and her daughter believed parents should listen to children.

The parents then reviewed the *options* list based on the mother's goals for her daughter and her and her daughter's needs, feelings, and so on. They decided that the daughter had a need to socialize with friends in a nonacademic setting, and the mother had a need to know the girl was safe and attending to academics enough to do well. The mother decided on a renegotiation of the rules and a compromise. She would acknowledge her daughter's need to socialize, and they might agree on 1 or 2 days a week. The daughter would call from the restaurant and from home when she arrived, and she would keep up with academics. This mother was not as concerned about safety as another mother in the group, who lived in a more dangerous neighborhood. Her option was to have the children go to their grand-mother's home near school to socialize, where they would be monitored by adults.

The parents got an idea that the model didn't have ready-made answers but rather that it provided some guides for decision making. They also learned that they could each make their own decisions and consider their own beliefs within this school program. In other words, there was no expert giving them all the same generic lecture or advice. They then went through the model again with a situation of a young boy who felt he knew a better way of solving a problem than his math teacher did and kept trying to show the teacher how the problems were done in his math enrichment classes. As a result of the model process, the boy's parent helped him focus on the teacher's needs and feelings. The boy stopped saying the teacher was wrong and instead said, "I have learned about another way of getting the answer. How do you feel about this method?" For the parents in this group, who were ethnically diverse, it was a little unusual not to get a lecture, but they were very responsive to a concrete discussion of their specific needs. They asked for more sessions like this one, as well as some written materials to take home. The counselor who directed this enrichment program mentioned on several occasions how use of this model helped her relate to her students and parents effectively.

GENERALIZATION OF THE PARENTING-CARING MODEL

■ What Would This Model Look Like in Schools?

The model has been very useful in many other situations. It is helpful not only in transitions from the expert-lecture model to getting parents actively involved in solving problems. For teachers, parenting educators, school counselors, special education teachers, social workers, and other practitioners, the model provided an objective and empowering way to relate to parents. In more than 20 years of using this caring model of decision making in schools in the city and suburbs of Chicago, I have found it to be a unifying construct for an entire school. Teachers also use the model to relate to each other, parents, students, and the community.

Teachers use the model in cooperative learning activities with students to evolve a class set of rules for relating to each other. Teachers also point out the model in many readings in literature, history, and social studies. Rather than reading extra books on caring, students apply the mindful questions of the model to any curricular materials. For example, what could have been another option for soldiers that would have been considerate of the dignity, rights, needs, and feelings of Native Americans?

Teachers use the model in science to generate options for caring for the environment, in health and sex education for caring for the body, and in virtually any

Photo by Cara Tetzner.

Mother meets with teacher to plan family science event for school parents and families.

school subject or process. Teachers also use the model when they help students choose high schools or colleges and to plan and implement tutoring, mentoring, or community service projects. They also use it to involve parents and the community in the school. Figure 6.3 provides an outline of caring parent-teacher planning.

SUMMARY AND CONCLUDING THOUGHTS

In a major study on caring, Ianni (1992) found that the effectiveness of a community in making students feel cared for correlates positively with how well that community coordinates its efforts with other systems, including schools, homes, and organizations. Kohn (1991) described "caring kids" and the Developmental Studies Center Caring School Community model founded in 1980, which puts a spotlight on caring as well. The Bookins Elementary School in San Jose, California, is another Cornerstone Project that involves parents in helping create a caring school climate. Parents using the Search Institute Developmental Assets training focus on caring not only for their own children but for other children in the school and community. The focus is on making more-caring connections. Heath and McDermott's caring model (McDermott, 2006) is unique in that it adds the parenting-caring connection to a focus on a caring school as well as a more detailed description of the parenting-caring process. It also adds the teaching of parenting-caring to youth within schools,

Parent-school collaborations might include:

- Parent-teacher conferences or parent-teacher discussions throughout the school year
- Working with parent volunteers in school
- PTA meetings and events
- Board meetings
- Neighborhood and community projects and concerns
- Advocacy efforts
- Individual Education Program plans

I. Plan*

Situation

- What are the circumstances of the meeting?
- In your thinking, ask

 Is it in anticipation of something, is it to receive or give support or solve a problem related to an ongoing situation, or is it in reaction to an immediate problem or crisis?

 If needed, does the school have a cultural guide to represent a parent's perspective or help with communication in the primary language spoken by this parent?

 Who has or will assume leadership for this collaboration? Parents? Teachers? Both?

 What time limitations exist?

 What personal and material resources are available to everyone?

Options

 What are all our ways of approaching this parent-teacher collaboration? (In brainstorming, the goal is to produce as many different ways of dealing with the situation as the group can. Calling out all ideas without judging produces the most choices.)

Guidelines for Making a Plan for the Collaboration and Deciding Which Option Is Most Appropriate

 Identify which choices from your brainstormed list would support your goals, deal with feelings and needs, and take into consideration the characteristics of those involved.

A. Goals

- It is recommended that before the school year begins, parents, teachers, and administrators meet and discuss the long-term goals they have for a particular child, class, or school situation. These goals should be written down and referred to in any collaboration.
- During the session on goals, the group should decide the following:

 What attitudes, information, and skills do people have to have to be able to attain this goal? If applicable, what attitudes, abilities, or knowledge do we want our children to obtain?

- Once goals have been identified, discuss the following:

 Are our goals conducive to healthy child development?

 Are our goals realistic under the circumstances, including the children's developmental level?

 How flexible can we be about goals?

 Do goals for one party conflict with goals for another party? If so, how do we reach consensus?

 What are the reasons for choosing the goals? Do they meet adult needs? Child needs?

 Are goals of equal importance? Should they be? If so, how do we work to make sure that they are?

 How are everyone's beliefs and values represented in each of our goals?

 Can time and curricula be reorganized to work for each goal?

 How can we understand the implications of each goal for everyone involved?

- During this discussion, goals may be modified or even withdrawn.

- At the end of the discussion, an agreed-on list of goals, with their definitions, should result.

  Once the group has identified its goals, members need to consider what attitudes, information, and skills people would have to have to be able to attain each goal; the developmental stages for attaining the attitudes, information, and skills related to each goal; and how to work into the school curriculum a program for teaching them. These goals should be referred to often during any collaboration.

B. Feelings

- How do teachers and parents feel about parent-teacher collaboration?
- How do we consider the feelings of all involved?
- Are the feelings about the issue at hand separated from or confused with the feelings about the persons involved? How can we work to keep them separate?

C. Needs

- What needs of children, parents, and teachers should be considered?
- How do we handle conflicting parent-child-teacher needs?

D. Individual Characteristics

- How do the following characteristics of all the parties involved figure into the situation? attitudes, gender, health, temperament, developmental level, learning and thinking style, interests, and previous experiences

E. Resources

- How much time, energy, and financial resources do all parties have?
- What community resources are available?

When a plan has evolved from the process, make sure that

- You have the needed resources for completing it. If the parent or teacher does not have them, he or she must work to get them before a plan is put into action.
- Make sure that when responsibilities have been assigned, all are in agreement.
- Agree on a time frame and specify when feedback will occur.

II. Do

- Decide on an option and do it.

III. Reflect and Assess

With all stakeholders, and possibly individually, consider the following questions:

- What goals were achieved? What do we need to work on further?
- What worked well? Why did it work well?
- How can we improve this process next time?

  Record the process if it will be needed for future collaboration.

Figure 6.3   Using the Caring Process to Plan for Parent-School-Community Collaborations

SOURCE: This exercise is based on my own expansion and development of Heath's Parenting Process (2001, "Planning: The Key to Mastering the Challenges of Parenting") outline as applied to schools and on the information in Figure 6.2.

*Before you begin the process in individual situations with parents, make time to meet with school colleagues and describe your current school situation. Are there written or unwritten policies for parent-teacher collaboration? If not, can you develop one? What style of communication between families and school currently exists? Does it match your written materials on what parent-school collaborations should be? Analyze everyone's goals, feelings, needs, and the other factors of the model regarding parent-school collaborations using the caring process of decision making.

which is an ideal way to teach caring and human development literacy (Brazelton & Greenspan, 2000; Eisler, 2000; Heath, 1995).

There are complex cognitive and affective dimensions to caring and to parenting. The abilities involved in the parenting-caring process can be taught. The caring decision-making process is the best skill we can teach children for coping successfully, socially and academically. If parents and teachers use this same process in their interactions with each other, all relationships will be greatly enhanced. Whether a teacher is in early childhood education, in a K–12 setting, doing home visiting, or working with special needs children or teen parents, this system will work well.

Some Activities and Questions for Investigation, Reflection, and Action

Think

1. How does the caring model facilitate adult learning?

2. Describe the connections between adult learning principles and modes of learning, meta-parenting, caring, and mindfulness.

3. Go through the model using one of your own concerns. Describe the process and outcome.

Reflect

4. Please journal on how a teacher could use this model to establish a classroom discipline policy.

Plan

5. How could a teacher use this model in planning to meet parents to discuss a child's problematic behavior? Or to discuss a student's falling grades in the middle of the grading period?

6. How might a principal use this model when senior citizens in the neighborhood complain that children are swearing loudly on the way to school and leaving cans and empty chip bags on their property?

7. Think about role-playing a situation with someone who says she dreads the upcoming parent-teacher conferences. What kind of "mindful" questions might you ask that will help her make a plan that produces less anxiety and will be helpful for all parties?

Chapter 7

Understanding Parents' and Teachers' Concerns

Parents and educators need to talk with each other, and with students, about their mutual concerns, needs, interests, responsibilities, and goals for students' learning and development.

—Epstein and Sanders, 2002, p. 430

Some of the questions this chapter addresses:

- What are some of the concerns and needs of parents of all socioeconomic statuses?
- What concerns and needs might be unique to certain groups?
- How do concerns about children parallel concerns about parents and teachers?
- What are some of the obstacles to accomplishing everyone's goals?

AUTHOR'S NOTE: Special thanks to the parents who participated in the focus groups and interviews that inform this chapter and to Denise Grogan and Jamie Ford, former graduate students in the School of Education at Loyola University of Chicago, for their qualitative analyses of the focus groups and their help writing the narrative. Thanks also to former Loyola graduate student Melanie Golden for her support in developing programming in response to these focus groups and especially for her work on bullying and on a "transitions" parent newsletter. Thanks to Margaret Link, O.S.B., Rich Batten, Jamie Price, and Rebecca Peisig for their evaluations of the focus group data summarized on the Sage Web site for this text. Thanks especially to Dr. Joy Segal, who helped in analyzing focus group results for all grades and for her support on formative and summative evaluations of programs and services that evolved from this process.

CONCERNS OF PARENTS OF DIVERSE SOCIOECONOMIC BACKGROUNDS

There are several goals for this chapter. The first is to present a list of concerns of parents of all socioeconomic backgrounds that can be addressed by means of the parenting-caring process described in Chapter 6. One parenting concern will be used to demonstrate the applicability of this caring process to many situations.

Second, by isolating a few recurrent child development themes that seem to figure prominently in the experience of many of the adults in children's lives, this chapter focuses attention on similarities as well as differences. Some of these shared concerns are control issues, communication issues, and external threats to families and schools. These themes were identified through a long process of focus groups for grades K–12 in the model development school I studied for 5 years. A closer look at a focus group experience for parents of middle school children within this large urban school is shared to demonstrate not only the concerns that emerge when one asks parents to share and reflect but the support parents get even from these simple interventions.

Finally, some formats for how parents want to meet (the when, how, what, etc.) are included to better inform practitioners of the diverse situations, preferences, and needs of parents today.

In this chapter, triangulation is demonstrated by reporting and analyzing findings from focus groups of parents in one large urban school, having the parents check that analysis, then submitting the findings to researchers (see Appendix D3: Validity Study—Use of Concurrent Validity in Parental Needs Assessment, found on the Sage Web site for this book: www.sagepub.com/mcdermottappendices), comparing them with the experience of parent educators across the country, and finally, comparing our findings with those of other studies.

For years, parenting educators have been trying to sort out the issues that face parents of all socioeconomic backgrounds and the issues that are unique to different parent groups. While some of this information has been reported in previous chapters in this book, what is presented here are findings of several annual meetings of the National Institute for the Study of Parenting Education (NISPE) in Chicago, New Orleans, and St. Louis throughout the 1990s and into this century. A group of parenting educators from Seattle to Pennsylvania and even in some years from Hamburg, Germany, and Birmingham, England, had been meeting at annual conferences of several educational and family support professional organizations but had been disappointed that there were few conferences specifically for parenting educators. Conferences focused either on middle-class norms or on so-called at-risk parents, but not on all parents. Together, they developed NISPE, where they were able to discuss and report the latest theories and research in their field and to analyze what was similar and what was different about their school parents, whose children ranged from infancy through college age.

SOME COMMON CONCERNS

■ What Are Some of the Concerns and Needs of Parents of All Socioeconomic Statuses?

Some of the common concerns these parenting educators have discussed with parents of all backgrounds were presented by their NISPE study group (Reilly & Soto, 1998) and confirmed by participants in the Family Resource Coalition Annual Conferences and annual NISPE meetings. They are listed in the following box.

BOX 7.1   Concerns of All Parents

The following concerns were raised by groups of parents of all socioeconomic levels:

- Helping children succeed in school and in life
- External threats to the family from the media; children's increased access to violence and other negative influences via the Internet, among other media
- Lack of recognition of the importance of the parent role in society
- Not enough time for family activities (how to prioritize them)
- The impact of homework on children and families
- Lack of connection with children
- Lack of time for family traditions and rituals
- Isolation of parents from other parents
- Discipline and control issues
- Parent-child-teacher-peer communication issues
- Lack of good relationships with teachers and principals
- Bullying in schools
- Self-esteem issues
- Issues of testing, grades, and traditional ways to assess student learning
- Inability to affect the way schools are structured and function

(Continued)

BOX 7.1 (Continued)

- Generational differences between parents and children
- Safety issues
- Drug and alcohol concerns
- Life changes: divorce, death, stopping or starting work, unemployment
- Child development (is my child normal?)
- Learning disabilities, special needs children
- Emotional and behavioral development and issues
- ADHD; the spirited child
- Keeping contact with culture (knowing and appreciating cultural history)
- Blended-family issues
- Anger management
- Sex and gender issues
- Legacy of parenting (will our children carry on our values?)

What concerns and needs might be unique to certain groups?

As was seen in Chapter 1 (de Carvalho, 2001; Lareau, 2003) and Chapter 5 (Fischer, 1982), often the social class and education of a parent become better predictors of parent concerns and the treatment of parents and families than are factors like ethnicity. The following issues are some that were mentioned more frequently by middle- and upper-class parents:

- Worries about overscheduling of children
- Sometimes wanting to affect school curricula more than other parents (often the most educated parents found themselves closed out)
- Peer pressure and competition for both parents and children
- Materialism in children and other families ("affluenza")
- Myth that families with economic resources don't have parent needs or problems
- Major transitions from executive position to an "at home" mom or dad
- Lack of diversity (picture of world is different from that at more socially diverse schools)
- Difficulty of asking for help
- Eating disorders in children and parents
- Difficulty realizing and admitting they have a need

- Adult children not leaving the home because it's "too nice" and they cannot duplicate it on their own
- Being omitted from some programming because they are not seen as at risk
- Having so much success that their children don't even want to try to measure up to that level of accomplishment (how do parents help children figure out their own path?)
- Overindulgence of children
- Inability of parents, even with power and influence, to make children into what the parents want them to be
- Fear of any kind of conflict with their children
- Difficulty setting boundaries for their children

Some issues were mentioned more frequently by parents of lower socio-economic status:

- Concerns regarding employment, housing, neighborhood violence
- Concerns about loss of children to the neighborhood
- Concerns regarding finances and family health issues
- Parents with English as their second language not understanding school communications, goals, or expectations
- A strong belief that their children were getting fewer resources from the school than students at more-affluent schools were receiving
- A perception that teachers did not believe in their children's potential
- Not enough people to supervise children after school
- No car or easy way to travel to and from work, school, home, hospital
- Sometimes having too many boundaries or wanting them but being limited in power to maintain them
- Long hours of work and too little time for family life
- Children not listening to parents because the children feel they are smarter than the parents
- Own basic personal needs not being met
- Cultural history and traditions being lost

SOURCE: Reilly & Soto, 1998, and annual NISPE meeting findings.

Many of these issues merit their own books. Presenting them in list form demonstrates that schools need to understand that all parents have concerns and "work" to do on behalf of their children and their families and communities in addition to the work that schools want parents to do for students.

PARENTS' CONCERNS BY AGE AND GRADE OF CHILD

The parenting focus groups in the model development school I studied identified not only general parent concerns but also grade-related concerns, as well as when and how parents wanted to meet to discuss these concerns. Results from focus groups of parents with students in grades preK–12 of this large urban school were reported by McDermott and Segal (1998). That school project is also described in more detail in Chapter 8, and readers can review the background of the project in Appendix D1: Parent Education Initiative, found on the Sage Web site for this book (www.sagepub .com/mcdermottappendices). National studies have also identified diverse parent needs and concerns. While it is recommended that each school survey its parents and teachers as to their unique concerns, the results described in this chapter reflect many general developmental and environmental issues facing parents.

What Topics?

In terms of specific issues, parents of students in preK through Grade 5 were concerned about the impact of other parents' and teachers' values and of classmates' behaviors on their own young children. They were also concerned about academic pressure to compete filtering down to these early grades and about overscheduling of activities (which seemed to be the norm for this particular group of middle- and upper-class parents though not a main concern of parents of lower socioeconomic status, who tend to enroll their children in fewer activities [Lareau, 2003]).

Other concerns were how to manage everyone's daily activities and still find connectedness; how to cope in a competitive world; how divorce or single parenting is related to children's performance; how to rear boys with the characteristics of honesty and integrity; how to get the right level of discipline; how to enhance curiosity in children (not as much of an issue among parents of lower socioeconomic status); how to work effectively with teachers; how to cope with increasing violence in schools and communities; how to deal with drug abuse and drinking in younger and younger children; how to say no and set rules; how to handle allowances, chores, and responsibilities; how to foster a positive body image, self-esteem, and good peer relationships; how to encourage children to try new activities; and how to deal with serious illnesses or death of a parent or others in the child's family and neighborhood.

Parents with children in the middle school years (Grades 6–8) seemed as confused as their children. These parents were trying to understand their changing role in terms of homework—what was expected of them and of their children. They wondered about when to intervene in their children's academic and social problems. Because they were sought out less by the middle school than by the preK–5 school, they began to doubt themselves and needed a place to share their concerns with other parents. They were worried about cliques, issues of self-esteem and self-respect (especially in girls), healthy and safe adolescent development for boys and girls, peer pressure, school safety, and limits and boundaries.

Parents of children in Grades 9–12 worried about enforcing curfews, the gray areas where there were no simple answers for teens, academic and social pressures, and families' more heated arguments about their older children. Although their own teens discouraged them from talking with other parents, they felt the need to do so even more strongly than before. Some parents saw teachers in the higher grades as less accessible than teachers in earlier grades and as thinking that parents had no legitimate role in helping when problems arose. Many wanted reassurance (perhaps from a professional parent coordinator) that their relationships with their children, though changing, were not ending. Because of concerns of high school parents, this model school extended parent support through their children's transition to college

Photo by Katie Montell.

Parents meet to discuss how to strengthen resiliency in their children.

or work, and the Parent Education Initiative brought in parents of children who had graduated from high school. These parents were seeking new ways of relating to their young-adult children. Other issues of concern were drugs, sex, peer pressure, academic work, and transition to work or college.

Parents of infants and toddlers were curious about all the new research on brain development. What should they be doing? They were concerned about the impact on the parent-child relationship of their working outside the home most of the day. Some were concerned about their child's health and safety in group or family day care. They were concerned about the impact of single parenting, divorce, or both parents working. Many of them did not have extended family nearby. They were also concerned about the impact of their own stress on their babies and about pressure from society to make sure even their toddlers were preparing for school.

A study by DeBord, Kirby, and Mead (1996) of more than 600 parents from several states (39% European American, 38% African American, 10% Hispanic, and the remaining Native American and other categories) asked the parents to note topics of interest to them. The topics with the highest salience for the parents surveyed were children's self-esteem, 63%; child stress, 61%; children and respect, 56%; child behavior, 56%; drugs and alcohol, 54%; talking about sex, 54%; and violent behaviors, 52%. We can see that these topics are similar to those noted already, and we can also see that some were of concern to parents nationwide.

In addition to these widely shared concerns regarding children of various ages and cultural contexts, parents of special needs children often have additional concerns. Santelli, Turnbull, Marquis, and Lerner (1997) studied 240 parents randomly sampled from 190 parent-to-parent programs across the United States and found that no matter their children's age, the parents needed emotional support, which often involved simply having someone listen to them and help them feel less isolated. They also needed informational support about their child's specific disability, about living with and caring for their special needs child, and about finding and getting the best possible services and resources for the child and the family. As the children got older, the parents had less need to know about the disability but more need for respite care and financial assistance.

When and Where?

Because of the way work and school schedules are set up in many countries, including the United States, there are no ideal times for parents to meet at school or near school. Many parents often have to begin work before their children begin school, and some finish their workday after their children are asleep. Some working parents at the model development school preferred to meet at 7:15 a.m. or 7:15 p.m., while others preferred to come when school was starting so they could bring their children to school and then stay for a meeting and, with their employer's permission, be a little late for work. Others preferred meeting before school was released. Some noncustodial parents had more time because they were not primarily responsible for their children. One noncustodial parent received a newsletter from the parent coordinator and started communicating regularly from 1,300 miles away. Several programs connect parents at a distance and even in prison with their children (Palm, 2001). Some parents felt torn; they wanted to connect with other parents, but they didn't want to give up their evenings or weekends to do so because that was their only time with their children. Some parents felt face-to-face meetings were preferable but thought the school Web site or other parent support Web sites might be their only chance to connect.

Many schools across the country, such as the Families and Schools Together Program, arrange family evenings and provide child care (McDonald, 1999). Other parents, although not able to attend physically, were very pleased when they were involved by being asked by their children to share family stories, traditions, and values as part of school assignments. Other ideas were scheduling joint parent-teacher meetings and inservices on topics of mutual concern, such as bullying, violence, and discipline. Finally, parents and teachers in some grades wanted joint parent-teacher-student meetings during the school day or in the evening (with child care) on topics such as sexuality or peer pressure. Parents also suggested that when their issues were very individualized and sensitive, they looked forward to meeting individually with a parent educator or coordinator who could act in a psycho-educational role. These meetings could take place in person or by phone or e-mail. Other parents preferred in-home meetings with either parenting educators or peer parents, a preference also documented by Wood and Baker (1999).

How?

During the 5-year study at the model development school, we began to see some differences emerge. Very educated parents in professional positions preferred to call the meetings *conversations* or *dialogues* and thought of the sessions as opportunities for sharing. Parents from some cultural backgrounds, whether highly educated or not, had been socialized to see the coordinator as the "expert" and would come only to lectures. In certain cultures, a coordinator who asked for parent solutions would be seen as incompetent. Less educated parents may have experienced top-down relationships with other institutions but were open to other ways of meeting, as was also seen in Hurtig's work (2005).

> **A Practitioner's Reflection**
>
> For many Mexican mothers new to Chicago, my "expert" status in the public schools where I studied and worked in the late 1980s and early 1990s was only a temporary inequality. They were very open to ideas regarding methods and content, but they wanted to attach that information to their own beliefs and values and be the final decision makers. In working-class communities, where I had worked on a parent development project 5 years earlier, more-educated parents who had full-time jobs in addition to work at home sometimes seemed less motivated than poorer parents were to do the "work" required of them by the school. The more affluent parents often wanted a quick solution from an expert.

Thomas and Footrakoon (1998) described three types of parenting education curricula used with parents in schools and agencies to address many of the concerns noted already in this chapter. Some parenting programs are what they described as *transmission models,* or the familiar sage-on-the-stage programs. Many of these curricula are designed to transmit knowledge, attitudes, or skills (e.g., communication skills) assumed to improve the way parents relate to children. The second type is a *transactional model,* designed to foster growth of the learner's capacities. In this type, the educator and the parent are both learners, and often the learning is about broad themes rather than specific skills. As mentioned in Chapters 2, 3, and 4, the *transformational model* provides opportunities for parents to think very differently about themselves and their role in their community. Parent-learners look at their social context and work toward changing themselves, their families, and their communities. Doherty's focus on community-engaged parent education (Doherty & Carlson, 2002) and Cochran's work on empowerment (1988) are examples of this approach.

Why?

Bowman's review (1994) of the reasons parents seek out parenting information and support sheds more light on the type of curriculum parents desire. He credits Dr. Paul Dokecki for identifying these categories. The first is the *prospective mode,* in which parents look to the future and anticipate possible changes. They are open to new information. Such a program can help parents assess their current ways of relating to their children and ways that worked in the past and may continue to work. It may also review new modes of relating that make sense as children develop new capacities. Groups of parents with children in similar grade levels worked best in this mode.

The next mode is called the *resource mode;* in it, parents may be looking for specific information. They may be more interested in a topic than in the way the information is delivered, and they may want to apply the information immediately. They may be able to use the information without support from a group or a parent educator. Parents in this mode may have many questions for the parenting educator, which might unsettle leaders who prefer a more collaborative and transactional mode.

In the *collaborative mode,* parents are looking for support and help in problem solving and are willing to support other parents in the same endeavor if they feel they have something to offer. Many parent groups are in this mode. In the Parent Education Initiative model school project, we were able to recruit these parents for the longer-term group discussions that used, for example, Heath's parenting curriculum guide (2001).

The *reactive mode* is the most difficult because parents are looking for immediate help for pressing concerns. They may not be willing to listen to others unless the others can give them solutions to their particular problem. One-on-one conversations very often work best in this situation. However, some large meetings about drugs, neighborhood safety, and similar issues were helpful for these parents as well.

In sum, we learned that over time, few parents wanted only the lecture format, some were open to group discussions, and many were open to methods not traditionally used in schools. Most of the parents in this preK–12 school were well educated. The study by DeBord et al. (1996), which involved more than 600 educationally and culturally diverse parents in North Carolina, Texas, Ohio, and Delaware, ages 16–65, found these parents tended to prefer groups of 10 or fewer, evenings over daytime, and weekends, especially Saturdays. Most parents in this study were more comfortable going to a meeting with someone they knew. Differences emerged in terms of education level and gender. Parents with higher levels of education and mothers were more comfortable in groups of people they did not know than were fathers and parents with less education. Fathers preferred going with a partner to going alone. One fourth of the parents needed transportation, and one third preferred bringing their children with them. Wood and Baker (1999), studying parenting education preferences of parents of lower socioeconomic status, found few differences in expressed desire to attend parenting programs in schools, but there were differences in actual attendance. Factors like a lack of transportation and child care figured into low attendance by parents of lower socioeconomic status.

DeBord (1996) found among 1,800 parents from several states and several parent support sites that parents with 2 years of college or more preferred newsletters, books, and magazines, whereas parents with less formal education preferred home visits, videos, and computer-assisted learning. Garton, Hicks, and Leatherman (2003), however, found, as others have in the past (Bogenschneider

& Stone, 1997), that newsletters can be effective for a wide population of parents. Wood and Baker (1999) also found that parents of lower socioeconomic status often preferred videotapes for the home, print materials, and parent-to-parent meetings over formal lectures. Wood and Baker also cautioned that packaged programs used in schools are often not responsive to cultural differences among parents and often do not take the cognitive and developmental level of the parents into consideration. Therefore, when practitioners design a parenting education and support program for a school, group format preferences and the parents' developmental levels and cultures should be determined in advance and catered to in order to guarantee successful participation.

Parents of children with special needs often do well in parent-to-parent programs in which a parent partners with a veteran parent who has experience to share and who provides understanding of the situation (Santelli et al., 1997). In their study of 240 parents of mildly and severely disabled children, Santelli and colleagues found that emotional support or someone to listen to their concerns, whether parent-to-parent or in groups, was welcome by parents in the study. Parents of children with severe disabilities preferred telephone warm lines to in-person meetings, perhaps due to the difficulty of logistics and getting someone to care for their child.

DeBord and Reguero de Atiles (1999) found in a multistate sample of 760 Latino parents who responded to a questionnaire on parent needs that doctors were the preferred source for support, with family in second place. They also found that small, family-like settings were acceptable. They valued learning about parenting from someone they knew, so they were less likely to come to a large meeting with an expert in the field than to meetings with someone they trusted already. Schools should think about partnering with those professionals who are most often approached by parents for information and support. In my own experience with adult college students who were also ethnically diverse parents, higher socioeconomic class was a good predictor of less reliance on doctors and more reliance on the Internet as a source of information about many parenting issues.

An example of a small-group format that worked well at the model development school was the book group. Some parents might be too embarrassed to come to a talk about children with drug or body-image problems but would participate in a book group on the topic. If they could not read well or lacked time, they would be no less welcome to come and join the discussion. Others wanted in-home parent meetings or meetings outside the school building about either school issues or community issues such as safety and drug abuse and in which parents, teachers, and students could partner as colearners. Large community meetings, however, might be overwhelming for many parents. However, opportunities to meet after large meetings to discuss the event have been found useful and even essential to involve parents of some cultural backgrounds.

The description in Box 7.2 of parents from middle- and upper-class backgrounds struggling to figure out how to stay connected with their children is an appropriate conclusion for this section. Hurtig's description (2005) of the perspective of parents of lower socioeconomic status and Lareau's excellent book (2003) *Unequal Childhoods: Class, Race and Family Life* are invaluable. My own experience of the past 4 years teaching parenting classes to very diverse parents at DePaul University has convinced me that all groups experience the same developmental changes and that all teachers will benefit from awareness of the concerns of all ages of students and their parents.

BOX 7.2 Middle School Parents Share Their Experiences

Understanding the Experience of Parents of Middle School Students

Excited, threatened, isolated, unsure, surprised, confused, wary, wonderful, stressed, curious, infuriated, and scattered: These are just a few of the emotions that, though rarely acknowledged, are experienced by parents and teachers on a daily basis. Adolescents do not experience changes in a vacuum, and the adults close to them are often strongly affected by the new challenges they face. Parents participating in school focus groups shared a wealth of insight into the complexity of parenting adolescents.

Supportive and Intrusive, Endearing and Unbearable, Excited and Horrified: Conflicting Feelings

Parents often feel that their adolescent, the principal, the coach, or a teacher views them as supportive one minute and intrusive the next. They are never sure when their involvement is just right. Parents in our focus group said they and their children saw each other as sometimes endearing and sometimes unbearable. One parent stated, "I'm finding it a very intense time to be a parent."

As parents (or teachers) see how a child is growing and changing, they may have very conflicting emotions. For example, "She's her own independent person with very strong opinions, which I just love. So I sort of see this individual beginning adult emerge. It's very exciting—and horrifying!" This parent can admire her child for the independent qualities she is developing, but she also sees how this independence may make things harder for caregivers. Adolescents often think in black-and-white terms and go from listening to all authority figures to needing to make all their own decisions. When

(Continued)

BOX 7.2 (Continued)

families with teens come to the United States from countries where such independence is not allowed, new problems emerge for parents and children.

Wonderful, Lucky, and Confused: Parents' and Children's Changing Relationship

As a child begins to become a young adult, parents must adjust to changing roles and developing personalities. In focus groups, some parents spoke of seeing their child as more of an equal partner, someone they could communicate with on the same level. One parent described beginning to see her daughter as an individual. "She's not a clone of my husband and myself." Parents find they must change the way they communicate with their teenage children. Instead of simply telling the child "No," many parents at the model development school said they discussed reasons for decisions they made that involved the child with their child. Many parents talked about being confused by their child's ambiguous feelings of dependence: "Sort of 'let me cross the street, but still hold my hand, and now don't hold my hand.'" It is a confusing time for both child and parent, and cultural variables add to the complexity, for while some children are expected to become independent, a number of parents expect their children to grow more interdependent.

Confused, Wary, Nervous, Unsure: Parallel Emotions

In preschool and elementary school more than in middle school, teachers are more comfortable advising parents regarding child development and ways to respond to situations. Parents also advise their children. But a middle school parent said, "You begin to let your children go a little bit in middle school, and it is the same thing with the parents. They tell you to let go of your child's hand, and they let go of yours also, and you find yourself spinning in the wind." Parents spoke often of understanding that their role with teachers would change, but they hoped it would not end. This is what experts say of children and adults as well. Life is too overwhelming to go it alone. Parents and children want to try to fashion a new role. Like the new pedagogy of Palmer (1998) and others, they wanted to be part of a circle of caring people, including teachers and students, looking in at a subject like independence together. What is it, and what is it not? What do adults mean when they say, "With freedom comes responsibility"? Perhaps the interdependence fostered in other cultures should be better understood. In the wake of the events of September 11, 2001, interdependence is something students will likely be open to discussing with the adults in their lives.

Concerned, Isolated, Pressured, and Frustrated: Influence of Others on Parenting

As children gain more independence, the conventional wisdom goes, they begin to be less influenced by their family and more by others. In fact, research has shown that teens still want to know how their parents and teachers feel about important issues (Simpson, 2001). As outsiders, such as teachers and peers, begin to have more influence on a child, parents must learn how to both interact and collaborate with those outsiders and deal with the resulting changes in their child.

Middle school children are often characterized as being cruel to each other. When preschool and elementary school children fight with a friend, a parent can help them make up. When a middle school child comes home sad, angry, or discouraged, a parent's intervention with the friend or the friend's parent may only make things worse. This leaves parents feeling concerned but helpless and frustrated because they cannot rescue or protect their child as they might have in the past. A third influence on a parent's ability to effectively parent an adolescent is the group of parents of the child's peers. With younger children, many parents are more involved in arranging play dates and transporting children. Smaller children want their parents around more, so when the children are together, the parents get to know each other as well. Adolescents may want more independence; consequently, the parents lose touch with each other. One mother noted:

> When the children were infants, you had moms-and-tots groups, you saw people outside of school. It was very easy to compare notes and know what they were doing and how other people were doing in a range of activities. By the time you get to middle school, because they're more independent, you lose contact with what is going on in anybody else's family.

Thus, the child's report of what "everyone else is doing" becomes a parent's primary source of information about other families. Adolescents become aware of the different rules that their friends' parents enforce and complain to their own parents about any perceived injustice on issues such as curfews, supervision, and so on. This leads many parents of adolescents feeling like "the meanest parents in the whole world" and wondering, "Am I really out to lunch?" Situations also arise when parents realize that other parents have differing parental values. Parents find themselves in situations in which an activity is deemed appropriate by one set of parents but inappropriate by another. The combination of children's complaints, parents' self-doubt, a lack of contact with other parents, and differing parental values

(Continued)

BOX 7.2 (Continued)

leads many parents to criticize and disagree with other parents, which leads to further alienation. Schools can be a tremendous help in supporting reflective dialogue on these issues between parents and with teachers as well.

Help Me! Support Me! Guide Me! Implications for Practice

Adolescence may be a difficult time for a child, but as any parent can tell you, adolescence is often a difficult time for a parent, too. It can be a time of overwhelming and confusing emotions, changing relationships, and new influences on the family. The child's experience seems to be vastly more studied, supported, and written about.

As the parents cited here have shown, there is a need for more information and support for parents of adolescents and every age of childhood. Ironically, developmental theories that overemphasize independence have an effect of minimizing the parent role. It is also the case that as children get older, the problems they experience are often more serious, and the shame factor impedes some parents from seeking support just when they need it most. Finally, for many working-class parents, children spend more time with extended family than with other families. This entails different dynamics, avoids some problems, but brings on others.

In his now famous article "The Three Worlds of Childhood," Bronfenbrenner (1985) described the interdependence of school and home. He noted that the family influences a child's capacity to be effective and profit from what he or she will experience or learn in other settings, including school. Likewise, the capacity of the family to care and help children learn to care depends in part on other systems, such as schools and communities.

The natural place for parents to seek education about contributing positively to the child and the school is at school with other adults. Focus groups in schools help bring to light and consciousness some of the concerns of parents. The goal of all these interventions is to help parents, students, and teachers feel supported and understood. This is not an end in itself. Emotional literacy is a very important first step to development and competence of the whole person. It is important to create a place for parents to stay connected, reduce isolation, and figure out an appropriate role that meets everyone's needs, a place where parents and teachers can learn and grow along with the adolescents in their care. Many home-school misunderstandings and many of the characterizations of parents as hostile and over- or underinvolved come from our not seeing parents as learners and not starting by looking at context, beginning with feelings. We know how fear affects a student's or a new teacher's performance. Underneath parental "hostility" is often fear, confusion, and frustration. Facing feelings, rather than avoiding them, helps us see we have more similarities with others than differences. Affect awareness is a necessary step for growth for parents and teachers, and the big beneficiaries will be the students who see empathy and emotional literacy modeled.

CONTROL: A COMMON CONCERN FOR ALL PARENTS

An issue that emerged for parents and teachers in these focus groups and of all socioeconomic backgrounds was control. Even though some parents with more material resources could pay for afterschool care or tutors and all kinds of resources to help children, parents were similar in terms of their realization of their limited ability to control their children when the children were not with them. To grapple with this issue with parents in the model school setting, we met with each other and listened to each other, met with students, brought in experts in the field, and read material by many authors on the topic. In discussing goals with parents, we often got to the insight that the issue was not so much about control but more about how parents could prepare children to make wise and moral decisions in varied environments (Berkowitz & Grych, 1998). The body of research by Grolnick (2003) on control is especially informative. First, we looked at how control was defined in the literature on parent and teacher socialization of children. Grolnick has written as follows:

> If control is conceived of being "in control"—that is exercising authority as a parent, maintaining high standards, and confronting and holding children accountable for misbehavior—then there is strong evidence that this type of control is beneficial to children. . . . On the other hand, I have argued that when control refers to pressuring, intrusive behavior, and motivating children through bribes and other external inducements, then control undermines children's motivation to achieve. It also harms children's sense of themselves as competent and in control and undermines the parent-child relationship. . . . We simply do not do well (or feel well) when we are made to feel like pawns to others, whether at work, at school, or in our personal relationships. (pp. 32–33)

We also found that concerns about children paralleled concerns about parents and teachers. People can hold each other accountable and have guides for relating that are respectful and good for children and adults, but everyone needs to feel competent, to feel that they are having an impact and are having some say in decisions.

What do the theories and research findings suggest children need to make good decisions as they grow and develop? Grolnick's theory (2003, p. 12) matches what we learned from early theorists in Chapter 2. First, children need to feel *competent,* as we saw in the theory of Robert White (1959). This means they feel they can do something, they can have an effect, and, therefore, they are willing to persist in spite of challenge. It is related to the "agency" Erikson spoke of (1963, 1968).

Second, they need to feel *autonomous,* that is, that their actions are their own, not someone else's. *Autonomous* does not mean independent or resistant to influence. Grolnick (2003, p. 12) cites theorists such as DeCharms (1968), who described it as children's need to initiate their own actions. Autonomy facilitates the self-regulation and personal responsibility so important for adult life. Grolnick describes self-determination theory (see Deci, Eghrari, Patrick, & Leone, 1994) as follows:

Individuals are born with the energy to pursue challenges and master the environment. Self-determination theory is an organismic theory because it assumes that humans engage their surroundings in an attempt to elaborate and expand themselves and thus to grow and develop. (p. 53)

Children should be encouraged to actively make their own meaning out of what they see and learn from us. They are not just passive clones of us, as the middle school mother observed in a school focus group. As she elaborated, they are their own person trying to choose which values they will name as their own and then live by, which Marcia (1980) referred to as being "identity achieved." They cannot do this if adults control all their choices. It is the same meaning-making process of parents and teachers as adult learners that parent educators should focus on in their work. They cannot make all the choices for parents.

Finally, children need to feel related and connected to others around them who support them in their efforts, as was seen in Adler (Dreikurs, 1989), Maslow (1969, 1970), and several of the theorists in Chapters 2 and 3.

Grolnick (2003, p. 28) also cited the research of Pomerantz and Ruble (1998), which found that parents who provided structure for children were effective when they did so to support their child's autonomy. If children know a parent tries to take their perspective and asks questions to help them think through their choices or situations, as in what Sigel, McGillicuddy-DeLisi, and Goodnow (1992) referred to as "distancing," then they feel supported. Their relationship needs were also met. If the parent tried to control them, however, they felt undermined. Kohn (2005) added the following observation:

It's harder to solve problems with them [children], to give them reasons for doing the right thing (let alone to help them formulate their own reasons), than it is to control them with carrots and sticks. "Working with" asks more of us than "doing to." (p. 118)

This of course applies to parenting educators and teachers as well in terms of how they relate to parents. Grolnick (2003) made the following observation about adaptive support:

Children need structure provided in a way that supports their autonomy and provides choice through development. Part of autonomy supportive parenting is taking the child's perspective and being sensitive to his or her desires to solve problems on his or her own. . . . At different ages, autonomy supportive parenting will look different. (p. 28)

As adult learners, parents and teachers also deserve autonomy supportive care and much latitude, along with children, in deciding what they learn, how they learn best, and how children are best prepared to be successful adult citizens and global citizens. Parents also need some say in how they choose to demonstrate parent involvement and solve problems in their children's lives and their own lives.

If autonomy is about having choices, then it is valued in diverse cultures (Ryan & Deci, 2003). If it is wrongly equated with independence, resisting influence, or asserting one's own needs to the exclusion of others' needs, then it would not be valued in more collectivist cultures (Kohn, 2005, p. 214). Some people have the stereotyped idea that parents and teachers with Asian or Latin American or other collectivist cultural backgrounds are controlling in the negative connotation of control and not autonomy supportive. Chao's research (1994; Chao & Tseng, 2002) has been very informative in identifying this misconception. Grolnick (2003) adds in describing Chinese parents,

The parental job, hierarchically at the top of the family's structure, is to provide training to the children in appropriate or expected behaviors—such as performing well in school. . . . Although the concept of training may evoke notions of controlling behaviors in Western culture, the concept of training, or *Chiao sun,* in China includes an extremely nurturing environment. (p. 76)

The ideal parent does not control to dominate but to guide the child into mature and responsible choices (Chao, 1994). So whether children are in an individualistic or collectivist cultural setting is not as important as is whether they are supported in thinking through and making choices.

Grolnick (2003) found that autonomy support held up in all cultures as having a positive outcome for children, even children in disadvantaged or dangerous neighborhoods. She and Kohn (2005, pp. 215–221) dispute the theory that parents of so-called disadvantaged children in dangerous environments need to be more controlling.

For children who are faced with difficult environments and who must negotiate peer pressure and the sometimes-coercive opportunities for engaging in deviant activities, the development of self-regulation and responsibility—both outcomes of autonomy supportive parenting—are just as necessary, if not more so than they are for children of advantage. (p. 74)

Research has found that parents of lower socioeconomic status are often more controlling and harsh in administering discipline than are middle- and upper-class parents—although we have seen that control is an issue for all parents. More-controlling behavior and harsher discipline are related in part to economic pressures and work status, as discussed earlier (Kohn, 1977; Pinderhughes, Dodge, & Bates, 2000), and in part to religious and ethnic beliefs. In spite of rationalizations by some that for many children, control through physical punishment is not perceived as necessarily negative, research studies in a context in which physical punishment was the norm have demonstrated some negative impact of that punishment on children (Rohner, Kean, & Cournoyer, 1991).

Parent and child goals, needs, feelings, and beliefs over time should be considered when control is discussed in its various forms. If the caring process of decision making is used and the discussion of control is tied to parents' long-term goals for their children, parents are making the decisions. There are no easy answers, but there should be a place to talk and listen to each other about this issue. Control within the institution of the school is also a big concern of teachers and administrators.

OTHER FACTORS RELATED TO PARENTAL CONTROL

Why do not all parents work to support their children's sense of competence, autonomy, and caring relationships? We need to look at some of the social contextual factors that make it difficult to do. Grolnick (2003) found that if parents are fearful, as many, irrespective of social class, are, they are more controlling and less autonomy supportive than if they do not feel threatened (p. 74).

This observation does not imply that being controlling is the best choice, but merely the reality for many. Often there is a correlation between stress and controlling parental behavior as well (Conger, Xiaojia, Elder, Lorenz, & Simons, 1994). Stress is not always related to financial problems. The time pressures that affect many parents can lead them to do for their children rather than patiently wait for children to do something by themselves.

Parents who have power in their work setting and are on the top in a top-down environment may also control their children more than would be ideal (Greenberger, Goldberg, Hamill, O'Neil, & Payne, 1989). Parents who can control people through their material resources may also use these resources to achieve short-term goals of child compliance and performance. If, however, their long-term goal is that their children make good choices, control through rewards or punishments is not conducive to that outcome. Parents who have a lot of resources but who also are invested in their children's accomplishing specific goals that reflect well on the parents (i.e., the parents are extrinsically motivated) may be more controlling than parents who are intrinsically motivated to parent.

Extrinsically motivated parents have children for status, to reflect well on them, to have someone to care for them in their old age, and so on. Parents who are intrinsically motivated have children so that the children can grow and develop as individuals. Intrinsically motivated parents may be less motivated to control children (Whitbourne & Weinstock, 1979).

Another correlate of controlling behavior has to do with how parents view their children. (The questions in Chapter 5 about parental beliefs about children as trustworthy are relevant in this connection.) Kohn (2005) cites the research of Clayton (1985), which found in a study of 300 parents that those who thought negatively of human nature in general (e.g., that children are born bad or selfish) were likely to be very controlling toward their children. Often authoritarian parents, whether rich or poor, have been shown to speak disparagingly of others and to demand obedience from their children, not trusting their children's ability to make the right choices. Sadly, these parents' own childhood experience often was similarly controlled and marked by mistrust.

Parents whose thinking is characterized by a focus on their own needs were described earlier. These parents, of all socioeconomic backgrounds, have been shown to also attribute ill will to their children or think the problem lies in the nature of the child rather than the situation or their own expectations (Hastings & Grusec, 1998; Kohn, 2005, p. 107).

What about school contexts? Do they help support autonomy in children? Grolnick (2003, p. 150) suggested that parents face institutional obstacles to promoting autonomy in children. Many parents, if they can, choose challenging schools for their children in order to maximize their future choices for college or careers. Challenging schools often are competitive schools. If parents allow their children to make choices, their very talented athlete may decide not to play basketball because at the high school level, it is not fun anymore and the school places too much emphasis on winning. What should parents do? How do they change the whole high school sports system? What if the parent has invested a lot of money in this education and is hoping the child wins a scholarship that depends on performance in curricular and cocurricular activities, even though that parent thinks it is too much? Parents need to talk about these issues and look at the way institutions affect parents' ability to facilitate autonomous behavior in their children.

If parents have to rush children to early morning study groups or day care because the parents start their own job at 7:00 a.m., they may have to tie their children's shoes and dress them even if it would be better for the children to do these things themselves. Some parents even feel they need to do their children's homework because the family runs out of time in the evening but the parents do not want their children to fail. This may be the case especially if teachers grade homework. In cultures where what someone does is more important than who one is, some parents feel extra pressure to do for their children so the children will do better and supposedly feel better, even though we know children will not feel better if they cannot take credit for their work.

A case in point is a story about Daniel's first day in high school. He came home, and his mother made the mistake of asking him how he had done. He proceeded to lecture her that in Spanish class he learned that parents greet their children with "How are you?" not "How did you do?" This story leads to another common topic in all parent groups: communication.

COMMUNICATION: ANOTHER COMMON CONCERN

Whether they are concerned with how disrespectful their children are to families, teachers, or peers, or whether they find it impossible to speak with their child, their child's teacher, or the parents of a bully about a serious topic such as bullying, communication is on parents' minds. Another experience with the caring process of decision making involved parents, counselors, teachers, and students coming together to solve a serious school problem and open up communication lines between home and school. These kinds of meetings have been recommended by Epstein and Sanders (2002).

CASE STUDY: A COMMUNICATION SOLUTION

A group of mothers of middle school girls requested a meeting to address issues of bullying, friendships, and peer pressure and also provide an opportunity to socialize. (Rest assured, other meetings addressed similar topics for boys *and* girls.)

Many of the mothers had younger children as well and wanted to spare them the older siblings' difficult experiences. The parenting educator worked with the school counselor to design an informative and enjoyable evening of discussion and group problem solving about kindness and civility, including strategies for dealing with difficult social situations among classmates and friends. To prepare for this event, we did informal focus groups with seventh-grade students during the lunch hour to better understand specific issues confronting them daily. We asked them to describe times they felt people had been uncaring. We put those scenarios on overheads for use in the evening workshop. The meeting started with a short pizza party for mothers and daughters. Then everyone gathered in the library for the meeting.

Welcome and Introduction. The school counselor welcomed the group and introduced the topic of the meeting. Group process rules were talked about (everyone would have a chance to talk, and everyone would show respect for others), as well as the procedure for the meeting. Then the parenting educator explained that she had been working with the parents on a method of problem solving and decision making called the caring process and that the skills involved in good parenting were very useful in making any environment more caring. The students were congratulated for coming and told that the school and their parents would support them in their efforts to improve their lives. They were then asked to read to their mothers some of the scenarios they faced daily.

The Scenarios. All the scenarios (listed in Appendix B2: "You Can't Sit at My Table" Workshop—Scenarios, found on the Sage Web site for this book, www .sagepub.com/mcdermottappendices) were read aloud by volunteer students. Each scenario was displayed on an overhead projector.

Modeling the Procedure. After the final scenario was read, everyone was walked through the steps of the caring decision-making model on the issue the group chose to address first.

Scenario 1: Exclusion. The following quotation was put on an overhead for a student to read to the group:

> My daughter would just die to be in with the group of popular girls at her school. When they snub her or she's not included in one of their parties, it just destroys her. Sometimes they even make rude comments about her clothes and whisper when she passes them in the hall. It makes my daughter feel horrible about herself. It makes it difficult for her to concentrate at school. It affects her entire life. It's just so cruel when people exclude you and say unkind things about you.

An outline of the caring process was displayed, and students received a handout of the model, a list of needs based on the hierarchy of needs described in Chapter 6, and a list of feelings (see Figures 6.1, 6.2, and 6.3 in Chapter 6). We limited our discussion to goals, needs, and feelings because of time constraints, but we included resources for the entire model. The students and parents then developed the following response to Scenario 1:

Describing the Situation. Children are being rude to each other. A student hears there is a party and learns she is not invited. Shortly afterward, these same girls mock her clothes and openly whisper about her as they point at her. For the rest of the day, she can't concentrate in her classes. What are all the things she could do?

Brainstorming Options. We listed all actions, good or bad, including the following:

- She can approach others and ask why they are doing what they do.
- She can find different friends.
- She can point out why she is unique.
- She can ask why she should dress their way.
- She can evaluate the group and ask herself, do I really want to be part of it?
- She can be mean back.
- She can buy new clothing.
- She can focus on school and find different friends.

Describing the Student's Goals. She wanted to be accepted. She did not want to be embarrassed in public, excluded, or distracted in her schoolwork. The other students seemed to want to hurt her. She wanted to be assertive, self-confident, friendly, and kind.

Identifying Feelings. We went through a list of feelings. The students could see the girl would feel hurt, small, sad, angry, frustrated, hopeless, and so on. They also described the other girls as feeling powerful, superior, and possibly guilty.

Identifying Needs. The young girl has a social need to fit in, to belong. She also has a competency need to do well in school and a self-esteem need to feel unique and good about herself. Her friends also have a social need to belong. Her parents and teacher have a need to feel like they can protect her and be competent in their nurturing role.

Identifying Unique Characteristics. This group did not have time to go into more details, but when I am with parents and have more time, I share information on the meaning of friendship for 12- and 13-year-olds. (A newsletter on this topic is included on the Sage Web site for this text as Appendix C4: Friendship Newsletter—Some Thoughts on Friendship, www.sagepub.com/mcdermottappendices.) We could also talk more about the girl. If she is an extrovert, that is, she draws energy from being with others, then it is very important for her to find a group of friends. (Eleanor Roosevelt, an introvert, said that when excluded, she began to read and prepared herself in many ways to develop an inner life and resources, which later contributed to her greatness. She reflected that she might not have done this had she been popular with peers.) We would also look at the girl's size (sometimes small or underdeveloped children are picked on). And we would look at the girl's previous experiences and perhaps remind her of a similar time and how she resolved situations like this successfully before.

Deciding on the Best Option, Taking Everyone's Needs Into Consideration. The students felt that the girl should find other friends. Other choices ignored her needs and feelings. Going through the list of feelings helped them realize the impact of the group's actions. The students felt empowered by realizing the situation was not hopeless and that there was more than one choice for the victim and the bystanders. After the mothers and children reflected on their findings, they were encouraged to practice using this approach.

Breaking Into Small Groups. The mothers and daughters were asked to count off from 1 to 5 and form small groups by number. The library had several spaces for groups to work separately. No mother could be in the same group with her daughter. Each group was given one of the other scenarios to discuss and work through the process of defining the problem, identifying the needs of all involved, and then brainstorming the options for a solution. Each group had a flip chart to write answers on for presentation to the full group.

Re-Forming the Large Group. After about 20 minutes, the small groups were asked to gather again as one large group to discuss what they had come up with in their small groups. One mother and one daughter from each small group had to present to the large group. As each group made its presentation, its scenario was put on the overhead projector for everyone to see.

Conclusions and Follow-Up. Clearly the room was alive with excitement. Mothers got an insight into the world of their daughters without getting into privacy issues. The girls were relieved, and some were stunned at the impact of their actions on others. We gave each girl a journal so she could record her use of the caring process all semester. On the inside of the book was the caring process and "Goals for Me," a poem by Virginia Satir.

BOX 7.3 Goals for Me

I want to befriend you without clutching,
appreciate you without judging,
join you without invading,
invite you without demanding,
leave you without guilt,
criticize you
without blaming,
and help you without insulting.

If I can have the same from you
then we can truly meet and
enrich each other.

Making contact involves two people at a time
and three parts. Each person in contact with
himself or herself and each in contact with
the other.

SOURCE: Reprinted with permission from *Making Contact* by Virginia Satir. Copyright 1976 by Virginia Satir, Celestial Arts, a division of Ten Speed Press, Berkeley, CA, www.tenspeed.com.

Students were encouraged to practice using the model. They were given the option of discussing it with other girls, their mothers, their counselor, or me. A number of girls came by my office. Over the next several months, girls came in for some encouragement or to share the news of a breakthrough or relapse. We were at least talking. Their moms called with news of being occasionally consulted by their daughters now that they both had some common language and communication tools.

It was important to have this meeting because the intense feelings about bullying and uncaring behavior had to be confronted. How we communicate about such topics is very important. There is often the content of a message and then there are the feelings we associate with that situation. A parent, teacher, or student may feel very strongly about bullying or may be upset and fearful. Those negative feelings about an issue may lead children to think parents, teachers, or others feel negatively about them, which clearly impedes fruitful communication. Intense feelings about a situation often make parent-teacher-student discussions very difficult and confusing. Educators must also remember that in some cultures, it is almost impossible to separate the doer from the deed or one's feelings about the deed from one's feelings about the doer.

Communication is one of the workshops parents request most frequently. Appendix E2: Communication Guides, found at the Sage Web site for this text (www.sagepub.com/mcdermottappendices), provides an outline with some key themes I have used in discussions of communication with parents. A newsletter based on a presentation on communication at the model development school, Appendix C3: Communication Newsletter—Enhancing Effective Communication in Home, School, and Community, is available on the same Web site.

COMMUNICATION AND EXPLANATORY STYLE

Seligman's work on explanatory style (Seligman, 1995) is also very informative for parents and teachers as they cope with children who communicate more pessimism than optimism in their self-attributions in situations such as bullying. Parenting educators also are concerned with this type of communication in parents. Seligman has helped parents understand their own and their child's thinking and the personality trait of explanatory style, specifically in terms of optimism and pessimism. If parents themselves and their children tend to communicate more pessimism (often helpless or hopeless) than optimism (hopeful, positive, and persistent in challenging situations), then parents can find ways to catch themselves and their children and help the children evaluate how they might communicate their feelings and thoughts differently.

Seligman notes that when it comes to bad events in children's and adults' lives, pessimists tend to think those events are permanent (the cause will persist; e.g., "I will never have friends at this new school"), pervasive (the event will affect many situations; e.g., "I am stupid in everything I do"), and personal (they are the cause of the problem; e.g., "something about me just turns people away"). Optimists, on the other hand, tend to see bad events as temporary ("it will take time to find a friend at this school"), specific ("my friend is mad at everyone today"), and impersonal ("my dad is having a bad day"). Furthermore, optimists see good events as permanent ("I succeeded because I am a hard worker"), pervasive ("I'm a smart person"), and personal ("because I stood up to that bully, Dylan was not hurt"). Pessimists would tend to see good events as temporary, specific, and impersonal, thus attributing less of the success to their own innate qualities and more to factors external to themselves.

When parents or their children ascribe causes to bad events, parents can think of, and help their children think of, the events as often temporary, not permanent; specific, not global; and often completely or partially external, not always just internal. When it comes to good events, parents can encourage children to see the causes as permanent, global, and internal. One would not want children to think they always succeed because of luck rather than their hard work.

Parents and teachers can try to catch themselves or children when they are having negative thoughts about themselves, evaluate the situation, find more-accurate explanations (e.g., you did not do well today because you didn't practice), and help them to not always think the worst (what Seligman calls *decatastrophizing*). It helps if parents, teachers, and children keep reminding themselves that there may be many causes for events and many solutions. (This does not mean parents encourage their children to always externalize blame. When children have done something wrong, they certainly need to take responsibility.) Finally, parents need to help children plan for what they will do next time. Help them clarify what things they can personally control and make better and what things are caused by external factors they may have little control over, at least at certain times. Divorce, for example, is a situation in which children wrongfully blame themselves for a parent breakup or argument.

The body of work on learned optimism merits attention because the way one communicates to children, parents, and other teachers can have a huge effect on their sense of efficacy. If we can avoid *always* and *never* (as in "You always . . ." and "You never . . .") and stick instead with *sometimes, lately,* and *today,* we will communicate more accurately, with less devastating effect, and far more helpfully with children and adults. If we can catch parents when they say "I'll never be a good parent" and help them recall all the times they have been successful in nurturing their children, we can help them feel more positive about their role and potential for effectiveness in parent-child and parent-teacher relationships.

COMMUNICATION WITH PARENTS, TEACHERS, AND SCHOOLS

These effective ways of communicating are also very helpful in terms of parent-teacher communications. Does everyone know the other's real perception or interpretation of a communication? Does everyone have enough information? Is there a place for naming feelings? For asking for clarification? What about the cultural or gender rules about naming feelings? How does a teacher understand the meaning of silence from different families? (It may mean disagreement, agreement and support, or lack of understanding.) Teachers and parents must be persistent in determining how their communications are received.

Many educators have found the work of Virginia Satir (1976) very helpful in understanding communication issues within family systems and school systems. She addressed the disconnects among feeling, talking, and action in our communications. She identified the most typical but ineffective and alienating style of communication as *blaming,* sometimes called the "I am OK, you are not OK" mode, in which one party claims innocence regarding a problem and attributes it to the other party or the situation. Blaming is frequently seen in parent-school interactions and gets people nowhere. Satir defined *placating* as a communication mode in which a person feels a responsibility to keep everyone else happy and be agreeable no matter the circumstances ("You are OK, I am not OK"), avoiding issues that often should be dealt with.

The *super reasonable* person does not deal with an issue from the perspective of feelings but from a logical perspective ("I am not OK, you are not OK"). This person's words do not correlate with how anyone feels. The *irrelevant* stance would ignore the issue and change the subject ("I am not OK, you are not OK, nor is the situation or context OK"). Satir believed we should all strive for *congruent communication,* which means everyone's concerns have a place in the process and no one's are negated ("I am OK, you are OK," and the context is acknowledged).

Congruent communication involves people whose words match their feelings, their bodily expressions, and their actions. This kind of person is trusted by others and feels a sense of wholeness and effectiveness in life.

COMMUNICATION EXPERTS LISTEN TO PARENTS

In the model development school, parents and teachers worked with me to sponsor several visits from communication scholars and family therapists Drs. Kathleen Galvin and Charles Wilkerson during 1998. They first met with small groups of parent leaders representing different grades, listened to their concerns, then after a few days presented a plan for a workshop, asked parents whether their concerns had been heard, presented a workshop, and came back for a second visit and a smaller meeting with fathers. Thus, they countered the sage-on-the-stage model and developed a relationship among the facilitators, parents, and teachers.

One of their key points was that we can never not communicate. Even when we do not speak to our children or the adults in their lives, we are communicating. They also reminded the audience that most communication with children and others is functional communication (e.g., telling people what to do), and they encouraged us to instead make sure a good percentage of our communication was nurturing communication that strengthens relationships.

Communication also has meaning in terms of the larger family-school relationship. Drs. Galvin and Wilkerson talked with us one evening about "communication at the intersection of family and community" (April 13, 1998). Dr. Galvin caught our attention by saying that every community has a shared vision that members tap into. Her presentation can be summarized as follows: Parents, teachers, and staff at each school walk into a particular school history. We also add to it, challenge it, and enlarge it. Ideal community involves all the members. Sharing in our community should add up to connectedness. It also implies that each person needs to define commitment at each school. For many, it implies permission for all parties to say what needs to be said and at appropriate times to hold others in the community accountable. The overall goal of our increasingly diverse community is unity of often very different and unique individuals in support of some shared goals. This idea is also helpful as we think about the global community.

Dr. Wilkerson noted that a binding factor in communities is shared meanings, or situations in which teachers and parents would construe and evaluate a behavior or communication similarly. It takes work to get at these meanings. He also suggested it involves people's taking the risk of letting themselves be known. It can and should be a creative process. Based on our previous experiences and cultural backgrounds, it may be much harder for some than for others. Often parents and teachers will do that hard work because they are united in their concerns about the impact of today's often toxic environment on children.

EXTERNAL THREATS

Schools often plan events to address external threats from the media and from the larger society. The work by Walsh (2004) on the impact of the media is very helpful, as is the work on child safety in de Becker's book *Protecting the Gift* (1999), which provides good information for parents and communities on the topic of child and family safety. The media and the Internet often threaten parents' and teachers' ability to provide safety for children.

Sometimes parents and teachers are confused by the advice from so-called experts on the Internet, on television, and in books and can begin to doubt their own choices and judgment (Connell-Carrick, 2006). Connell-Carrick offers a critical thinking guide to help parents and teachers cope with this problem by asking questions such as, what are the unstated assumptions in this parenting advice? Is there evidence to support this advice? What other viewpoints exist that contradict this parenting method? Does this advice fit my beliefs about what infants and young children need and my goals for their well-being?

Martland and Rothbaum (2006) offer suggestions on critical thinking in Internet use and in assessing the trustworthiness of sources there. First, parents need to ask, do I know where this site is coming from? Government agencies (.gov) and educational institutions (.edu) are considered reliable. Second, who wrote this? One needs to question the credentials of the author. Third, where do these ideas come from? (p. 847). One needs to ask about the sources of the information (e.g., books or articles or referenced research). Parents and teachers often feel they are losing control of who is influencing children via the Internet, but they are less aware of who is influencing them in terms of advice. Information about the Tufts Child and Family Web Guide and other reliable sources is included on the Sage Web site for this text (www.sagepub.com/mcdermottappendices) in Appendix E3: Some Helpful Resources.

Many schools provide opportunities to meet and discuss ways to protect children. Teaching children the caring process of decision making while they are very young will allow them to make more-informed decisions in their later years. However, parents need to be vigilant and monitor who and what is influencing their children (Crouter & Head, 2002). Chapter 3 explained that monitoring is a role very important to parenting and good child outcome. Schools can be places where parents and teachers discuss how to monitor so as to provide the adult vigilance children need to manage all the input from the media, while still supporting the development of autonomy.

Schools and parents also consider some of the policies of government to be external threats to what may be done in communities and schools. To counter some of the threats on the macro level, such as our society's lack of protection for children in terms of health and safety, unfunded mandates, or unequal opportunities for all children to succeed in school, parents and teachers often have joined forces with many community organizations and social service agencies to multiply their effectiveness. This effort often means advocating for others who do not have the time, energy, resources, or skills to do so themselves at certain times in their lives. It also implies that parent and school engagement can also mean working to improve government policies and processes so that all children and families are priorities. And it might also mean that involvement for parents and teachers focuses much less on homework and more on building better human connections in their communities so they can do more for children.

Would all parents and teachers be inclined to do this? Recall the distinction discussed in Chapter 5 between parents who were socialized to focus on individual needs, goals, and rights and parents who were socialized to focus more on communal responsibilities, not only within their own family or group but within the larger democratic society.

Some parents and even professionals may not feel responsible for the school community of families and may in fact feel unconnected or even threatened by people of social classes, political ideologies, religions, and cultures different from their own. Flanagan (2001), in her cross-cultural research and literature review of youth and civic commitment, shares some interesting findings on this topic.

In terms of U.S. society, if parents socialize their children to be compassionate and to feel responsible for the well-being of others beyond their own family and for redressing societal inequities, their children are less likely to blame others for problems such as poverty, unemployment, and homelessness and more likely to hold the larger society accountable for inequities than are children of families who emphasize rugged individualism (Flanagan & Tucker, 1999). Could it be, then, that if a family valued being part of the human family, as recommended by many religions (see, e.g., Pax Christi, 2001; Yust, Johnson, Sasso, & Roehlkepartain, 2006), its view of what and who constitutes a threat might be affected?

If empathy were valued and nurtured in children, might it also prepare them to not only be able to but to *want* to take another person's perspective and understand that other person (Eisler, 1999; Gordon, 2005)? Flanagan (2001) believes the best preparation for global citizenship is for children to learn, interact with, and work with children very different from themselves. But Flanagan and Botcheva (1999) found in their study of 2,000 8th and 11th graders from 11 countries in western and eastern Europe and the United States that U.S. youth were the *least* likely to want to meet youth from other countries (p. 29)! This is discouraging when we consider the necessity for our youth to be socialized as global citizens. Flanagan contends that "self-interest and materialism are antipodal to social tolerance and the principles that sustain a democratic society" (p. 34).

She and her colleagues found that youth who "considered democracy in terms of individual entitlements and freedoms had higher materialist aspirations and were warned by their families to be vigilant about whom they could trust" (Flanagan, 2001, p. 33). Other youth in this study viewed democracy as "civil and political equality of all people, regardless of their social background" (p. 33). It was this latter group who described their schools as places where they "felt like they mattered, where teachers respected students' views and encouraged them to share opinions, even disagreements as long as they did so in a civil fashion" (p. 33). Thus, schools and homes where children can share their differing opinions are positively correlated with social tolerance in youth.

SUMMARY: HISTORICAL CONSCIOUSNESS

The theories and research cited in this chapter showed parents to have many concerns about their children and families, including concerns about control, communication, and external threats to the family. These issues are often interrelated, and parents' and teachers' own beliefs and values affect the way they view these issues. Several authors cited offer practical suggestions for dealing with these concerns in the home, at school, in the larger community, and even globally.

Meetings of parents and schools together to discuss control issues, communication concerns, and many other issues are nothing new. Cutler (2000) suggested that meetings of concerned citizens to address schooling and children have been recorded since at least the 1840s (p. 2). He also suggested that as early as the 19th century, schools realized parents and homes were not monolithic (p. 7). Debates about the value of homework were going on in the 1920s, when Patri (1923) recommended no homework for children under 10 and only enough for older children to tie up the loose ends of the day (as cited in Cutler, 2000, p. 168). Winship (1912) talked about the inequity of homework's disadvantaging children with few resources (p. 517, as cited in Cutler, 2003). Finally, educators have long emphasized the need for students to have schools that support them in preparing for their most important roles, as parents in the home and as citizens in their communities (Cutler, 2003, p. 159). In the 21st century, we are part of a global community as well. Preparing children for the parenting-caring role is addressed in Chapter 9. Appendix E3: Some Helpful Resources, on the Sage Web site for this book, www.sagepub.com/mcdermottappendices, includes a list of resources for parents, teachers, and schools regarding many of the concerns raised earlier in this chapter, as well as advocacy initiatives.

Some Activities and Questions for Investigation, Reflection, and Action

Think

1. How do parent concerns about children (control issues, autonomy, communication, external threats) parallel themes in this book regarding parents and teachers themselves?

2. Identify and connect at least one example of theory or research from Chapters 2, 3, 4, and 5 that relates to the findings on control summarized in this chapter. What conclusions do you draw?

Reflect

3. Take time to journal. What concerns do you share with parents?

Plan

4. Interview a parent from a lower socioeconomic status and a parent from an upper socioeconomic status. What are their three biggest concerns?

5. What one action can you take as a student or practitioner to address one of the concerns of parents?

6. Role-play a discussion with a teacher who is overwhelmed with the most recent cuts in funding for school programs. What "mindful" questions might you pose to help this teacher feel more in control?

Chapter 8

PROVIDING DEVELOPMENTAL OPPORTUNITIES FOR PARENTS AND TEACHERS

Mindfulness means stepping out of those grooves to explore new territory, and that can be difficult to do at times.

—Ritchhart and Perkins, 2000, p. 45

The more familiar we are with our inner terrain, the more surefooted our teaching—and living—becomes. . . . We must do something alien to academic culture: We must talk to each other about our inner lives—risky stuff in a profession that fears the personal and seeks safety in the technical, the distant, the abstract.

—Palmer, 1998, pp. 5, 12

How do we keep from choking on the world's despair and cynicism and instead serve as agents of hope and healing? One way is by trying to live from the "inside out" continually reflecting on and sharing who we are and what we believe, knowing what and who sustains our inner strength. From that place of perspective and hope, we can do practical things that contribute to the common good, putting together our unique desire to make a difference with others.

—Bliss Browne and Shilpa Jain (www.imaginechicago.org/home.html)

AUTHOR'S NOTE: Special thanks to Dr. Nancy Hogan for sharing the qualitative information from the first two groups of the Committee on Teaching and Learning, and to Dr. Alice Price, who coordinated the Committee on Teaching and Learning Project. These findings were presented at the 1999 annual meeting of the National Association of Independent Schools (McDermott, 1999).

Some of the questions this chapter addresses:

- How do teachers grow and learn together as they confront all the challenges of working with children, parents, administrators, and communities?
- Can parent and teacher journeys facilitate the growth and development of children?
- What are some best practice models to facilitate parent-teacher development?
- What are some exemplary parent support and development models around the country and the world?

NEEDS OF ADULTS CARING FOR CHILDREN

The preceding chapter painted a picture of the multiple concerns of the adults in children's lives. How do they manage all this? Parents and teachers need a place and opportunity to think about all the concerns mentioned in Chapter 7 and to think about how they can cope with them, alone or in collaboration, so that they can meet the challenges that face them and their children. This chapter presents some successful models for parent and teacher growth and development that should inform school reform. It includes much information from the Parent Education Initiative (PEI) I developed in Chicago between 1995 and 2000. You will hear about a model in one school for parent and teacher reflection on practice. You will also learn of ways for parents and teachers to grow through joint meetings, personal and joint writing, and storytelling, to name a few successful methods. Finally, you will learn of other school district models around the world and governmental initiatives focusing on the development of the adults in children's lives.

A Practitioner's Reflection

Many people now expect schools to be learning communities for all involved, including parents and teachers. In the school where I immersed myself for 5 years to make this happen, I did not know that a unique teacher learning and development project would begin about a year after the start of our parent learning and development project. It was a gift in that it demonstrated what was hoped for in the theory section of this book to happen. How parents and teachers could relate as described in this ideal situation can and should be considered for every school. This chapter provides a snapshot of some important parent and teacher development opportunities that were designed in a preK–12 urban school. It also describes some comprehensive family center models around the country and world that particularly focus on parent and teacher learning and development. It is hoped that more schools, including today's exemplary community schools, will incorporate this unique way of fostering parent and teacher development.

I developed the PEI based on best practices theories discussed in Part I of this book. The PEI's purpose was to meet the growth and development needs of parents. Rarely is an educator afforded the opportunity to do this. It helped me understand how hard it is for parents and teachers to develop personally.

The rationale for the development of a model preK–12 PEI, the mission statement, as well as the implementation and needs assessment process are included in Appendix D1: Parent Education Initiative (www.sagepub.com/mcdermottappendices). Guides for the actual focus groups to assess parents and school staff interests are included in Appendix D2: Focus Group Guides (www.sagepub.com/mcdermott appendices). It is unique in that the parents, teachers, and staff worked for 3 months to define the mission statement. The program served teachers and staff as parents and caregivers of their own children and families, be they elder parents, foster children, or others. Often teachers work so hard that they have less time for their own families than they would like. The model recognized this.

The PEI and the Committee on Teaching and Learning were funded by the model school, external grants, a family foundation, and parents of the school's alumni to create opportunities for learning and growth for the adults in students' lives. School board members and administrators were aware that in a hurried culture, parents, teachers, and students often found themselves performing their roles without the benefit of adequate time for reflection or support. Often their work was done in isolation. Reflection, as we know, helps learners derive meaning from their experience.

Today, for example, we grapple with information from a multitude of sources. Should teachers and parents simply accept this information overload and the associated rising expectations for students, parents, and teachers, or should they investigate the impact of this trend on all involved and reflect on how to respond as a community? This is one example of a concern that might be addressed by both parents and teachers.

Are parents really just looking for isolated skills to help them improve their child's test scores, as the content of most parent involvement programs assumes, or are some willing to use the school and parenting educators and resources to help them focus on the ongoing, adaptive, changing, reflective, lifelong learning process that many educators feel is essential? Kegan (1994) has described the open-ended process of thinking, born of the dynamic interaction of today's cultural demands and parents' mental capabilities. The school learning communities promoted today are an ideal place for this process to occur.

PARENTS AND TEACHERS SEEK GUIDANCE AND SUPPORT

The PEI supported teachers and staff with their own parenting and family concerns, and the information provided also helped them better understand key issues challenging families today, such as the lack of caring and even safety in homes, schools, and communities discussed in Chapter 7. The Committee on Teaching and Learning was created at this model development school to provide an opportunity for teachers across grades to meet regularly to reflect on their teaching and to further develop professionally, personally, and as a community. No one imagined initially how much this committee and the PEI would parallel each other, but parents and teachers have similarities in learning, and supporting both groups bolstered student development and school success in the long run.

Each year, a group of approximately one fifth of the school's teachers met regularly, so after 5 years, all teachers had this opportunity to consciously reflect on their role. The school's parenting coordinator was part of the first cohort of teachers. Those of us who reviewed the evaluation of our experience were struck by how often the word *parent* could be substituted for *teacher*. In fact, parents and teachers were seeking many of the same goals. Both concluded that in order to be generative caregivers of children, they must find ways to attend to their own personal and professional needs.

An elementary school parent remarked, "If you get enough time to talk to yourself, then you can talk to your kids. Reflecting and thinking about things helps you be open and prepared to do this with your children." Similar thoughts were voiced in First and Way's study (1995) of parents' transformative learning: "I need to make the change inside myself before I could deal with the kids" (p. 106). Some of the goals for this teacher group are listed in Box 8.1. They demonstrate how rich an experience the teacher initiative was, as well as how we came to see that parents and teachers are on a similar journey. That insight, combined with how teachers and parents viewed the PEI program in the school, became helpful qualitative data for assessing the overall effectiveness of the program.

BOX 8.1 Teacher Learning Goals

What Do You Feel You Can Gain From Thinking About Teaching and Learning With Your Peers?

- I will have a chance to learn more about my evolution as a teacher.
- I will have a chance to reexamine my teaching philosophy.
- I will learn from others, including colleagues, authors, and site visits.
- By reflecting on my teaching, I will learn what works and what needs improvement.
- I will have an opportunity to get out of my own world and share with others.
- I will gain openness to a variety of teaching styles, new ideas, and techniques.
- I will develop connections, exchanges, and community across preschool, elementary, middle, and high school levels.
- I will have an opportunity to share my ideas and have a place to discuss thoughts brewing.
- I will develop by reflecting more deeply on how and why I do things.
- I hope to gain a chance to step back and think about what I do in the midst of the hustle and bustle.
- I will gain a personal awareness of what being a teacher means.
- I hope to gain insight into my strengths and weaknesses as a teacher.
- I hope to have a chance to examine some of my assumptions or habits of teaching.
- I hope to gain some renewed spirit, to gain a renewed commitment to teaching.

FACULTY LEARN AND GROW TOGETHER

■ **How Do Teachers Grow and Learn Together as They Confront All the Challenges of Working With Children, Parents, Administrators, and Communities?**

Below are some responses from teachers in this model school studied as to how more time to meet together helped them to accomplish this task. Any model for supporting and engaging parents can and should parallel a model for supporting and engaging teachers. While each school that chooses to implement a similar initiative will be unique, the list of teacher and parent goals and experiences in this qualitative study provides a wealth of information in terms of justifying such a project or in planning school goals and objectives. Every teacher has a right to this learning experience. To that end, the following responses are shared. In reading them, you are encouraged to think about substituting the word "teacher" with "parent" and think about all the adult learning principles that are at work here. The teacher statements parallel material theorists said parents needed in Part I of this book.

In working with parents and teachers over the years, these very same themes have emerged continually for both groups. Themes had to do with examining one's philosophy and beliefs, learning from others, looking at one's role, identifying strengths and weaknesses, and renewing one's commitment to children. Many parents want to do what teachers are doing in reflection on practice groups in schools. What do they think will change? One gets an idea by listening to teachers:

BOX 8.2   What Teachers Hope to Change

What Do Teachers Think Will Change in Their Teaching as a Result of Meeting Together?

- My self-confidence will grow, and I will continue to grow and mature.
- I hope to have renewed energy.
- I hope that my teaching will develop new manifestations, new depth.
- I believe my ability to discuss and develop ideas with other faculty will improve, thereby improving my teaching by connecting with others.
- I would like to think I would be able to constructively criticize myself more effectively.
- I would like to think I could become more open to my students and find more ways to help them learn and be more successful.
- I would like to find ways to do things more efficiently and effectively so that neither my students nor I feel so rushed all the time.
- I would like to be more willing to try new ideas and learn from my mistakes.
- I hope that my teaching will be more focused and that my direction will be clearer.
- I will learn how to listen better to students and keep students goal directed.
- I will learn how to make clear my expectations every day.

Again, you are encouraged to substitute the word "parenting" for "teaching" for the comments just cited. These are some of the goals suggested for parent groups as well, such as more confidence, trying on new ideas in a supportive environment, being more open to others, and being more effective in listening and responding. Thus, it is not hard to see why a parenting educator would be needed to support parents of all socioeconomic backgrounds to reflect on their practice too. In the 5-year detailed chronological log of parent experiences at this model school, many of the identical themes voiced by teachers were shared as reasons parents attended and appreciated having a place for them in the school.

PARENTS, TEACHERS, AND STAFF GROW AND LEARN THROUGH THE PEI

We documented comments from parents and school staff over 5 years regarding both their hopes for and experiences with a PEI in their school. Gathering information from many sources, relating to others more effectively, and having time for reflection were frequent themes. While teachers and parents often see themselves as very different, both groups are seeking opportunities to learn and grow within the community. When asked what they hoped to gain from the PEI, their answers, shown in Box 8.3, corresponded very closely to the goals of parenting education and support programs and thus afford a picture of theory being informed by lived experience. *Parents did grow and learn together.*

BOX 8.3   What Can Be Gained From the PEI?

Question

What do you feel you can gain from taking advantage of the PEI?

Some Answers From Parents

- You will share needed information on human development for all ages with us and we can discuss this together.
- We need a "front porch" at school like our mothers had in our childhood in their neighborhoods. The parent initiative gives us this.
- You can be a resource . . . an expert . . . what do we need to know to make good decisions. . . . We can then attach on our own beliefs and still have the final say. We can share beliefs with each other.

(Continued)

BOX 8.3 (Continued)

- Like middle school students moving toward independence, the school is letting go of our hands and we are spinning in the wind. You can help us find an appropriate way to support our child(ren) and each other.

- Help us relate better to each other. In elementary school, we are upset if our children are the victims or perpetrators of bullying or exclusion. We are upset if our children's friends' parents have very different values. Help us understand and discuss these situations so they are a win-win for all.

- Help us understand our children's and our own normal transitions.

- We will be free to discuss things if we are not discussing our children's or families' problems in front of teachers or principals.

- I think we are embarking on a kind of more thoughtful decision making than we have done in the past.

- When our children are studying a subject (like cultures or other religions), we could do the same thing with you and other parents.

- We don't want to call school if it is not academic, but we could call you for ideas about concerns we have and not embarrass our children by calling the school.

- You are not giving our children a grade, so we feel more comfortable talking with you.

- Help us deal with stressfulness and find ways to lessen it.

- You can help us know there isn't a perfect parent model or one way to do it, but you can help us know it's okay to do it our way within our framework.

- It feels like so much is dictated by what's coming from outside the family, and I know parents can use some help in maintaining what's important.

- You can create an environment where it is not oddball but the norm for parents to call each other and build a sense of comfort between each other.

- My life as a lawyer is organized by rules, but my 5-year-old does not want to play by the rules. Help me deal with this.

- How do I figure out my role in homework?

- As a new parent in a school where parents seem connected, how do I find a place?

- I am a single parent. Sometimes I feel out of the loop. I do not even know what information I am missing. You could help me. What about support groups or Saturday groups for single parents or noncustodial parents or divorced parents?

- Help me figure out at what age you let children learn from their mistakes.
- Help me figure out how to deal with the parents of my children's friends who are more conservative (or liberal) than I am.
- Start parent growth discussions in the early grades so it won't be hard for you to keep them going in the later school years, when they are still needed.
- Help those of us who work and cannot get to all the afterschool events to find a way to stay connected with other parents.
- Facilitate some networks of support as we get to serious issues like drinking, curfews, and the like.
- Don't always have meetings about a problem. People won't come for fear of embarrassment.
- Help us understand the issue of conflict. Is some amount of it normal?
- Help me figure out the differences between control, guidance, limits, and boundaries.
- Help us understand how to encourage a talented child without pressuring him.

Faculty and staff had some expectations of a PEI that were similar to those of parents and some that were different.

From Faculty and Staff

- We need more information on how parents of diverse backgrounds view our communications.
- You could be an onsite resource to help us keep abreast of research on gender, child development, techniques to improve classroom climate and parent-teacher relations, and so on.
- You could help teachers explore how to better deal with parent anxieties.
- Help us work more effectively with parents so that students will make good decisions regarding peer pressure, alcohol, drug use, and so on.
- Help parents who can't come out at night access resources and parent discussion groups through an intraschool Web site and other external parenting resources and Web sites.
- You could provide parenting information and support to our alumni parents and students via print and electronic connections.

Later, we asked parents and teachers how the PEI had changed their experiences in the school, home, and community. The responses, shown in Box 8.4, were very positive.

BOX 8.4   What Changed as a Result of Involvement in the PEI?

Question

What do you think has changed as a result of your involvement with the PEI?

Some Answers From Parents

- I have less anxiety than before, knowing my child's situation is somewhat predictable.
- As an empty-nest parent, you allowed me to stay connected to the school as a lifelong learner who is learning how to stay connected also to my young adult child at college.
- You helped us learn how to talk more effectively with our children and the school.
- Your timely book group on adolescent female development was a great resource for me as a dad and a way for me to feel comfortable in a parent group.
- While I cannot come to many meetings, your informative newsletter [Appendix C4: Friendship Newsletter—Some Thoughts on Friendship, found on the Sage Web site for this book at www.sagepub.com/mcdermott appendices] on friendships helped me understand my child's perspective and what I could do as a parent to help.

School staff responses demonstrate the wide range of ways the PEI could be supportive to teachers, personally, as members of families, and professionally, in terms of professional skills, better understanding, and making connections with parents. Over the 5 years of model development, the following were shared by teachers:

From Faculty and Staff

- Your newsletter on transitions helped my spouse, who is retiring.
- Your newsletter on transitions [Appendix C5: Transitions Newsletter, available at the Sage Web site for this book, www.sagepub.com/mcdermott appendices] helped my wife better understand what new mothers face. She felt less isolated, and this helped her.

- My job as a school counselor was helped because students knew some-one else was helping their parents identify students' and parents' needs, and I was not running interference for them.

- You helped our staff, not yet parents, better sort out child, parent, and teacher needs.

- Your group for dads helped me, as a teacher and dad, get to know parents in another positive way.

- Your resources were very helpful for my graduate school project.

- I shared your newsletter on resiliency [Appendix C1: Resiliency Newsletter, available at www.sagepub.com/mcdermottappendices] with fellow school counselors, and they found it very helpful.

- My husband and I really appreciated your newsletter and the workshop on prevention [Appendix C6: Parenting for Prevention Newsletter, available at www.sagepub.com/mcdermottappendices]. It gave us hope and helped confirm our practices and beliefs, which we felt were not shared by school parents but which we learned at the workshop were.

REFLECTION ON PRACTICE BENEFITS EVERYONE

■ Can Parent and Teacher Journeys Facilitate the Growth and Development of Children?

Yes. In simultaneous school initiatives, the PEI and the Committee on Teaching and Learning, the caregivers of children within a school community identified a need and responded to support to meet that need. Those who participated in these initiatives soon became their best advocates. While one might consider both projects secondary to direct student support, one only has to review the teacher and parent goals and evaluations to be convinced of the positive ripple effect of such an adult intervention on student academic, social, and emotional development. By acknowledging their own growth needs, teachers and parents were better positioned to recognize and respond to student needs in all areas of development. We encourage other schools to take a similar journey because this process is essential to parent engagement initiatives.

PARENT-TEACHER DISCUSSIONS ARE ALSO HELPFUL

The efforts described above represent separate programs for parents and teachers. Other chapters describe how parents and teachers engaged in thoughtful discussions of topics such as helping children learn how to care or to resist peer pressure. Other discussions featured *Punished by Rewards* (Kohn, 1999), which deals with whether parents and teachers should reward and praise students or work toward intrinsic motivation. The author came to the school as a guest speaker to discuss caring, competition, and student motivation. A discussion by parents and teachers on excellence in schools is included in Appendix E4: What Is Excellence? An Example of a Joint Parent-Teacher-Staff Inquiry (see www.sagepub.com/mcdermottappendices) to demonstrate the process, progress, and learning that takes place when parents, teachers, and staff search for answers together. Teachers and parents also met to discuss a term that sometimes worries teachers: *advocacy*. A workshop on advocacy, with narrative and supportive references, is included in Appendix B3: Advocacy in Schools and Communities Workshop (see www.sagepub.com/mcdermottappendices).

STORIES AS A WAY THAT ADULTS IN CHILDREN'S LIVES LEARN FROM EACH OTHER

You have seen ways parents and teachers could grow and develop by talking to each other within groups. You also saw, in Chapter 7, how parents and teachers could benefit from reflecting together on a common theme such as peer pressure to further understand each other and evolve roles with which they were each comfortable. In addition, parents and teachers can learn and grow, personally and professionally, from the methods employed in writing groups.

Parents have used writing with great success to derive meaning from experience and achieve transformative learning, and educators are trying to extend this successful method to teachers. Hurtig, at a school's request, is beginning a writing project with teachers (2006, personal communication) similar to her project with parents described in Chapters 1 and 5. (Conversely, much of the work on professionals' reflection on practice [Campbell & Palm, 2004] can serve as an effective model for parents.)

■ The Use of Stories to Enhance Learning and Growth: What Are Some Best Practices Models to Facilitate Parent-Teacher Development?

In the field of family and parent support, Reyes's discussion (1995–1996) of stories as "the life force of an organization" has been very influential and reflects the need for mindfulness. He describes stories this way:

Some stories simply entertain, inform or teach us, while others move us deeply and challenge us to change or remove our entrenched ways of viewing situations.

A good story touches something familiar within us, yet shows us something new about our lives and how we experience our world. (p. 33)

Hurtig (2005) has provided an example of how stories worked for a parent educator still learning from the parents and teachers with whom she was working. A mother wrote a story about her kitchen (p. 264) and how happy she was that her children came home in the afternoon to sit around eating snacks in the kitchen and tell her stories of their day. She also wrote that when she was young in Mexico, her parents were often busy working, and it was not their habit to talk so intimately with their children. The mother noted that she mentioned this not out of disrespect for her parents but as a reminder to other parents to focus on the parent role of being there to listen to their children's stories. When Jeana, an educator, read this story, it resonated with something in her life. She had become a teacher because her mom, dad, and family were interested in her stories. She was the first in the family to go to college and bring home "the world," so to speak, to her mom and grandmother. She recalled her teen daughter coming into her bedroom and telling her a long story with more details than she cared to hear. Now she realized that she belonged to a generation in which her career world was more interesting than her daughter's story, but how could she not do for her daughter what her mom had done for her? So the Mexican American mother's story about kitchen talk with children reminded Jeana of the need to respect children and their stories because their stories help them find meaning and coherence in life.

Reyes (1995–1996) identified another role of stories:

Stories and metaphors can construct bridges of coherence and meaning between our personal identity (the authentic self) and the professional role we play. . . . Stories give voice to a morality that reflects the belief system of the storyteller. (p. 33)

Hurtig's example (2005, p. 255) of this role involves a mother who wrote a story about playing in trees and with objects in nature when she was a child because her family had no money for toys. The stories were not written for the parent writing group and their children because they felt sorry for themselves but so they could grapple with the materialism they saw in some people in the United States. The story revealed that while they wanted a better life for their children in terms of education and job opportunities, a better life had little to do with material goods. They wanted to retain the definition of a good life that included close family ties, love, and responsibility, not accumulation of wealth, and they wanted to impact the society in which they lived as well.

Jalonga (1992) encouraged teachers to draw on stories as professionals in law and medicine draw on "cases" to help them better understand their world, their role, and their profession's best practices. Weiss, Kreider, Lopez, and Chatman (2005) have done this with the Web site for teachers, finenetwork.org, and their book, *Preparing Educators to Involve Families,* which recommends using case studies and stories as objects for discussion and reflection. Stories have been found to be an ideal way to process information. Jalonga (1992) discussed reports that found that teachers become the stories they tell, so a preponderance of pessimistic or complaining stories might indicate a strong need for renewal and reflection.

Stories are a good vehicle for teachers to get at their beliefs about children, families, and teaching. Stories can be a teacher's road to "discovery" of what it is they do as teachers and why. Many personal stories of daily teaching and interactions with students and parents can provide teachers with ideas about what their own theories of good teaching and parenting are. It becomes important data they can use to develop theories of how children learn best and how teachers and parents can help.

Jalonga (1992) also notes that stories can become metaphors for change as teachers think about how they have interpreted and reinterpreted the same situation differently over time. Stories, she says, also demonstrate an ethic of care. As teachers have a chance to talk to each other about the right amount of care teachers should give students or whether they are becoming too sensitive or too insensitive to a student's needs, they are able to think about their motivations for teaching. Often teachers have found that sharing stories about caring can help them endure the numerous questionable curricular or administrative changes that come and go over the years. The stories remind them why they are teachers, and that sustains them.

Echoing the issues that parents report, teachers often feel isolated from other teachers and lack time for reflection. Writing and telling stories are suggested as useful tools for counteracting both these problems. At our model school, each of us in a reflection group for teachers wrote about our own philosophy of education, and then we read our paragraphs to each other, first in pairs and then in larger groups. We had a lot of time to weave our stories together. The process was very helpful and led to many interesting discussions and much learning from one another. We ended up with a document that incorporated many of our ideas, which we shared with the school and with the school parents. It was another way for the parents to get to know us better.

Teachers often have more opportunities to reflect on practice than parents do. Parents are asked to be involved by doing things, not focusing on their evolving identity as a parent. Many opportunities are needed for parents to gather together and with teachers, students, and community members to reflect on their role and their hopes and dreams for children.

OTHER MODELS TO SUPPORT
PARENT AND TEACHER DEVELOPMENT

■ **What Are Some Exemplary Parent Support and
Development Models Around the Country and the World?**

While many schools today offer multiple family services, some stand out for the opportunities they offer for parent development. One model for parent engagement provides a parenting and family center to serve a school district, as is the case with the 30-year-old Family Center in Clayton, Missouri, a model for other districts in the state and around the country. This center is open to parents of infants for drop-ins and classes, has a preschool on the premises, and also provides school families (parents, teachers, and staff with children through Grade 12) with counseling or educational activities for and within the schools. It also is a base for the highly successful state-sponsored Parents as Teachers program, which involves parent educators working with parents of children from infancy through age 5, providing home visits, yearly developmental screenings, and programming to support parents in those crucial early years. The staff has read Kegan (1994), Holden and Hawk (2003), and other parenting theorists and researchers, invited some of them to speak with parents and teachers, and helped convene the first annual meeting of the National Institute for the Study of Parenting Education. Staff members apply the theories of these authors in their work daily. For example, they work with parents of young children in families anticipating transitions. They work with parents of all school-age children in anticipating, assessing, problem solving, planning, and reflecting.

That same interest in linking current theory and research to practice is demonstrated by the parent-community coordinators in Catholic schools in Sydney, Australia. Coordinators are each assigned to a school region, and they also meet regularly to support each other and the leaders of the Federation of Parents and Friends Association. They also bring in parenting educators from the area and from around the world to support parents, teachers, and staff in understanding how to work effectively with parents and families with diverse cultural experiences. They were especially concerned, when I visited in 2005, with understanding how forced migration from the Sudan impacted many of their newest parents. (Educators in Australia, at certain points in their careers, receive a 3-month leave for renewal and professional development. Recently I met with an educator from Tasmania who came to the United States to improve his work on the development of community schools. Teachers in the United States could certainly benefit from such an opportunity to learn from others around the world.) The parent educators in Australia also worked with parents, university educators, and researchers to

Photo by Katie Montell.

Parents of infants meet at Clayton Family Center to support each other in the early years of child rearing.

develop position papers to transform the way schools work with families. (See McConchie, 2004, cited in Chapter 1 of this text.)

Additional position papers and other materials on parenting education can be found at the National Parenting Education Network Web site (NPEN.org). This site provides a place for anyone working with parents around the country and the world to support each other, think about best practices for supporting parents and families, and find ways to network and elevate the importance of parenting education in the United States and around the world. Cooke (2006) has described the history of parenting education, the competencies needed to be effective, and the movement to elevate this professional field. The state of North Carolina has described how it set up a network to support parenting educators and professionals from all settings across the state to alleviate their own isolation as they work to support diverse parents (Bryan, DeBord, & Schrader, 2006).

England has also done a good deal to support parenting educators and schools in helping families. The Parenting Education and Support Forum is a national umbrella body for people working with parents to promote best practices, keep members informed of improvements in the field, provide chances to network, and educate the public as to how to provide comprehensive and supportive services to parents and families. Jackson, Hill, and Clarke (2004) prepared a document titled *Government Policy and Practices Regarding Parenting Support,* which is impressive for the

Photo by Mary Anne O'Neill.

Parent group at St. Ursula's in Kingsgrove, NSW, Australia, reviews a survey of new high school students on what stresses them.

understanding it conveys of the many areas in which parents need support. It was also impressive in that its primary goals were to counteract the top-down approach of most services to families, including schools, and replace it with a bottom-up approach.

The Parenting Education and Support Forum (www.parentinguk.org) provides excellent materials for people working with parents and for parents who want to improve their understanding of parent and child developmental needs. These initiatives also address the comprehensive needs of families, including family-friendly policies in the workplace and health care needs. While these are just a few samples of international work and come from predominantly English-speaking countries, they reflect countries that have a history of receiving a large number of culturally diverse families, working to support and learn from these families, and attempting to improve those efforts.

Other parent education and support programs using the theories and research on parent developmental needs in Part I have originated in hospitals like the Parent Center at Children's Hospital New Orleans. It supports parents and collaborates successfully with universities, schools, city agencies, and work settings on behalf of parents and families. It reaches parents through its outreach services in businesses, and it has reached all parents in New Orleans through its warm line, which has been a model for other family centers.

After the devastation of Hurricane Katrina, director Barbara LeBlanc and her staff went on the road to find parents wherever they could and offer support to them and their children. Now she is spearheading a movement to make family support agencies, hospitals, schools, and communities much better prepared to provide ongoing services to families who experience threats from the external environment and assaults to their own sense of self-efficacy and well-being. She not only gives parents essential resources but also helps them cope with experiences like the impact of having a special needs or chronically ill child without a wheelchair, medications, or support services. Her work attests to the need for schools to collaborate and coordinate services with diverse agencies to provide the complex solutions children and parents often need not just to survive but to thrive.

SUMMARY AND CONCLUDING THOUGHTS

These are just a few of the initiatives that are especially impressive in terms of staff understanding of the developmental needs of parents, teachers, and families. Certainly many other programs mentioned in this text, including all the early childhood and family education programs (http://ecfe.mpls.k12.mn.us/) universally accessible to parents in Minnesota, are exemplary.

It is clear that the first step in a caring model of parent-teacher-child-community relationships is more preservice courses on working with parents. After reading this book, an increasingly large number of teachers should appreciate the benefits of having a parenting and family life educator at each school or school district and should advocate for having them. Likewise, more students and teachers should be inspired to enter the profession of parenting education. Other ways to accomplish parenting education involve family support agencies working within or with schools to provide support to moderate all the environmental events that affect parents and families, such as isolation, too few parental resources, inadequate educational experiences and employment opportunities, lack of health care, and lack of afterschool care. Many outstanding parent support programs are described in *Putting Parent Engagement Into Action* (Williams, 2002). The National Parenting Education Network and Prepare Tomorrow's Parents are other catalyst organizations that serve to link states and countries together to focus specifically on parent and family support. See Appendix E3: Some Helpful Resources, at www.sagepub .com/mcdermottappendices, for a list of helpful organizations for parents and the professionals working with them.

Readers have learned about numerous examples of new initiatives and best practices from the perspective of the growth of the whole child and the growth of parents and other adult caregivers of children. Many other parent involvement and engagement models are added to the Web resource of Harvard's Family Involvement Network of Educators (finenetwork.org) monthly.

Preparing Educators to Involve Families, by Weiss et al. (2005), also discusses opportunities for student teachers and current teachers to develop professionally and reflect on parent involvement cases or situations to anticipate challenges and ways to succeed in involving parents.

Educators also need to be aware of the support needed from others to succeed. How can teachers do their job if a child comes to school without access to good dentists or doctors? How can parents do their jobs as parents if they are busy fighting dangers in their neighborhoods, dealing with their own personal challenges, or struggling to find decent employment?

Everyone involved must make sure governments don't forget nonvoting children, who need advocates. Many organizations (e.g., the Coalition for Community Schools) are working with the legislature now to better support full-service schools, which address the multiple needs of families so that schools can focus on being innovative and creative contributors to our knowledge society.

Of course, education would be enriched by the rich family and community influences such as the ones you have read about in this book. Sharing the success stories through appreciative inquiry (what does a school or a community or government initiative look like when it is succeeding in supporting parents and teachers?) should enable everyone to envision more-caring communities at home, school, and in their neighborhoods.

Some Activities and Questions for Investigation, Reflection, and Action

Think

1. What five statements by teachers about their group learning experience are activities that parents should ideally be doing as well? Explain why you think this is the case.

2. What five comments by parents in terms of their learning and experiences would also be important for teachers? Explain why you think this is the case.

3. Read Appendix D1: Parent Education Initiative (at www.sagepub.com/mcdermottappendices), which provides information on the implementation of the PEI. What got your attention

(Continued)

(Continued)

in this model? What in this process relates to what you have read about adult learning?

Reflect

4. Write a story or describe an experience that indicates how you think a teacher or parent should relate to children. It can be a good or bad experience but one that provides insights into what would be ideal.

5. As you journal, tell a story or describe an experience that helps you understand how parents and teachers should ideally relate to each other. The experience can be either good or bad.

Plan

6. Read the advocacy workshop in Appendix B3: Advocacy in Schools and Communities Workshop, at www.sagepub.com/mcdermott appendices. What are your own thoughts on how you might encourage parents or other teachers to advocate in the future?

7. Role-play this exercise: You walk into the faculty lunchroom in November, right after parent-teacher conferences, and notice most of the talk reflects negatively on parents. Suggest some mindful questions you might ask to help the teachers gain some perspective on what's happening.

Chapter 9

ENSURING THAT THE NEXT GENERATION OF PARENTS IS PREPARED FOR THEIR ROLE

It is important to help children learn as much as possible about parenting to help prevent social problems like premature child bearing and child neglect and abuse. Now that we know more about brain development in the very young, it is critical that we teach our future parents the important role that parents play in stimulating and nurturing their children, and in preparing them to reach their full potential in school and in later life.

—Zigler, 1999, Testimony to the
Connecticut Committee on Children

Certainly parenting courses for adults are important. But the adults who need these the most, are often the least likely to take them. So this schooling has to start much earlier, not only through a partnership process (which makes it possible for all children to experience real one-to-one caring from their teachers) but also through the opportunity to experience the giving of caring themselves. This experiential learning of caring and care-giving behaviors as part of the school curriculum is important for all children, but it is essential for neglected and abused children as well as for children who, in their homes, have learned to associate caring with fear, coercion, and violence.

—Eisler, 2000, pp. 232–233

AUTHOR'S NOTE: This chapter draws on my earlier articles on this subject. See McDermott (2003–2004), "Building Better Human Connections: Parenting/Caring Education for Children and Teens in School," in *Childhood Education, 80*(2), 71–75 (reprinted with permission), and McDermott (2006), "The Complex Dimensions of Caring in Parent, Teacher and Student Relationships," in *International Forum on Teaching and Studies, 1*(2), 30–37 (reprinted with permission).

It may well be that the nation cannot survive—as a decent place to live, as world-class power or even as a democracy—with such high rates of children growing into adulthood unprepared to parent. . . .

—Douglas W. Nelson, Executive Director,
Annie E. Casey Foundation, (as cited in Gleick, 1996)

Some of the questions this chapter addresses:

- What does parenting education in schools look like?
- Why does parenting education need to start so early?
- What has the research shown to be the benefits of these programs?
- What potential and challenges does this movement face?

BACKGROUND AND RATIONALE

In the previous chapters, you learned of all the challenges parents and teachers face in our society. They are daunting for the strongest adult. What if parents and teachers are not adequately prepared to understand the needs of children? With smaller families, and with families scattering all over the country to find jobs and separated from extended family, how do people learn how to do all that parents need to do? On-the-job training is insufficient in the face of all we know about the importance of the early years. Even in a climate of no extras in schools, many are convinced that teaching parenting in our schools is the only strategy that will contribute significantly to improved schools today and tomorrow. It is a logical focal point for caring-school and violence-prevention initiatives. It also teaches cognitive skills and affect awareness that children need in order to succeed in schools and as adults.

■ What Does Parenting Education in Schools Look Like?

In 1987, several educators, including myself, were trained by Harriet Heath at Education for Parenting in Philadelphia. We viewed parents and infants visiting in Philadelphia's Germantown Friends School and in center-city public schools. Parents and infants in the program visited a classroom once a month for the entire school year. Students charted the infants' development and observed how a parent had to adapt to a changing infant from month to month and minute to minute. This focus on adaptation was in line with Holden's theory of parenting (1997), discussed in Chapter 6. We were amazed at how much social and academic learning took place. Students planned for the visit, participated in the visit, and reflected on

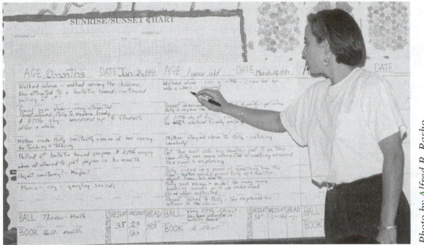

A teacher charts physical, language, social, emotional, and cognitive development of infants during a monthly visit.

how it went. Then during the month until the next visit, they discussed themes that related to the experience.

A typical topic discussed was needs. Teachers would focus in an early visit on how an infant gets its needs met when it cannot speak. The class would then discuss ways children communicate their needs and might relate the discussion to what the students were reading in literature. In *Ramona and Her Father,* for example, Ramona and her sister were worried about their dad, who had lost his job and who smoked. Though her parents were preoccupied with their own concerns, Ramona realized she needed to find a way to communicate her needs and fears to them, including her fear that smoking could kill a person, as well as her fears for her dad's competence and safety needs.

PARENT-INFANT VISITS: A POWERFUL TEACHING TOOL

Parent-infant visits are powerful teaching tools. They give parents a legitimate role in the school. Furthermore, the parents play an authoritative role. They are the specialists who know their individual children, and teachers are more like generalists (Weissbourd, 1994) who know about child development. Ideally, of course, teachers also hope to know children as individuals. In the visits, parents care for their children, talk about their children, answer questions, and model caring as they respond to their child in a caring manner in the classroom. They demonstrate the importance of responsibility, and they illustrate respect, both in the way they relate to their child and in the way they respond to the students.

Below are a collection of comments from visiting parents from the many parenting programs around the country and world with whom I share findings through the international networking organization Prepare Tomorrow's Parents (PTP). Some of these quotations come from my own research with parent volunteers from 1989 to 2000 (Coohey, Heath, & Murphy, 1992; Coohey & Murphy, 1990; McDermott, 2003–2004) and cover the reasons parents participate in these programs. Additional research findings are available on the PTP Web site (www.preparetomorrowsparents.org):

The students get a realistic view of parenting. They see how much time, effort, money, etc. goes into parenting. I participate because so many young girls have babies and are really not ready to be a good parent. . . . Positive interaction with others is something I feel is needed for children. It has made me feel good about my parenting skills. . . . I would love to see this program in every school. I think it would help the young adults make some important decisions.

I can show these children what it is like . . . facing reality on having a baby, doing what is right. If you are on the bottom, get back on top, get back in school and finish.

It was a great sharing experience. It helped my wife and me get to know many more students in an intimate setting. It was very positive, in a prideful way for my older son who was a student in the class, and that was good to see firsthand.

I enjoyed participating in the program. Since I have quit work to raise my children, I have needed to be involved in activities that allow me to feel I am still contributing to the outside world. It helped me to focus on the importance of my job as a parent. It also allowed me the opportunity to observe the way younger children view growing babies. This helps me to communicate and relate better with my children. I also notice that the students like to tell stories about their younger siblings. I wonder if the program helps them understand their own brothers and sisters and parents.

I volunteer to overcome my shyness.

Since I volunteered I have decided to continue studying child development in college . . . something I once began but could not finish.

I come to share my experiences as a mom (good and not so good) . . . to help students discover what they'd do in certain situations.

It made me want to go to school and eventually teach children.

It helped me to be more outspoken.

I faced a group and was able to speak to a group that was supportive.

It was a challenge to me and my daughter.

I am a scientist and was very impressed with the analytical skills being taught in the [Educating Children for Parenting] program. It's impossible for kids to see what their own parents do within the family. This program gives them an objective look at what's involved in taking care of a child. Planning the questions they would ask, the things they wanted to observe, measuring the baby's growth, and comparing and discussing what they learned are all fundamental parts of the scientific process.

Photo by Alfred B. Rasho.

Students use the scientific method as they participate in parent-toddler observations over the school year.

I wanted to bring my two-year-old son in the classroom because many of the children in this school do not have fathers in their homes and I want to show them how being a father is part of being a man and that maturity includes nurturing roles. I want the boys in this school to see that a man can bond with his child and keep involved with his child's life, and I want to show the girls that not all men leave their families and that they don't have to expect this to happen to them.

SOURCE: Prepare Tomorrow's Parents, www.parentingproject.org/students.htm. Used with permission.

As can be seen from their comments, the parents hoped children in the program would be better prepared to care for their own children. Parents were also growing as individuals through this program. Parents and teachers underestimated the powerful impact these classes would have on students' social-emotional development, their empathy, and their excitement about learning.

A Practitioner's Reflection

What amazed me when we implemented these visits in Chicago and in other states and countries was how immediately students applied what they learned about nurturing and caring from the baby visits to their classrooms and homes. A teacher in a middle school in Cleveland, where one of my former students, a middle school science teacher, had monthly parent-infant visits, reported that for weeks after these visits, students were noticeably kinder to each other. According to this teacher, these students brought all their fellow students, not just popular students, into classroom decision-making processes. They took fellow students' needs into consideration more often and were generally more considerate and respectful to everyone in their school.

THE MANY REASONS FOR TEACHING PARENTING AND CARING

Portes (2005) talks of teaching parenting in the schools as a way to lessen the disadvantage gap in achievement for many children. His rationale is that the subject of families is an area, unlike math, reading, or science, in which middle-class students are not way ahead of everyone else. Nurturing children as parents do is an intrinsically relevant body of information that few children have mastered. Also, he reasons that if children learn what is involved in parenting in the very early years, they will be more prepared to provide the caring environment that will allow their own children to succeed academically and socially, so teaching parenting is early prevention as well.

Many educators (Meier, Kohn, Darling-Hammond, Sizer, & Wood, 2004; Merrow, 2002) warn us of potential dire consequences of No Child Left Behind: "No child may be left whole." Under the regimen of No Child Left Behind, teachers have little time to expand programs on diversity, character education, or affective education. They must prepare children to be better mathematicians, readers, and test takers. Students may be able to build better bombs, but will they be able to build better human connections? In describing "the irreducible needs of children," Brazelton and Greenspan (2000) see human development literacy to be even more important in schools than math and reading, which are subjects mandated for testing in the No Child Left Behind legislation. They advocate the teaching of parenting as an excellent way to accomplish human development literacy (pp. 76–77). Preparing children and teens for the most important job most of them will ever have has a great deal of support because it addresses their immediate social and emotional needs and the familial and societal needs of a more socially and emotionally fit next generation.

Comer (2001) reminds us of the purpose of education:

> Given the purpose of education—to prepare students to become successful workers, family members, and citizens in a democratic society—even many "good" traditional schools, as measured by high test scores are not doing their job adequately. . . . A good education should help students to solve problems encountered at work and in personal relationships, to take on the responsibility of caring for themselves and their families, to get along well in a variety of life settings, and to be motivated contributing members of a democratic society. Such learning requires conditions that promote positive child and youth development. (p. 1)

And Bronfenbrenner (1979) made a similar point:

> It is now possible for a person eighteen years of age to graduate from high school without ever having had to do a piece of work on which somebody else truly depended . . . without ever having cared for, or even held, a baby . . . without ever having comforted or assisted another human being who really needed help. . . . No society can long sustain itself unless its members have learned the sensitivities, the motivations, and skills involved in assisting and caring for other human beings. (p. 53)

However, schools are focusing more on competition than on caring. Tests often compare students' performance to one another's. Yet despite all the money infused into schools and the heroic efforts of teachers, great academic improvements are not in evidence. Some blame stresses in students' lives (e.g., poverty, violence, ineffective and unprepared parents, uninvolved parents). Others say children will not learn unless there is a caring environment for learning at home, at school, and in the community and unless what they learn in school is meaningful to them (Kohn, 1991, 1999). Noddings (1992) notes, "Surely the care of children should be a central topic in the education of all students" (p. 106). She adds the point that emotional and academic achievement are not mutually exclusive:

> I have argued that education should be organized around themes of care rather then the traditional disciplines. All students should be engaged in a general education that guides them in caring for self, intimate others, global others, plants,

animals, and the environment, the human-made world, and ideas. Moral life so defined should be frankly embraced as the main goal of education. Such an aim does not work against intellectual development or academic achievement. On the contrary, it supplies a firm foundation for both. (p. 173)

All these educators have for decades been wisely suggesting that learning to care in homes and schools is essential preparation for citizenship not only in one's neighborhood but in a global society, where students should be welcoming of differences rather than fearful of them.

ADVOCATES FOR THE CAUSE

PTP, a grassroots organization founded by parents, educators, and citizens in the public and private sectors, has identified programs that teach children how to be caring students today and caring parents tomorrow. This national organization promotes parenting education as the yeast to grow schools that develop whole students who are successful intellectually, personally, socially, and emotionally. Today's students may be limited in their capacity to learn because of unprepared parents or because of school settings that are not responsive to their complex needs. Some, due to parental neglect and lack of adult awareness of their needs as infants, may never be able to learn as well as others. If schools have resources to add only one program, it should be teaching parenting. Not only will such programming teach students caring skills crucial in today's violent world (Eisler, 2002), but this generation of students will know what their own children will need to learn and grow. Think of how this knowledge will help future teachers do their work.

Effective parenting and caring enhances children's potential for healthy human relationships. In learning about parenting, students grow to understand that "nurturing emotional relationships are the most crucial primary foundation for both intellectual and social growth," according to Brazelton and Greenspan (2000, pp. 2–3), who explain the necessity of early nurturing in this way:

It's this early reciprocal dialogue with emotional cueing, rather than any cognitive stimulation like flash cards, that leads to the growth of the mind and the brain and the capacities to reason and think. Both emotional and intellectual development depend on rich, deep, nurturing relationships early in life, and now continuing neuroscience research is confirming this process. (p. 9)

As Chapter 2 illustrated, the most important word in the study of adult and child development is not *success* or *achievement;* it is *relationships.* All future parents must get this information. Observing nurturing parents firsthand, thinking about what all babies need, caring for others, and reflecting on that caring provides students of all learning styles an equal opportunity to learn and grow.

WHAT CHILDREN LEARN IN PARENTING-CARING CLASSES

Teaching students how to care by observing how parents care for constantly changing infants not only prepares the students for parenting but improves their own mental health and well-being by eliminating many destructive behaviors toward themselves and others (Schiffer, 2002, p. 27). In learning to understand the needs, feelings, and temperaments of infants and parents, students learn about their own needs and feelings and those of others in their lives. Focusing on others and grappling with the self, as many parenting programs allow, can be more effective for students' social-emotional learning than can studying virtues in the abstract, as some character education programs do. Consider some of the comments from students in New York describing their experience in Lou Howort's class on child development in New York City's High School for the Humanities (www.parentingproject.org/students.htm):

> I learned that using language to express your feelings teaches the child to do the same. This is very important for good communication between parent and child throughout life.

> To really know your child, your family, even friends, you have to understand yourself.

> I've learned to be patient with smaller children and to show them support. To love and take care and protect your child. I can't really tell you how much this class made me a better person.

> As I was learning about child development, I was understanding why my parents are the way they are.

> My relationships with my sisters as well as my grandmother have really improved since I now know a little more about the feelings of kids and what parents go through.

We who are part of PTP believe the essence of parenting—the ability to empathize with and nurture others—forms the basis for a child's character development and cannot be left to chance. Youngsters with empathy skills are less violent and less likely to abuse others (Schonert-Reichl, Smith, & Zaidman-Zait, 2004). Teaching these skills early, before boys see them as a female trait, is essential

(Miedzian, 2002). But having the skill of empathy is not enough. Educators (Mayeroff, 1971; Noddings, 1984, 1992) believe children must be encouraged and motivated to care. Caring is defined by Noddings as "stepping out of one's own frame of reference" (1984, p. 24). Mayeroff talks about having the development of the other in mind (p. 1). How different the post–September 11, 2001, world would be if more people could do this. Kohn (1991) suggests that imagining how someone else thinks, feels, or sees the world not only fosters caring but also promotes cognitive problem solving. It would also promote more peaceful relations globally. Rolheiser and Wallace (2004) found that teaching empathy in a parenting class facilitates social-emotional and cognitive development, and Zins, Weissberg, Wang, and Walberg (2004) have shown that social-emotional learning facilitates academic learning. In sum, instituting caring-parenting programs in our schools has broad developmental implications for children.

Heath's curriculum titled *Education for Parenting: Learning How to Care* (1995), now being revised, helps students develop the cognitive and affective parenting skills that also facilitate success academically and interpersonally. The questions asked about the parent-infant relationship involve the same *parental thinking skills* in her theory on parenting, described in Chapter 3: *anticipating, brainstorming, causal reasoning, deductive reasoning, descriptive reporting, empathizing, evaluative thinking, imaginative thinking, inductive reasoning, interpretive thinking, judging, noting differences, noting similarities, sequencing, solving problems, planning, reflecting, and relational thinking.* All this learning takes place in connection with one of the most meaningful topics for students: families and relationships. It is no wonder Heath's use of this program in English as a second language and family literacy classes is so well received. If our schools teach these critical thinking skills to young children, they in turn will know the right questions to ask about their children. Appendix E5: Thinking Skills in Parenting (at www.sagepub.com/mcdermott appendices) provides a chart from Heath's curriculum (1995) with the guiding questions for each of the thinking skills mentioned above.

The Right Questions Project (www.rightquestion.org) helps parents think critically about their children's needs and how to advocate for them by knowing what to ask of decision makers. It also helps parents come up with their own solutions through a brainstorming process much like the one we teach students in the program described in Chapter 6 and in the parent-infant school visits. We feel these skills are better taught before people have children than as interventions afterward.

While most teachers appreciate having a program that addresses violence prevention, pregnancy prevention, child abuse and drug abuse prevention, human development literacy, and cognitive skill development, they need empirical data to justify such a program in their school. Many parenting program evaluations have been described on the PTP Web site and in the organization's advocacy guide

(Schiffer, 2002). Many programs effective in teaching parenting and caring skills exist (the next section describes a few), but institutionalizing them in schools nation-wide will require a paradigm shift.

INTERNATIONAL MOVEMENT FOR PARENTING IN SCHOOLS

In England and Australia, momentum is also building. Tomison (1996) notes, "In New South Wales . . . education is strongly involved in preparing young people to function in society, rather than working to educate on a purely academic agenda" (p. 40). Tomison (1998) described the Starting Out Project, in Burnside, New South Wales, whose "purpose is to prevent abuse by educating young people about child development and the impact of abuse on children. The project . . . enables them to reflect on the way they were parented and to begin to think about how they want to parent" (pp. 13–14). Mary Gordon has also brought her program Roots of Empathy to Australia.

In 1990, O'Connor wrote, "Education for Parenthood has for many years been a neglected, low status area of school curricula, despite a professed belief in the family as a stabilizing influence on society" (p. 86). She advocated that such programs, though varying in format and the way they are integrated into curricula, need to be consistent in terms of buy-in by school staff. Hope and Sharland (1997) concur. Their comprehensive study found that programs were most successful when they were built into personal and social-emotional education programs that were highly valued by school personnel and the government.

Sadly, while these programs are growing around the world, many are being cut from U.S. schools, in spite of encouraging reports such as this one on parenting education programs for middle and high school students begun in 1994 in Manchester, England (Hope & Sharland, 1997, p. 69): Parent education in five pilot schools showed a measurable positive impact on students' knowledge, skills, and attitudes toward parenting. The majority of students showed an increased understanding of the roles and responsibilities of parenthood. The majority saw the importance of reading to children and asking for help in coping with a baby's crying. There were few differences in interest in children by gender or ethnicity. Parents saw the program as practical, relevant, useful, and interesting and wished they had had these programs when they were students.

There is also strong support among U.S. parents for parenting education for young people. A national survey by independent researchers (Lake Snell Perry & Associates, 1999) found that Americans strongly favored relationship and parent preparation for young people: 88% favored it in high schools, 82% in middle schools, and 69% in elementary schools.

TEACHING PARENTING THROUGHOUT THE SCHOOL YEARS

■ Why Does Parenting Education Need to Start So Early?

Experts believe that to be effective, parenting courses should have a redundancy component geared toward children's changing learning capacities. The National Children's Bureau describes parent education as a "continuous process, starting with birth and early childhood and going through school days, adolescence and committed relationships, pregnancy and parenthood itself" (O'Connor, 1990, p. 85), with education tailored appropriately to developmental tasks. Others believe one high school intervention is helpful but not adequate to prepare for such a difficult role (Luster & Youatt, 1989, p. 13).

Gaudin (1993) is one of many prevention experts who believe parenting education in schools will have invaluable and widespread benefits:

> Schools are in a key position to offer preparation for parenting and life skills development beginning with very young children in kindergarten through critical preteen and teenage years and for young adult parents through extended hour programs. Curricula should include child development and child care skills, interpersonal skills, problem-solving and decision-making skills, budgeting, health maintenance/physical fitness, and identity enhancement skills. . . . Development of these critical life skills would do much to prevent neglect in the current and next generation of parents. (p. 63)

RESULTS DEMONSTRATE STUDENT LEARNING

Ideally all schools would have an onsite parenting educator, family life educator, or Family and Consumer Science (FACS) teacher well qualified to teach parenting. FACS teachers were and are the backbone of these courses, but some of their positions are threatened by the emphasis placed on reading and math. Some parenting and child development courses are being reduced to brief coverage in a physical education class. Yet parents and educators continue to advocate increasing the number of these courses. With all that is learned in the parenting-caring process, it is also strongly recommended that teachers in pretraining learn of the many benefits of such courses for their students.

■ What Has the Research Shown to Be the Benefits of These Programs?

Educating Children for Parenting® *(ECP)*. Besides FACS classes, this was one of the earliest parenting education programs in the United States for the elementary grades. This program's early evaluations (Masterpaqua, 1992) of fifth- and sixth-grade students in seven schools in Pennsylvania and New York found that children in ECP classes had a significantly larger number of solutions to parent-child problems than controls did. The program participants also had a significantly greater number of solutions reflecting positive caring of young children than controls did. Students were able to generate solutions, an important parenting-caring and life skill. There was also a trend for students to see physical punishment as less desirable than they had seen it previously. Many of these findings were replicated in other ECP studies in 1996 and 1998. Often students showed increased skills in observation, questioning, and interpersonal problem solving—all skills highly relevant to academic and interpersonal learning.

Education for Parenting: Learning How to Care (Heath, 1995). I have used this curriculum since 1985. It was evaluated by Murphy, D'Anna, D'Anna, Heath, and Towey (1994) when taught to 474 students in two Chicago public schools. In a sample of fifth to seventh-grade students who took pre- and postmeasures in the first (predominantly Spanish-speaking) school, students observed and described infants and their needs more accurately at the posttest and generated more developmentally appropriate solutions than before the program. For example, prior to the program, for almost any infant scenario presented, students answered, "Give her a bottle and put her to bed." After the program, these students had an improved appreciation of the parent role and showed modest gains in knowledge of the physical and social dimensions of child development. In a pretest story told to pictures, when an infant was exploring a closet of dangerous cleaning products, students gave the "bottle" solution. After the program, they saw a "curiosity need" and suggested finding safe toys for the infant to explore.

In the other school, which was predominantly African American, junior high students were interviewed and kept journals. A content analysis of the journals and interviews (Coohey & Murphy, 1990) found that students reported infant safety and the responsibilities of parenthood as the most important information learned. Teachers in both schools believed parenting classes should be part of a school initiative on caring. Their logic was that if a school values the teaching of caring and personal and social-emotional education, teachers would be able to incorporate parenting classes successfully. Teachers in Chicago, New York, Ohio, Alaska, and Philadelphia with whom we worked believed the same caring process taught in these parenting classes should be used in classroom discipline; in the ways teachers, parents, and students relate; and in how parents are encouraged to relate to their own children and toward schools and communities. (See also Chapter 6 and McDermott, 2006.)

In urban and suburban Chicago public and private schools in the late 1990s, I helped develop a caring school model with parent visits as the centerpiece. These programs succeeded when the principal believed in them. Unfortunately, some of these inner-city schools, despite showing great progress in caring, were closed due to Catholic school consolidations. Public school programs were cut because of pressure for improvements in math and reading. Thus, longitudinal research efforts were interrupted. The following comments from participating Chicago inner-city public school teachers reflect the power of parenting classes within a caring school model. From one teacher we heard,

> Because of parenting education, there has been an increased sensitivity to the needs of infants and others. There has been an increased understanding of one's dependency on others for varying needs. My students have been very willing to share their thoughts and feelings.

Another informative comment was, "I feel students are more aware of each other as individuals. They appear to be more accepting of differences. . . . My class got to observe a loving, caring mom who is really involved with her children's development." Another teacher remarked, "Their observation skills were increased. They can now appreciate what adults do for them . . . how much time and effort is taken to rear a child or teach a student."

The following student comments match key objectives in these programs. One objective is that students will realize the responsibilities involved in parenting. From a Chicago public school seventh-grade student, we heard

> The parenting program has good benefits towards kids. It scares the kid to death knowing that parents go through that much responsibility. It teaches them that having a baby isn't fun or a joke, it's real and they have to deal with it no matter what. A baby needs love, care, and a place to live and keep warm. The program could be important because besides it scaring you, it teaches you responsibility.

From other public school students, we heard about babies' needs, including love, curiosity, and competency:

> I have learned that taking care of a baby is very hard work and that babies need people who love them and who would take care of them. . . . It is a big responsibility. . . . The babies never stay still and they are never still because they want to see and experience new things.

> I have learned to take care of babies and let them explore.

> Another frequent comment had to do with a baby's need to feel safe and secure.

> Parents need to know that they should not play with guns, matches, knives, drugs, or leave on hot things like irons. Kids and babies need to be safe and you need to always love them.

Children also learned about the uniqueness of each baby.

The thing I liked the best was when I got to observe the baby because all babies are different.

Finally, when asked how to improve the program, students mentioned having more visits and the need to see more fathers. In the Learning How to Care Curriculum, teaching children how to care parallels the principles of the character education many feel is essential for holistic student development (McDermott & Heath, 2002). Appendix E6: Parenting Education and Character Development (at www.sagepub.com/mcdermottappendices) provides more details.

Roots of Empathy (ROE). Gordon (2005) introduced the concept of parent-infant visits to Canada in the ROE program. Recently a study evaluating ROE by Rolheiser and Wallace (2004) demonstrated that using parent-infant visits to teach students how to care and be empathic was in fact related to enhancing the core social-emotional learning competencies of social awareness, self-awareness, relationships, responsible decision making, and self-management (p. 61). Life skills were also enhanced.

Gordon received support for her program that rivals anything we have received in the United States for similar programs. This program has as its mission to "build caring and peaceful citizens through the development of empathy in children and adults." (See www.rootsofempathy.org/research.html and http://ncab.nssfbestpractice .org.au/resources/resources.shtml for more supportive data.) On this Web site, you

Photo by Alfred B. Rasho.

Students requested that more fathers visit schools to demonstrate their love, sensitivity, and commitment to their children.

will also find evidence for significant positive associations between teaching these social-emotional skills in parenting programs and increases in academic test scores, enthusiasm for learning, decreases in behavior problems, and increases in cognitive functions, as Heath's program also demonstrated (Liff, 2003). Gordon's program and ECP differ from Heath's in that rather than teaching teachers how to facilitate these visits and weave themes into curricula throughout the month, Gordon and ECP train professionals to do these visits in schools. Having both models allows schools to choose the method that best matches their needs. It is exciting seeing these programs receiving attention from international audiences who also recognize the need for increased empathy in the next generation to counteract the global mistrust and fear that seem to predominate.

Parents Under Construction™. This is a preK–12 parenting education program that has been evaluated in several separate independent studies over the past decade (see www.childbuilders.org; Hawkins & Backscheider, 2002). This program's goals are to show students the relationship between a parent's practices and a child's mental health. Students learn about parenting, child development, positive discipline practices, and nonviolent conflict resolution. This next generation of parents will be more aware of a child's needs and more capable of meeting them. These skills also can prepare students for global citizenship.

In many of Parents Under Construction's studies, the organization found significant increases in knowledge of child development and more-positive attitudes toward children. Recently they initiated their first 5-year follow-up with a small sample of the high school students who had taken the course in middle school. A more extensive study is in progress. They found knowledge and attitudes remained at the posttest range for the students 5 years after the courses. In interviews, they found that students were using the information in the way they cared for infants and children in their own families. Students also said that what they learned helped them not lose control in peer interactions. Many students saw physical punishment as a less viable option after the program than they had before.

Other studies immediately after the initial program, in spite of small numbers of responses and problems with control groups, reported positive results in terms of empathy, prosocial behavior, and caring. Furthermore, teacher ratings of treatment group students' improvements in empathy and prosocial behavior were very often significant and positive. Teachers also felt the programs improved their own caring skills, something also reported in England (Hope & Sharland, 1997, p. 38). These results support Parents Under Construction's Logic Model (see Culler & Ostaszewski, 2005), which predicts that the program will help not only children but parents who do activities with their children, and teachers who use the materials to improve classroom climate and even their own relationships at home.

These programs also involve training teachers, school counselors, and nurses to lead the classes. There are parent-student activities in every lesson of each curriculum, and all the curricula are available in Spanish as well as English.

Baby Think It Over®. Now part of an organization called *Realityworks*®, Baby Think It Over and Real Care® Baby provide hands-on learning experiences to help youth understand and feel the reality of life's key decisions and focus on students who learn best through concrete experience and active experimentation. Classroom debriefings allow for reflective observation and generalizations of learning. The program uses a computerized infant simulator to teach students the responsibilities of parenting. Several independent studies have found the program has a significant impact on students in terms of realizing parenthood was much more difficult than they had thought and should be delayed. In dealing with infant crying, students in this program often refer to the need for patience and tolerance in caring relationships, attributes related to competent parenting and citizenship (see Chapter 3). Informal comments from teachers at conferences and schools indicated that infant simulators lure male students into elective parenting and child-care classes.

There has been a good deal of research on infant simulators (see www.reality works.com for an extensive review). Roberts and McCowan (2004) found the program was effective in teaching high school students child-care skills and the time, commitment, and patience involved in parenting. Roberts, Wolman, and Harris-Looby's study (2004–2005) of a culturally diverse group of students ages 14–20 showed increases in empathy and in the students' realistic expectations of the skills they would need to parent, as well as the dramatic changes parenting would bring to their lives.

STUDENTS CONTRIBUTE MEANINGFULLY TO THEIR COMMUNITY

Dads Make a Difference. Like Baby Think It Over®, this program has often been used in family and consumer science classes or afterschool programs. It educates students about the importance of fathers in children's lives. The curriculum for middle school, led by older teens, focuses on the legal, financial, and emotional responsibilities of caring as a parent, and the program for older teens focuses on relationship skills and life planning. Several independent research studies (e.g., Professional Data Analysts, 2001/2002) showed that students from rural, urban, and suburban schools retained new knowledge regarding parenting, paternity, and attitudes about delaying parenting until ready. There were no differences between genders or geographical areas. Student leaders showed even more permanent change than student participants did.

Especially impressive is the qualitative research study by Hayne (2000), which highlighted key areas of program impact on the teen leaders, trained in the cross-age teaching paradigm. The study followed a sample of 13 teen leaders ages 17–22 representing the diversity (age, location, gender, ethnicity, etc.) of the 55 teens trained in the program to that point. Through extensive interviews, the following themes emerged:

1. Improved skills and improved feelings of self (self-confidence and self-esteem). Students' own learning was enhanced in teaching others. They improved their communication (actively listening, responding, and reflecting on what is being said), decision making (including accepting responsibility for one's actions), and problem-solving skills (getting information, using resources, working through a process to reach a resolution).

2. Relationships with caring adults (guidance during training and daily life).

3. An increased knowledge of Dads Make a Difference concepts, and informal sharing of that information (a sense of expertise extending beyond school to family and community; students were sought out or shared information frequently).

4. Future planning and connecting actions to consequences. Students felt the need to plan ahead if they were going to be successful. Students also felt the need to think about an outcome of a choice before they did something.

5. A change in attitude and behavior (increased understanding of responsibility of parenthood).

6. Youth teaching youth, and a feeling of contributing to the community (enhanced self-esteem derived from improving lives of other students and one's community).

7. Fun (especially having an impact).

8. Reflections on their dads or other males (often new appreciation).

9. A sense of belonging to something important (coming together as a group for something worthwhile).

10. A belief in the message (especially the importance of dads to their children).

This program is flexible and can be adapted to a variety of student groups, and students also gained a feeling that what they learned could be applied to other future adult roles. Frequently the youth were nominated by their communities for recognition. With this came more-positive visions for their futures than they had before the programs. The main drawback in terms of program effect is that programs like this need an ongoing strong commitment from funding sources and school administration in terms of freed-up time for advisers and for students and resources for ongoing training. Educators and parents need to make the case more strongly that students, in learning content of meaning and interest to them in terms of life skills, will simultaneously learn other skills like critical thinking that can be generalized to traditional academic subjects as well. Communities do well to remember that how well students do often depends on how well schools and communities combine efforts to support them.

PARENTING COURSES AS A REQUIREMENT FOR HIGH SCHOOL GRADUATION

The programs mentioned in the preceding section are usually one of many tools used by successful family and consumer science classes in high schools, middle schools, and, it is hoped, elementary schools. In Connecticut, the Coalition for Parenting Education has been working for legislation to mandate parenting education in schools. In May 2005, Congressman Bob Filner advocated for parenting education on the floor of the U.S. House.

The PTP advocacy guide (Schiffer, 2002) includes the FACS education standards for teaching parenting education provided by Marilyn Swierk. She has worked in this area for several years, has been training teachers on the brain development of infants for years (Swierk & Moore, 2000), and has helped develop materials for the PTP Web site. Assessments for the thousands of parent education classes being taught by FACS teachers are tied to standards and scope-of-instruction guidelines. Rarely have there been funds to do additional evaluations as assessment is built into FACS class activities.

The state of New York now mandates that every student take a parenting class before high school graduation. Based on collaborations between educators and parents, the state education department developed a Parenting Education Resource Guide. Heath and McDermott prepared materials for the teachers on the rationale and best practices for teaching and assessing these courses (McDermott, 2002b). Heath matched her curriculum to the scope and sequence requirements in the state for the subject matter.

A few independent university studies demonstrate the effectiveness of general parenting classes in high schools taught by FACS teachers. They focus on helping students know the resources available to parents in their communities, which is crucial information. A study by Luster and Youatt (1989) tested 138 students from eight high schools serving as the experimental group and 26 controls. The goals of the program were to increase students' knowledge of child development, their understanding of how to provide a supportive environment for children, and student awareness regarding the resources and level of commitment needed to function effectively as parents. Students were given information on community resources for parents and vital health care practices for child growth.

Pre- and posttests were administered in an English class the students shared. The tests, given at the beginning and the end of the semester, measured knowledge of child development, student beliefs about appropriate child-rearing practices, and beliefs about the extent to which parents influence child development. Students in the treatment group were significantly more knowledgeable about child development than the controls were, significantly less likely than controls to believe infants are "spoiled" by responsive and affectionate care, and more likely to emphasize the importance of talking and reading to children. Students in the program were more likely to believe infants needed considerable leeway in exploring the environment and were less likely than the controls to be authoritarian in their discipline views. Finally, they were significantly more likely than the controls to believe that parents exert considerable influence on the developing child. Control students' scores decreased over time on this measure. From what we know from research with parents (see Chapter 3), the posttest beliefs of the treatment group are those related to positive child outcome and parental competence (Luster, Rhoades, & Haas, 1989).

Tulloch and Omvig (1989) studied a random sample of upper-level Kentucky high school students taking a one-semester course on parenting. All teachers used a similar parent education curriculum from the Kentucky Department of Vocational Education. These students were compared with students taking family and consumer science courses least likely to address parenting. Students taking parenting showed a significant change in attitudes toward timing of parenthood, wanting to delay it until older. There were few changes in terms of behavior, as there had been in an earlier study by Dittman and Anderson (1987), in which high school students showed significant gains in knowledge, problem solving, and self-confidence. Tulloch and Omvig, like many others (e.g., Cooke, 1991), conjectured about the lack of significant findings in terms of behavior. There is great variability from teacher to teacher in how and how much a program is implemented. Length of programs also varies. Many researchers (Gaudin, 1993; Luster & Youatt, 1989; O'Connor, 1990) point out the need to stretch parenting education programs across many years of schooling.

SUMMARY

The key benefit of teaching parenting and caring in schools is to teach children the skills they need to succeed academically and to foster their social-emotional development by means of a subject of intrinsic interest to them. The goal is to get teachers to think mindfully about such programs.

■ What Potential and Challenges Does This Movement Face?

People would need to put aside beliefs that parenting is not the business of schools and think about the whole process as a way to integrate parents in a meaningful way into a school and to use life experience as a resource for learning to help students avoid the alienation they often feel with respect to school subjects and practices. More important, parent-infant visits or any variation of parenting classes are the best way to teach students how to care. Join that with teaching children to care for each other, for teachers, for the environment, and so on, and children get a coherent and consistent message from the school that it is a place to help them learn how to contribute and to feel connected to others and cared for. Even in this time of high-stakes testing and program cuts, many educators (e.g., Noddings, 2006) continue to make the case for teaching parenting in schools.

The PTP advocacy guide (Schiffer, 2002) and the updated Web site provide much more in terms of programs, references, and guides for getting a program started. The positive impact of these courses is clear. Teachers no doubt know about the capacity of children to care and how it can get lost in the competitive climate of schools. A child's success in school cannot flourish until parents and teachers advocate for systemic change in schools, which would include opportunities for children to learn what is meaningful to them and to be connected to the community, not isolated from it.

Some Activities and Questions for Investigation, Reflection, and Action

Think

1. What thinking skills learned in these classes could advance academic learning?

2. Describe at least five ways graduates of these programs will be better prepared to be involved in their communities and schools as adults.

3. Take a look at Table 3.1 in Chapter 3. What competencies described as necessary for effective parenting could be learned in these parenting classes?

Reflect

4. Please journal about how parenting classes might help in class and schoolwide discipline concerns, character education, and violence prevention.

(Continued)

(Continued)

Plan

5. Role-play: One student plays a teacher or parent volunteer who hears parenting education will be offered in school and describes it as an extra that will interfere with academic learning. Another student plays a teacher or parent who makes some "mindful" comments that will help the first teacher or parent understand why that description is not accurate.

Epilogue

RELATIONSHIPS AS A UNIFYING THEME

In the first part of this book, we looked at parents and teachers as lifelong learners, embedded within a variety of sociocultural contexts and challenges but all with the potential to grow and develop personally and professionally as they care for children. You learned that children's development and success depended on the quality of their relationships with others and on the relationships between adults in their lives within all systems, starting with the parent-child relationship and moving on to a commitment from extended family, neighborhoods, schools, whole cities or towns, governments, countries, and the world to building better human connections on which children can build a better world for their own children (Eisler, 2000; McDermott, 2003–2004).

As can be seen in the chapters in Part II of this book, a caring model of decision making and parenting education and support initiatives can be helpful to teachers and parents in many ways. Both involve parents and teachers looking inward in terms of their own concerns, attitudes, beliefs, and values and looking outward to see how they could individually and jointly counter societal institutions, culture, and media that are not supportive of families.

Ideally a parenting educator in each school, aware of and continually reviewing the relevant theories and research in human development and human services, could help teachers and parents learn more about children's and adults' developmental needs, tasks, and abilities across the lifespan. In the theory-to-practice model described in this book, we worked from a model that takes into consideration the impact of the environment on parents, teachers, and students; thus we were also able to provide a realistic view of the challenges faced by all. If people look at teachers and parents out of the context in which they were reared and live and work, our schools will be the worse for it.

A parenting educator is in a great position to support the whole school and not just one constituency. Because they are there to work with all parents, teachers, and staff over a period of years, parenting educators provide continuity, picking up on areas of parent or teacher interests after meetings and presentations and doing follow-through. How many times have teachers and parents come to sage-on-the-stage lectures after which nothing happens to build on the new information? At the model school I studied for 5 years, new parents of prekindergartners, with support from a parenting educator, formed a support group to take them through the school years together; middle school parents got to know each other better and began trusting each other enough to stick together through the difficult high school years; and high school parents found a place to discuss the more serious issues that their children faced—much to the relief of many of their children. In this book, you also looked at certain educational and parental goals and methods of relating to children and families based on what is known about how children become confident, autonomous adults with the competencies they need to survive and thrive in a global society. Those competencies go beyond reading, science, and math literacy.

FINAL REFLECTIONS

A Practitioner's Reflection

One of the reasons the particular urban K–12 school was chosen for the Parent Education Initiative (PEI) model development was that, unlike most schools, it had a counselor, a nurse, and an affective education teacher in each school, as well as strong parent leaders who truly appreciated this approach to working with parents, and when the study was over, it was hoped, this infrastructure would have been influenced by the PEI parent development philosophy. The hope was that all three principals, from the elementary, middle, and high school, would opt to continue a version of the PEI. As often happens in schools, however, new administrators, who had not been involved from the beginning, came in and brought with them different priorities. I had collaborated on several projects with support staff over the 5 years, focusing on the needs of parents, children, families, and teachers in a very different way than they had experienced in their professional training. Many of us hoped and believed that this exposure to a more mindful look at parents would have a long-lasting impact.

In addition to such an infrastructure, a parenting initiative coordinator is needed in all schools or school districts to coordinate and advocate for systemic and continual efforts at engaging parents and in educating and supporting students as future parents. Before I worked at the model development school, I had been involved in components of a PEI at schools that were facing so many "competing urgencies," or pressures from the school system and government, that they were not able to test the model's full potential or sustain it after the funds for the project were exhausted. The model school, however, was in a position to sustain the PEI if all principals and administrators chose to do so.

I am continually grateful for the openness of many parents, teachers, and staff to being part of this new paradigm. They took risks, exposed their own parental or teacher fears and concerns, and did the hard work needed to succeed in their roles. Perhaps it also helped that the teachers were reading Parker Palmer's book *The Courage to Teach* (1998). Some of the lessons learned are the following: While one gets interest and participation from many teachers, often the teachers who are most interested are also the busiest and most overextended. Time and those competing urgencies become a personal enemy. A paradigm shift in the way a school institutionalizes support for parents and teachers to collaborate needs buy-in and structural change on all levels, but most importantly from the top, to be sustained. There still is too much resistance from administrators (Graue & Brown, 2003; McConchie, 2004; Shartrand, Weiss, Kreider, & Lopez, 1997), and that must change for programs like the PEI to be institutionalized.

In the 1980s and 1990s, I had introduced components of the caring school decision-making model to Chicago public schools and to a small parochial school (240 children, toddlers through eighth graders) in Rogers Park, an inner-city neighborhood in Chicago, which has been described as one of the most diverse neighborhoods in the United States. The principal was completely supportive and recruited teachers who also were open to this approach. We had retreat days on the philosophy of the school and the caring school approach described in this book, and teachers had an opportunity to be involved in planning. We had many other meetings with individual teachers and small and large groups throughout the first year. We then gradually implemented the components of this model, based on teacher interest. They suggested we begin with parent-infant visits, as described in Chapter 9, as a new way to involve parents. We also involved the older students in teaching this caring process to younger students. Then mixed-grade parent groups met to learn the adult version of the caring process of decision making. These parents were selected by the principal because they represented all levels of school engagement, self-confidence, and self-efficacy, from none at all to confident full-time volunteer.

Some of the school parents also used the caring process of decision making as they challenged the Chicago Catholic Archdiocese, which ultimately closed the school because it lacked funds to pay off huge building-repair loans. Unfortunately, the decision was made without sufficient awareness or recognition of the good things that had been happening in the school. Because of the financial exigencies, parents in this urban school did not have enough opportunities to convince the decision makers that what the school community was providing the children and the adults was very exceptional.

That principal went to another school, where we again incorporated components of the caring school model, but we never forgot the group of teachers and parents at that small school in Rogers Park who were united and truly growing together. Ironically, at the time of the school closing, we had been making wonderful progress in working collaboratively with the local university and local community agencies (the Loyola University Family Literacy Program and the Child Assessment, Child Care and Counseling Services) to provide additional needed support to these parents and to the neighborhood community council offering help with family services. Similar important collaborations have been described recently by Sanders (2005). We ran out of time at the Rogers Park school, but parents, teachers, and children were changed, with the principal's leadership and school support, and are no doubt having an impact wherever they are. This story is mentioned because it is important to understand that while the principal's leadership is critical, external threats may prevail, even when a program is very successful. Efforts early on to involve the whole community are essential. With community support *and* principal leadership, commitment, and courage, great things can happen.

Having at least one staff person in each school or school district with a credential in parenting is very important. Many Family and Consumer Science teachers are qualified and prepared to teach these courses, but with the current focus on testing and the so-called basics, they are often cut from school faculty. The National Parenting Education Network Web site lists other programs offering degrees and certifications in parenting education. Currently the master's degree in Parenting Education and Support developed at DePaul University finds that more than half the students are teachers wanting to enhance their understanding of and work with parents and children. Because of the complexity of parenting, as you have seen in this book, it is hard to imagine making progress in terms of child and adult outcome unless we move in the direction of parenting education and support. In the meantime, I hope that the content of this book will help family-serving professionals have a better understanding of the developmental challenges of parents and families and a better idea of how to collaborate with families more effectively.

I once read an article about how to help our children have hope in a time of nuclear threats. The author quoted a little boy, who said, "It will be okay, because my dad goes to a peace meeting each month." We do need to help our children be hopeful by showing them that although it is hard, we will never stop working together in a caring and collaborative manner on their behalf, even if it means the difficult work of structural changes in the way schools and all our institutions and governments operate and relate to parents and families. This brings us back to appreciative inquiry, discussed earlier in the book. Bliss Browne, an expert in this field, left the corporate world and founded Imagine Chicago more than a decade ago to connect youth to older, more experienced community members—whom she called the "glue" of the community—in order to facilitate dialogues across generations, races, incomes, cultures, and so on, and to "cultivate hope in both generations" (www.imaginechicago.org/). Please look at her work, which has now been replicated around the world, to get creative ideas about ways to involve youth and their parents, families, and communities in imagining themselves as creators of a better and more civic society. Her visioning process is akin to the assets-based community-building approach, but it hinges on young people seeing themselves as leaders in community change, not just part of a problem. This view has also been supported and described further from a global perspective by Flanagan (2001). Browne's success stories of parents and youth are inspiring. In opposition to the deficit approach and in line with successful strategies of adult learning, she focuses on people better understanding what is, imagining what could be, and creating what will be. Let us think mindfully about all the good work we do and can do to advance these efforts toward creating more caring homes, schools, and communities.

References

Abbeduto, L., Weissman, M., & Short-Myerson, K. (1999). Parental scaffolding of the discourse of children and adolescents with intellectual disability: The case of referential expressions. *Journal of Intellectual Disability Research, 43*(6), 540–557.

Ada, A., & Beutel, C. (1991). *Participatory research as dialogue for action.* Unpublished manuscript. San Francisco: Univeristy of San Francisco.

Ainsworth, M., & Bowlby, J. (1991). An ethological approach to personality development. *American Psychologist, 46,* 333–341.

Almonte, B. (1996). A practitioner's view of cultural competence. *Family Resource Coalition Report, 14*(3 & 4), 5.

Auerbach, E. (1990). *Making meaning, making change.* Boston: University of Massachusetts Press.

Baker, H., & Baker, M. (1987). Heinz Kohut's self-psychology: An overview. *American Journal of Psychiatry, 144,* 1–9.

Ball, M. (1987). *The micro-politics of school.* London: Methuen.

Bandura, A. (1989). Human agency in social cognitive theory. *American Psychologist, 44,* 1175–1184.

Bandura, A. (1997). *Self-efficacy, the exercise of control.* New York: W. H. Freeman.

Barrett, F., & Fry, R. (2002). Appreciative inquiry in action. The unfolding of a provocative invitation. In R. Fry, F. Barrett, J. Seiling, & D. Whitney (Eds.), *Appreciative inquiry and organizational transformation* (pp. 1–26). Westport, CT: Quorum.

Baumrind, D. (1989). The permanence of change and the impermanence of stability. *Human Development, 32,* 187–195.

Baumrind, D. (1996). The discipline controversy revisited. *Family Relations, 45,* 405–414.

Bavolek, S. (Ed.). (1997). *Multicultural parenting education guide: Understanding cultural parenting values, traditions and practices.* Park City, UT: Family Development Resources.

Beaver, P. (1983). *An internalization model to evaluate affective behavioral skills in the workplace.* Unpublished doctoral dissertation. Wayne State University, Detroit, MI.

Belenky, M., Bond, L., & Weinstock, J. (1997). *A tradition that has no name: Nurturing the development of people, families and communities.* New York: Basic Books.

Belenky, M., Clinchy, B., Goldberger, N., & Tarule, J. (1997). *Women's ways of knowing.* New York: Basic Books. (Original work published 1986)

Belenky, M., & Stanton, A. (2000). Inequality, development and connected knowing. In J. Mezirow & Associates (Eds.), *Learning as transformation: Critical perspectives on a theory in progress* (pp. 71–102). San Francisco: Jossey-Bass.

Bell, R. (1968). A reinterpretation of the direction of effects in studies of socialization. *Psychological Review, 75,* 81–95.

Belsky, J. (1984). The determinants of parenting: A process model. *Child Development, 55,* 83–96.

Belsky, J., & Barends, N. (2002). Personality and parenting. In M. H. Bornstein (Ed.), *Handbook of parenting: Vol. 3. Being and becoming a parent* (2nd ed., pp. 485–508). Mahwah, NJ: Erlbaum.

Belsky, J., Crnic, K., & Woodworth, S. (1995). Personality and parenting: Exploring the mediating role of transient mood and daily hassles. *Journal of Personality, 63,* 905–931.

Belsky, J., & Vondra, J. (1985). Characteristics, consequences, and determinants of parenting. In L. L'Abate (Ed.), *Handbook of family psychology and therapy* (pp. 523–536). Homewood, IL: Dorsey.

Benard, B. (1996). *From research to practice: The foundations of the resiliency paradigm.* Retrieved April 5, 2000, from www.resiliency.com/research.htm.

Benedek, T. (1970). Motherhood and nurturing. In E. J. Anthony & T. Benedek (Eds.), *Parenthood: Its psychology and psychopathology.* Boston: Little, Brown.

Benson, P. (1997). *All kids are our kids.* San Francisco: Jossey-Bass.

Berkowitz, M., & Grych, J. (1998). *Fostering goodness: Teaching parents to facilitate children's moral development.* Retrieved January 29, 2007, from http://parenthood.library.wisc.edu/Berkowitz/Berkowitz.html.

Berrera, I. (1994). Thoughts on the assessment of young children whose socio-cultural background is unfamiliar to the assessor. *Zero to Three, 14,* 9–13.

Bigner, J. (2006). *Parent-child relations: An introduction to parenting* (7th ed.). Upper Saddle River, NJ: Prentice Hall.

Black, M., & Teti, L. (1997). Promoting mealtime communication between adolescent mothers and their infants through videotapes. *Pediatrics, 99*(3), 432–437.

Block, J., & Block, J. (1980). The role of ego-control and ego-resiliency in the organization of behavior. In W. A. Collins (Ed.), *Minnesota symposium on child psychology: Vol. 13* (pp. 89–101). Hillsdale, NJ: Erlbaum.

Bloom, B. (1956). *Taxonomy of educational objectives.* New York: D. McKay.

Bogenschneider, K., & Stone, M. (1997). Delivering parent education to low and high-risk parents of adolescents via age-paced newsletters. *Family Relations, 46,* 123–134.

Bornstein, M. (2002). *Handbook of parenting* (2nd ed., Vols. 1–5). Mahwah, NJ: Erlbaum.

Bowman, T. (1994). *Matchmaking: The variety of needs and learning styles.* Minneapolis, MN: Family Information Services, ISSN 1042-0878, January, 1–4, Methods & Materials.

Bowman, T. (1996). Empowering parents is mining diamonds in the rough. *Family Resource Coalition Report, 15*(2), 27–28.

Brazelton. T. B., & Greenspan, S. I. (2000). *The irreducible needs of children: What every child must have to grow, learn and flourish.* Cambridge, MA: Perseus Books.

Brems, C., Baldwin, M., & Baxter, S. (1993). Empirical evaluations of a self psychologically oriented parent education program. *Family Relations, 42,* 26–30.

Breslin, F., Zack, M., & McMain, S. (2002). An information processing analysis of mindfulness: Implications for relapse prevention in the treatment of substance abuse. *Clincial Psychology: Science and Practice, 9*(3), 275–299.

Brody, G. (2003). Parental monitoring: Action and reaction. In A. C. Crouter & A. Booth (Eds.), *Children's influence on family dynamics: The neglected side of family relationships* (pp. 163–169). Mahwah, NJ: Erlbaum.

Brody, G., Flor, F., & Gibson, N. (1999). Linking maternal efficacy beliefs, developmental goals, parenting practices and child competence in rural single parent African American families. *Child Development, 70,* 1197–1208.

Bronfenbrenner, U. (1979). *The ecology of human development: Experiments by nature and design.* Cambridge, MA: Harvard University Press.

Bronfrenbrenner, U. (1985). The three worlds of childhood. *Principal, 64*(5), 7–11.

Bronfenbrenner, U. (1986). Ecology of the family as a context for human development: Research perspectives. *Developmental Psychology, 22*(6), 723–742.

Bronfenbrenner, U. (Ed.). (2005a). *Making human beings human: Bio-ecological perspectives on human development.* Thousand Oaks, CA: Sage.

Bronfenbrenner, U. (2005b). The bioecological theory of human development. In U. Bronfenbrenner (Ed.), *Making human beings human: Bioecological perspectives on human development* (pp. 3–15). Thousand Oaks, CA: Sage.

Brookfield, S. (1986). *Understanding and facilitating adult learning.* San Francisco: Jossey-Bass.

Brookfield, S. (1995). Adult learning: An overview. In A. Tuinjman (Ed.), *International encyclopedia of adult education and training* (pp. 375–380). Oxford: Pergamon Press.

Brookfield, S. D. (1987). *Developing critical thinkers: Challenging adults to explore alternative ways of thinking and acting.* San Francisco: Jossey-Bass.

Brooks, J. (2006). *Parenting* (7th ed.). Boston, MA: McGraw-Hill.

Brown, N. (2001). *Recommended practices: Parent education and support.* Retrieved February 2007 from http://ag.udel.edu/extension/fam/recprac/part1.pdf.

Brown, R., Mounts, N., Lamborn, S., & Steinberg, L. (1993). Parenting practices and peer group affiliation in adolescence. *Child Development, 64,* 467–482.

Browne, B., & Jain, S. *Living from the inside out.* Retrieved January 27, 2007, from www.imaginechicago.org/livinginsideout.htm.

Brufee, K. (1993). *Collaborative learning.* Baltimore: The Johns Hopkins University Press.

Brunnquell, D., Chrichton, L., & Egeland, E. (1981). Maternal personality and attitude in disturbances of child rearing. *American Journal of Orthopsychiatry, 51*(4), 680–691.

Bryan, G., DeBord, K., & Schrader, K. (2006). Building a professional development system: A case study of North Carolina's parenting education experiences. *Child Welfare, 85*(5), 803–818.

Buehler, C., & Gerard, J. (2002). Marital conflict, ineffective parenting, and children's and adolescents' maladjustment. *Journal of Marriage and the Family, 64,* 78–92.

Buhrmester, D., Camparo, L., Christensen, A., Gonzalez, L., & Hinshaw, S. (1992). Mothers and fathers interacting in dyads and triads of normal and hyperactive sons. *Developmental Psychology, 28,* 500–509.

Burchinal, M., Follmer, A., & Bryant, D. (1996). The relations of maternal social support and family structure with maternal responsiveness and child outcomes among African American families. *Developmental Psychology, 32,* 1073–1083.

Calabrese Barton, A., Drake, C., Perez, J., St. Louis, K., & George, M. (2004). Ecologies of parental engagement in urban education. *Educational Researcher, 33*(4), 3–12.

Campbell, D., & Palm, G. (2004). *Group parent education: Promoting parent learning and support.* Thousand Oaks, CA: Sage.

Canberra: Commonwealth Department of Education, Training and Youth Affairs. Retrieved January 10, 2006, from http://www.dest.gov.au.

Capaldi, D. (2003). Parental monitoring: A person-environment interaction perspective on this key parenting skill. In A. Crouter & A. Booth (Eds.), *Children's influence on family dynamics: The neglected side of family relationships* (pp. 171–179). Mahwah, NJ: Erlbaum.

Carey, W. (1997). *Understanding your child's temperament.* New York: Macmillan.

Carlson, B., Healy, M., & Wellman, G. (1998). *Taking care of me so I can take care of my children.* Seattle, WA: Parenting Press.

Caspi, A., & Roberts, B. (2001). Personality development across the life course: The argument for change and continuity. *Psychological Inquiry, 12,* 49–66.

Cassidy, J., & Shaver, R. (1999). *Handbook of attachment theory, research and clinical applications.* New York: Guilford Press.

Cervero, R., Wilson, A., & Associates. (2001). *Power in practice.* San Francisco: Jossey-Bass.

Chao, R. (1994). Beyond parental control and authoritarian parenting style: Understanding Chinese parenting through the cultural notion of training. *Child Development, 65,* 1111–1119.

Chao, R., & Tseng, V. (2002). Parenting of Asians. In M. H. Bornstein (Ed.), *Handbook of parenting: Vol. 4. Social conditions and applied parenting* (2nd ed., pp. 59–94). Mahwah, NJ: Erlbaum.

Chen, C., & Uttal, D. (1988). Cultural values, parents' beliefs, and children's achievement in the United States and China. *Human Development, 31,* 351–358.

Chess, S., & Thomas, A. (1984). *Origins and evolution of behavior development: From infancy to early adult life.* New York: Brunner/Mazel.

Chess, S., & Thomas, A. (1999). *Goodness of fit: Clinical applications from infancy through adult life.* Philadelphia: Taylor & Francis, Psychology Press.

Christian, L. (2006). Understanding families: Applying family systems theory to early childhood practice. *Young Children, 61*(1), 12–20.

Christopher, S., Dunnagan, T., Duncan, S., & Paul, L. (2001). Education for self-support: Evaluating outcomes using transformative learning theory. *Family Relations, 50*(2), 134–142.

Christophersen, E., & Mortweet, S. (2004). *Parenting that works: Building skills that last a lifetime.* Washington, DC: American Psychological Association.

Cicchetti, D., Toth, S., & Bush, M. (1988). Developmental psychopathology and incompetence in childhood: Suggestions for intervention. In B. B. Lahey & A. E. Kazdin (Eds.), *Advances in clinical child psychology: Vol. 11* (pp. 1–77). New York: Plenum.

Clabby, J., & Elias, M. (1987). *Teach your child decision making.* Garden City, NY: Doubleday Press.

Clayton, L. (1985). The impact upon child-rearing attitudes, of parental views of the nature of humankind. *Journal of Psychology and Christianity, 4*(3), 49–55.

Coalition for Community Schools. (2003). *Making the difference: Research and practice in community schools.* Retrieved January 29, 2007, from http://www.communityschools .org/mtdhomepage.html.

Cochran, M. (1988). Parental empowerment in family matters: Lessons learned from a research program. In D. R. Powell (Ed.), *Parent education as early childhood intervention* (pp. 23–50). Norwood, NJ: Ablex.

Cochran, M. (1993). Parenting and personal social networks. In T. Luster & L. Okagaki (Eds.), *Parenting: An ecological perspective* (pp. 149–178). Hillsdale, NJ: Erlbaum.

Cochran, M., & Walker, S. (2005). Parenting and personal social networks. In T. Luster & L. Okagaki (Eds.), *Parenting: An ecological perspective* (2nd ed., pp. 235–273). Mahwah, NJ: Erlbaum.

Coleman, J. (1966). Equal schools for equal students. *Public Interest, 4,* 70–75.

Coleman, M., & Churchill, S. (1997). Challenges to family involvement. *Childhood Education, 73*(3), 144–148.

Coleman, P., & Karraker, K. (1998). Self-efficacy and parenting quality: Findings and future applications. *Developmental Review, 18*(1), 47–85.

Comer, J. (1988). *Maggie's American dream.* New York: Penguin Books.

Comer, J. (1989). Parent participation in schools: The School Development Program as a model. *Family Resource Coalition Report, 8*(4–5), 26.

Comer, J. (2001, April 23). Schools that develop children. *American Prospect, 12*(7). Retrieved January 29, 2007, from http://www.prospect.org/web/page.ww?section= root&name=ViewPrint&articleId=4704.

Comer, J., Ben-Avie, M., Haynes, N., & Joyner, E. (Eds.). (1999). *Child by child: The Comer process for change in education.* New York: Columbia University Teacher's College.

Comer, J., & Schraft, C. (1980). Working with black parents. In R. R. Abidin (Ed.), *Parent education and intervention handbook* (pp. 322–348). Springfield, IL: Charles C Thomas.

Conger, J., Rueter, M., & Elder, G. (1999). Couple resilience to economic pressures. *Journal of Personality and Social Psychology, 76,* 54–71.

Conger, R., Xiaojia, G., Elder, G., Lorenz, F., & Simons, R. (1994). Economic stress, coercive family processes, and developmental problems of adolescents. *Child Development, 65,* 541–561.

Connell-Carrick, K. (2006). Trends in popular parenting books and the need for parental critical thinking. *Child Welfare, 85*(5), 819–836.

Conners, N., Bradley, R., Mansell, L., Liu, J., Roberts, T., Burgdorf, K., & Herrell, J. (2004). Mothers with serious substance abuse problems: An accumulation of risk. *American Journal of Drug and Alcohol Abuse, 30*(1), 85–100.

Coohey, C., Heath, H., & Murphy, D. (1992, September 11). *Parents: A vital component for healthy infant development*. Paper presented at the Bi-Annual Meeting of the World Association of Infant Psychiatry, Chicago.

Coohey, C., & Murphy, D. (1990). *Report of the Education for Parenting Development Grant to the I. Harris Foundation, The Northern Trust and the United Way of Metro Chicago*. Unpublished document.

Cook, S. (1979). *Parental conceptions of children and childrearing: A study of rural Maine parents*. Unpublished master's thesis, Tufts University, Boston, MA.

Cooke, B. (1991, January/February). Teaching and evaluating courses in parenthood for adolescents. *Illinois Teacher, 86*–88.

Cooke, B. (2006). Competencies of a parent educator: What does a parent educator need to know and do? *Child Welfare, 85*(5), 785–802.

Cooperrider, D. (2001). Positive image, positive action: The affirmative basis of organizing. In D. Cooperrider, P. Sorensen Jr., T. Yaeger, & D. Whitney (Eds.), *Appreciative Inquiry: An emerging direction for organization development* (pp. 31–76). Champaign, IL: Stipes.

Cowan, C., & Cowan, P. (2000). *When partners become parents: The big life change for couples*. New York: Basic Books.

Cox, M., Owen, M., Lewis, J., & Henderson, V. (1989). Marriage, adult adjustment and early parenting. *Child Development, 60,* 1015–1024.

Crnic, K., & Law, C. (2002). Everyday stresses and parenting. In M. H. Bornstein (Ed.), *Handbook of parenting: Vol. 5. Practical issues in parenting* (2nd ed., pp. 243–267). Mahwah, NJ: Erlbaum.

Crockenberg, S. (1988). Social support and parenting. In H. Fitzgerald, B. Lester, & M. Yogman (Eds.), *Theory and research in behavioral pediatrics: Vol. 4.* (pp. 141– 174). New York: Plenum.

Cross, K. (1981). *Adults as learners*. San Francisco: Jossey-Bass.

Cross, T. (1995/1996). Developing a knowledge base to support cultural competence. *Family Resource Coalition Report, 14*(3 & 4), 2–7.

Crouter, A., & Head, M. (2002). Parental monitoring and knowledge of children. In M. H. Bornstein (Ed.), *Handbook of parenting: Vol. 3. Being and becoming a parent* (2nd ed., pp. 461–483). Mahwah, NJ: Erlbaum.

Crouter, A., & McHale, S. (2005). The long arm of the job revisited: Parenting in dual earner families. In T. Luster & L. Okagaki (Eds.), *Parenting: An ecological perspective* (2nd ed., pp. 275–296). Mahwah, NJ: Erlbaum.

Culler, R., & Ostaszewski, P. (2005). *Teaching children parenting skills: May 2005 follow-up study of students receiving the Parents Under Construction program 2000–2001*. Retrieved January 29, 2007, from http://www.childbuilders.org/programPUCResearch.htm.

Cummings, E., & Cummings, J. (2002). Parenting and attachment. In M. H. Bornstein (Ed.), *Handbook of parenting. Vol. 5: Practical issues in parenting* (2nd ed., pp. 35–58). Mahwah, NJ: Erlbaum.

Cummings, E., & Davies, P. (2002). Effects of marital discord on children: Recent advances and emerging themes in process-oriented research. *Journal of Child Psychology and Psychiatry, 43,* 31–63.

Cushman, K. (1998). The family and essential schools: Mobilizing democracy toward equity. *Horace, 15*(1), 1–11. Retrieved September 11, 1999, from www.essentialschools.org/horace/15/v15n01.html.

Cutler, W. W., III. (2000). *Parents and schools.* Chicago: University of Chicago Press.

Cutrona, C. (1984). Social support and stress in the transition to parenthood. *Journal of Abnormal Psychology, 93*(4), 378–390.

Cuttance, P., & Stokes, S. (2000). *Reporting on student and school achievement.* Retrieved January 29, 2007, from http://www.dest.gov.au/sectors/school_education/publications_resources/other_publications/reporting_on_student_and_school_achievement.htm.

Daloz, L. (1986). *Effective teaching and mentoring: Realizing the transformational power of adult learning experiences.* San Francisco: Jossey-Bass.

De Becker, G. (1999). *Protecting the gift: Keeping children and teenagers safe.* New York: Dial Press.

DeBord, K. (1996). Parent preferences for learning: A study of Euro-Americans, Hispanic, Native American, Asian, and African American parents. *Forum for Family and Consumer Issues, 1*(2). Retrieved May 27, 2006, from http://www.ces.ncsu.edu/depts/fcs/pub/parents.html.

DeBord, K., Heath, H., McDermott, D., & Wolfe, R. (2000). Sharing the wisdom of parenting. *America's Family Support, 18*(14), 23–27.

DeBord, K., Kirby, J., & Mead, J. (1996). *Parent education: Parental preferences for learning methods and parenting educator.* Retrieved August 9, 2001, from http://www.agnr.umd.edu/nnfr/parented/Parbr3.html; research brief retrieved January 29, 2007, from http://www.ces.ncsu.edu/depts/fcs/human/resbrief3.html.

DeBord, K., & Reguero de Atiles, J. (1999). Latino parents: Unique preferences for learning about parenting. *Forum for Family and Consumer Issues, 4*(1). Retrieved January 29, 2007, from http://www.ces.ncsu.edu/depts/fcs/pub/1999/latino.html.

De Carvalho, M. (2001). *Rethinking family–school relations: A critique of parental involvement in schooling.* Mahwah, NJ: Erlbaum.

Deci, E., Eghrari, H., Patrick, B., & Leone, D. (1994). Facilitating internalization: The self-determination theory perspective. *Journal of Personality, 62,* 119–142.

DeCharms, R. (1968). *Personal causation.* New York: Academic Press.

Demick, J. (2002). Stages of parental development. In M. H. Bornstein (Ed.), *Handbook of parenting: Vol. 3. Being and becoming a parent* (2nd ed., pp. 243–270). Mahwah, NJ: Erlbaum.

Deutsch, H. (1945). *The psychology of women. Vol. 2.* New York: Greene & Stratton.

DeVito, C., & Hopkins, J. (2001). Attachment, parenting, and marital dissatisfaction predictors of disruptive behavior in preschoolers. *Development and Psychopathology, 13,* 215–231.

Dinkmeyer, D., McKay, G., Dinkmeyer, D., Jr., & McKay, J. (1987). *Leader's guide, the next STEP: Effective parenting through problem solving.* Circle Pines, MN: American Guidance Service.

Dittman, J., & Anderson, E. P. (1987). An evaluation of parenting education for teenagers. *Journal of Vocational Home Economics Education, 5*(1), 1–12.

Dix, T. (1992). The affective organization of parenting: Adaptive and maladaptive processes. *Psychological Bulletin, 110,* 3–25.

Dix, T., & Branca, S. (2003). Parenting as a goal-regulation process. In L. Kuczynski (Ed.), *Handbook of dynamics in parent-child relations* (pp. 167–187). Thousand Oaks, CA: Sage.

Doherty, W. (1997). *The intentional family: How to build family ties in our modern world.* Reading, MA: Addison-Wesley.

Doherty, W., & Carlson, B. (2002). *Putting family first: Successful strategies for reclaiming family in a hurried up world* (chap. 13, pp. 160–175). New York: Henry Holt.

Dreikurs, R. (1969). *Children the challenge.* New York: Hawthorn Books.

Dreikurs, R. (1989). *Fundamentals of Adlerian psychology.* Chicago: Alfred Adler Institute.

Drummond, K., & Stipek, D. (2004). Low-income parents' beliefs about their role in children's academic learning. *Elementary School Journal, 104*(3), 197–213.

Duncan, S. F. (1998). *Take care of yourselves so you can care for your children.* Retrieved January 10, 1999, from www.montana.edu/wwwpb/home/61798fam.html. Retrieved February 14, 2007, from https://www.ext.vt.edu/offices/southwest/answers/nov98.html.

Dunlap, L. (2002). *What all children need: Theory and application.* Lanham, MD: University Press of America.

Dunst, C., & Trivette, C. (2006, March 27). *Measuring the quality of family resource programs and their benefits for children, parents and families.* Symposium presented at the 11th Biennial International Conference of Family Support America, Chicago, IL.

Dunst, C., Trivette, C., & Deal, A. (1988). *Enabling and empowering families: Principles and guidelines for practice.* Cambridge, MA: Brookline Books.

Eccles, J., & Harold, R. (1996). Family involvement in children's and adolescent's schooling. In A. Bloom & J. F. Dunn (Eds.), *Family-school links: How do they affect educational outcomes?* (pp. 30–34). Mahwah, NJ: Erlbaum.

Ehrensaft, D. (1987). *Parenting together.* New York: Free Press.

Eisenberg, N., & Valiente, C. (2004). Elaboration on a theme: Beyond main effects in relations of parenting to children's coping and regulation. *Parenting: Science and Practice, 4*(4), 319–323.

Eisler, R. (1999). *Spiritual courage.* Retrieved January 29, 2007, from http://www.partnershipway.org/html/subpages/articles/spirtitual.htm.

Eisler, R. (2000). *Tomorrow's children: A blueprint for partnership education in the 21st century.* Boulder, CO: Westview.

Eisler, R. (2002). *The power of partnership.* Novato, CA: New World Library.

Elias, M., & Schwab, Y. (2004). What about parent involvement in parenting? *Education Week, 24*(8), 39–41.

Elias, M., Tobias, S., & Friedlander, B. (1999). *Emotionally intelligent parenting.* New York: Harmony Books.

Epstein, J. (1995). School, family, community partnerships: Caring for the children we share. *Phi Delta Kappan, 77*(9), 701–712.

Epstein, J., & Salinas, K. (2004). Partnering with families and communities. *Educational Leadership, 61*(8), 12–18.

Epstein, J., & Sanders, M. (2002). Family, school and community partnerships. In M. H. Bornstein (Ed.), *Handbook of parenting: Vol. 4. Social conditions and applied parenting* (2nd ed., pp. 407–438). Mahwah, NJ: Erlbaum.

Erikson, E. (1963). *Childhood and society* (2nd ed.). New York: Norton.

Erikson, E. (1968). *Identity, youth, and crisis.* New York: Norton.

Family Resource Coalition. (Fall/Winter 1995–1996). *Culture and family-centered practice.* (ERIC Document No. ED393594)

Feinberg, M. (2002). Co-parenting and the transition to parenthood: A framework for prevention. *Clinical Child and Family Psychology Review, 5*(3), 173–195.

Feshbach, N. (1987). Parental empathy and children's adjustment/maladjustment. In N. Eisenberg & J. Strayer (Eds.), *Empathy and its development* (pp. 271–291). Cambridge, MA: Cambridge University Press.

Field, T. (1995). Psychologically depressed parents. In M. H. Bornstein (Ed.), *Handbook of parenting: Vol. 4. Social conditions and applied parenting* (pp. 85–100). Mahwah, NJ: Erlbaum.

Fincham, F., & Hall, J. (2005). Parenting and the marital relationship. In T. Luster & L. Okagaki (Eds.), *Parenting: An ecological perspective* (2nd ed., pp. 205–233).

Finn-Stevenson, M., & Zigler, E. (1999). *Schools of the 21st century: Linking childcare and education.* Boulder, CO: Westview.

First, J., & Way, W. (1995). Parent education outcomes: Insights into transformative learning. *Family Relations, 44*(1), 104–109.

Fischer, C. (1982). *To dwell among friends: Personal networks in town and city.* Chicago: University of Chicago Press.

Flaherty, J. (1999). *Coaching: Evoking excellence in others.* Boston: Butterworth Heinemann.

Flanagan, C. (2001). Families and globalization: A new social contract and agenda for research. In J. Myers-Wall & P. Somalai (with R. Rapoport; Eds.), *Families as educators for global citizenship.* Burlington, VT: Ashgate.

Flanagan, C., & Botcheva, L. (1999). Adolescents' interest in other cultures: Patterns across eleven countries. In F. Alasaker & A. Flammer (Eds.), *The adolescent experience: European and American adolescents in the 1990's.* Hillsdale, NJ: Erlbaum.

Flanagan, C., Gallay, L., Gill, S., Gallay, E., & Nti, N. (2005). What does democracy mean? Correlates of adolescents' views. *Journal of Adolescent Research, 20,* 193–218.

Flanagan, C., & Tucker, C. (1999). Adolescents' explanations for political issues: Concordance with their views of self and society. *Developmental Psychology, 35,* 1198–1209.

Flavell, J. (1963). *The developmental psychology of Jean Piaget.* Princeton, NJ: Van Nostrand.

Florin, P., & Dokecki, P. (1983). Changing families through parent and family education: Review and analysis. In I. Sigel & L. Laosa (Eds.), *Changing families.* New York: Plenum Press.

Fogel, A., & Melson, G. (Eds.). (1986). *Origins of nurturance: Developmental biological and cultural perspectives on caregiving.* Hillsdale, NJ: Erlbaum.

Foucault, M. (1977). *Discipline and punish: The birth of the prison.* New York: Pantheon.

Freud, S. (1936). *The problem of anxiety* (A. H. Bunker, Trans.). New York: Norton.

Frieri, P. (1970). *Pedagogy of the oppressed.* New York: Herder & Herder.

Fuller, B., Caspary, G., Kagan, S., Gauthier, C., Huang, D., Carrol, J. & McCarthy, J. (2002). Does maternal employment influence poor children's social development? *Early Childhood Research Quarterly, 17*(4), 470–497.

Furstenberg, F., Cook, T., Eccles, J., Elder, G., & Sameroff, A. (1999). *Managing to make it: Urban families and adolescent success.* Chicago: University of Chicago Press.

Gadsen-Dupree, R. (with Elleby, G., & Pritchett, V.). (2006). *Family partnership agreements workbook for Headstart and Early Headstart programs* (2nd ed.). Bowling Green, KY: Training and Technical Assistance Services.

Galinsky, E. (1987). *The six stages of parenting.* Reading, MA: Addison-Wesley.

Galinsky, E., & David, J. (1988). *The preschool years.* New York: Ballantine Books.

Galvin, K., Bylund, C., & Brommel, B. (2003). *Family communication, cohesion and change* (6th ed.). Boston: Allyn & Bacon.

Galvin, K., & Wilkerson, C. (1998). *Communication at the intersection of family and community*. Workshop presented at Latin School, Chicago, April 13.

Garanzini, M. (1995). *Child-centered, family sensitive schools: An educator's guide to family dynamics.* Washington, DC: National Catholic Education Association.

Garbarino, J., & Bedard, C. (2001). *Parents under siege.* New York: Free Press.

Garbarino, J., Bradshaw, C., & Kostelny, K. (2005). Neighborhood and community influences on parenting. In T. Luster & L. Okagaki (Eds.), *Parenting: An ecological perspective* (2nd ed., pp. 297–318). Mahwah, NJ: Erlbaum.

Garton, M., Hicks, K., & Leatherman, M. (2003). Newsletters: Treasures or trash? Parenting newsletter series results in positive behavior change. *Journal of Extension, 41*(1). Retrieved May 29, 2006, from http://www.joe.org/joe/2003february/rb5.shtml.

Gaudin, J. M., Jr. (1993). *Child neglect: A guide for intervention.* Washington, DC: National Center—Child Abuse and Neglect, with Westover Consultants.

Gerris, J., Dekovic, M., & Janssens, J. (1997). The relationship between social class and childrearing behaviors: Parents' perspective taking and value orientations. *Journal of Marriage and the Family, 59,* 834–847.

Gesell, A., & Ilg, F. (1946). *The child from five to ten.* New York: Harper & Row.

Gestwicki, C. (1999). *Home, school and community relations* (3rd ed.). Albany, NY: Delmar Learning.

Gestwicki, C. (2003). *Home, school and community relations* (5th ed.). Clifton Park, NY: Delmar Learning.

Giles, H. (1998). *Parent engagement as a school reform strategy*. Retrieved April 15, 2006, from www.ed.gov/databases/ERIC_Digests/ed419031.html.

Ginott, H. (2003). *Between parent and child* (Rev. ed. by A. Ginott & H. W. Goddard). New York: Three Rivers Press. (Original work published 1965)

Glaser, B. (1978). *Theoretical sensitivity: Advances in the methodology of grounded theory.* Mill Valley, CA: Sociology Press.

Glaser, B., & Strauss, A. (1967). *The discovery of grounded theory.* Hawthorne, NY: Aldine.

Gleick, E. (1996, June 3). The children's crusade. *Time.* Retrieved from http://www.time .com/time/magazine/article/0,9171,984640-1,00.html.

Goldberg, W., & Easterbrooks, M. (1985). Role of marital quality in toddler development. *Developmental Psychology, 20,* 504–514.

Goleman, D. (1995). *Emotional intelligence.* New York: Bantam Books.

Gonzalez-Mena, J. (1997). *Multi-cultural issues in child care* (2nd ed.). Mountain View, CA: Mayfield.

Goodnow, J. (2002). Parents' knowledge and expectations: Using what we know. In M. H. Bornstein (Ed.), *Handbook of parenting: Vol 3. Being and becoming a parent* (2nd ed., pp. 439–459). Mahwah, NJ: Erlbaum.

Goodnow, J., & Collins, A. (1990). *Development according to parents: The nature, sources and consequences of parents' ideas.* Hillsdale, NJ: Erlbaum.

Gordon, M. (2005). *Roots of empathy: Changing the world child by child.* Toronto, Canada: Thomas Allen & Son.

Gordon, T. (1975). *Parent effectiveness training.* New York: New American Library.

Gordon, T. (1991). *Discipline that works.* New York: Plume.

Gorman-Smith, D., Henry, D., & Tolan, P. (2004). Exposure to community violence and violence perpetration: The protective effects of family functioning. *Journal of Clinical and Adolescent Psychology, 33*(3), 439–449.

Gottman, J. (1998). *Raising an emotionally intelligent child.* New York: Simon & Schuster.

Graue, M. E. (1998). *Representing relationships between parents and schools: Making visible the force of theory.* Retrieved January 30, 2007, from http://parenthood.library .wisc.edu/Graue/Graue.html.

Graue, E., & Brown, C. (2003). Preservice teachers' notions of families and schooling. *Teaching and Teacher Education, 19,* 719–735.

Gray, M., & Steinberg, L. (1999). Unpacking authoritative parenting: Reassessing a multi-dimensional construct. *Journal of Marriage and the Family, 67*(3), 574–587.

Greenberger, E., Goldberg, W., Hamill, S., O'Neil, R., & Payne, C. (1989). Contributions of a supportive work environment to parents' well-being and orientation to work. *American Journal of Community Psychology, 17,* 755–783.

Greenfield, P., & Suzuki, L. (1998). Culture and human development: Implications for parenting, education, pediatrics and mental health. In I. E. Sigel & K. A. Renninger (Eds.), *Handbook of child psychology: Vol. 4. Childhood in practice* (5th ed., pp. 1059–1109). New York: Wiley.

Greenspan, S., & Greenspan, N. (1985). *First feelings: Milestones in the emotional development of your infant and child from birth to age four.* New York: Viking.

Grolnick, W. (2003). *The psychology of parental control: How well-meant parenting backfires.* Mahwah, NJ: Erlbaum.

Gross, D. (1996, July/August). What is a "good" parent? *Maternal and Child Nursing, 21,* 178–182.

Grossman, F., Pollack, W., & Golding, E. (1988). Fathers and children: Predicting the quality and quantity of fathering. *Developmental Psychology, 24,* 82–91.

Grusec, J. (1992). Social learning theory and developmental psychology: The legacies of Robert Sears and Albert Bandura. *Developmental Psychology, 28,* 776–786.

Grusec, J., & Goodnow, J. (1994). Impact of parental discipline methods on the child's internalization of values: A re-conceptualization of current points of view. *Developmental Psychology, 30,* 4–19.

Grusec, J., & Ungerer, J. (2003). Effective socialization as problem solving and the role of parenting cognitions. In L. Kuczynski (Ed.), *Handbook of dynamics in parent-child relations* (pp. 211–228). Thousand Oaks, CA: Sage.

Grych, J. (2002). Marital relationships and parenting. In M. H. Bornstein (Ed.), *Handbook of parenting: Vol. 4. Applied issues in parenting* (2nd ed., pp. 203–225). Mahwah, NJ: Erlbaum.

Grych, J., & Fincham, F. (1992). Interventions for children of divorce. Towards greater integration of research and action. *Psychological Bulletin, 111,* 434–454.

Harkness, S., & Super, C. (1996). *Parents' cultural beliefs systems: Their origins, expressions, and consequences.* New York: Guilford Press.

Harkenss, S., & Super, C. (2002). Culture and parenting. In M. H. Bornstein (Ed.), *Handbook of parenting: Vol. 2. Biology and ecology of parenting* (2nd ed., pp. 253–280). Mahwah, NJ: Erlbaum.

Hastings, P., & Grusec, J. (1998). Parenting goals as organizers of responses to parent-child disagreement. *Developmental Psychology, 34*(3), 465–479.

Hauser, S., Powers, S., & Noam, G. (1991). *Adolescents and their families: Paths of ego development.* Northampton, MA: Free Press.

Hawkins, J., & Backscheider, A. (2002). *Teaching children parenting skills: A final evaluation of the Parents Under Construction Program 7–12 curriculum and parent intervention component.* Houston, TX: University of Houston Department of Educational Psychology. Summary report available at http://www.childbuilders.org/programPUCResearch.htm.

Hayne, J. (2000). *The experiences of Dads Make a Difference teen trainers: An interpretive study.* Unpublished master's thesis, College of Education and Human Development, University of Minnesota.

Haynes, N. M., & Comer, J. P. (1996). Integrating school, families and communities through successful school reform. *School Psychology Review, 25*(4), 501–506.

Heath, D. (1994). *Schools of hope: Developing mind and character in today's youth.* San Francisco: Jossey-Bass.

Heath, D. (with Heath, H.). (2005). *Growing more mature: Insights from the lives of highly achieving men and women.* Philadelphia: Conrow.

Heath, H. (1995). *Education for parenting: Learning how to care.* Philadelphia: Conrow.

Heath, H. (1998). *Choosing parenting curricula based on the interests, needs and preferences of the parents who will use it.* Retrieved January 30, 2007, from http://parenthood.library.wisc.edu/Heath/Heath-q2.html.

Heath, H. (2000). *Using your values to raise your child to be an adult you admire.* Seattle, WA: Parenting Press.

Heath, H. (2001). *Planning: The key to mastering the challenges of parenting.* Philadelphia: Conrow.

Heath, H. (2002). *Being culturally sensitive—answering the questions.* Minneapolis, MN: Family Information Services, ISSN 1042-0878, January, Methods & Materials, 4–6.

Heath, H. (2004). Assessing and delivering parent support. In M. Hoghughi & N. Long (Eds.), *Handbook of parenting: Theory, research and practice.* Thousand Oaks, CA: Sage.

Heath, H. (2006). Parenting: A theory of competence. *Child Welfare, 85*(5), 749–766.

Heath, H., & McDermott, D. (2006). Educating students for their future role as parents. *America's Family Support.* Available at www.preparetomorrowsparents.org.

Heath, S. (1990). The children of Trackton's children: Spoken and written language in social change. In J. Stigler, R. Schweder, & G. Herdt (Eds.), *Cultural psychology* (pp. 496–519). Chicago: University of Chicago Press.

Heckman, P. (1996). *The courage to change: Stories from successful school reform.* Thousand Oaks, CA: Corwin Press.

Heinicke, C. (2002). The transition to parenting. In M. Bornstein (Ed.), *Handbook of parenting: Vol. 3. Being and becoming a parent* (2nd ed., pp. 363–388). Mahwah, NJ: Erlbaum.

Henderson, A., & Mapp, K. (2002). *A new wave of evidence: The impact of school, family and community connections on student achievement.* Austin, TX: Southwest Educational Development Laboratory.

Hinde, R. (1989). Ethological relationships and approaches. In R. Vasta (Ed.), *Annals of Child Development: Vol. 6* (pp. 251–285). Greenwich, CT: Jai Press.

Hirschman, A. (1970). *Exit, voice, and loyalty.* Cambridge, MA: Harvard University Press.

Ho, D. (1994). Cognitive socialization in Confucian heritage cultures. In P. M. Greenfield & R. R. Cocking (Eds.), *Cross-cultural roots of minority child development* (pp. 285–313). Hillsdale, NJ: Erlbaum.

Hoffman, L., & Hoffman, M. (1973). The value of children to parents. In J. T. Fawcett (Ed.), *Psychological perspectives on fertility.* New York: Basic Books.

Hoffman, L., & Saltzstein, H. (1967). Parent discipline and the child's moral development. *Journal of Personality and Social Psychology, 5,* 45–57.

Holden, G. (1983). Mothers as tacticians in the supermarket. *Child Development, 54*(1), 233–241.

Holden, G. (1997). *Parents and the dynamics of child rearing.* Boulder, CO: Westview.

Holden, G., & Hawk, C. (2003). Meta-parenting in the journey of child rearing: A cognitive mechanism for change. In L. Kuczynski (Ed.), *Handbook of dynamics in parent-child relations* (pp. 189–210). Thousand Oaks, CA: Sage.

Holden, G., & Miller, P. (1999). Enduring and different: A meta-analysis of the similarity in parents' child rearing. *Psychological Bulletin, 125*(2), 223–254.

Holden, G., & Ritchie, K. (1988). Child rearing and the dialectics of parental intelligence. In J. Valsiner (Ed.), *Child development within culturally structured environment* (pp. 30–59). Norwood, NJ: Ablex.

Holden, G., & Zambarano, R. (1992). Passing the rod: Similarities between parents and their young children in orientations towards physical punishment. In I. E. Sigel, A. V. McGillicuddy-DeLisi, & J. J. Goodnow (Eds.), *Parental belief systems: The psychological consequences for children* (2nd ed., pp. 143–172). Hillsdale, NJ: Erlbaum.

Hoover-Dempsey, K., Bassler, O., & Brissie, J. (1992). Explorations in parent-school relations. *Journal of Educational Research, 85,* 287–294.

Hoover-Dempsey, K., & Sandler, H. (1997). Why do parents become involved in their children's education? *Review of Educational Research, 67*(1), 3–42.

Hope, P., & Sharland, P. (1997). *Tomorrow's parents: Developing parent education in schools.* London: Turnaround.

Hurtig, J. (2005). Resisting assimilation: Mexican immigrant mothers writing together. In M. Farr (Ed.), *Latino language and literacy in ethnolinguistic Chicago* (pp. 247–275). Mahwah, NJ: Erlbaum.

Ianni, F. (1992, February). *Caring and the community* (Working paper of the Chapin Hall Center for Children). Chicago: University of Chicago.

Institute for Responsive Education Parent Leadership Exchange Project. (2002, April). *Supporting parents as leaders: Stories of dedication, determination and inspiration.* Retrieved January 10, 2003, from www.responsiveeducation.org/pdf/supporting.pdf.

Izard, C. (1991). *The psychology of emotions.* New York: Plenum Press.

Jack, D. (2000). Ecological influences on parenting and child development. *British Journal of Social Work, 30,* 703–720.

Jackson, N., Hill, N., & Clarke, A. (2004). *Government policy and practice regarding parenting support.* London: Parenting Education and Support Forum.

Jaffe, P., Sudermann, M., Reitzel, D., & Killip, S. (1992). An evaluation of a secondary school primary prevention program on violence in intimate relationships. *Violence and Victims, 7*(2), 129–146.

Jalonga, M. (1992). Teacher's stories: Our ways of knowing. *Educational Leadership, 68–73.*

Jeynes, W. (2005). A meta-analysis of the relation of parent involvement to urban elementary school student achievement. *Urban Education, 40*(3), 237–269.

Johnson, G., Heath, H., & McDermott, D. (2006). *Mindfulness: Uses and benefits for parenting education, family support practice and your stressed life.* Workshop presented at the 11th Biennial International Conference of Family Support America, Chicago, March 27.

Johnson, J. (1997). Units of analysis for the description and explanation of personality. In R. Hogan, J. A. Johnson, & S. R. Briggs (Eds.), *Handbook of personality psychology* (pp. 73–93). San Diego, CA: Academic Press.

Jordan, J., Kaplan, A., Miller, J., Stiver, I., & Surrey, J. (1991). *Women's growth in connection.* New York: Guilford Press.

Katz, L., Aidman, A., Reese, D., & Clark, A. (1996, November). Preventing and resolving parent-teacher differences. *ERIC Digests.* (ERIC Document Reproduction Service No. ED401048)

Kearn, C. (2000). *Affecting the future: The role of appropriate scaffolding in the development of social competence.* Retrieved January 14, 2006, from http://ceep.crc.uiuc.edu/pubs/katzsym/kearn.html.

Kegan, R. (1994). *In over our heads: The mental demands of modern life.* Cambridge, MA: Harvard University Press.

Kessler, R. (2000). *The soul of education.* Washington, DC: ASCD.

Knowles, M. (1980). *The modern practice of adult education.* New York: Cambridge University Press.

Kohn, A. (1991). Caring kids: The role of the school. *Phi Delta Kappan, 72*(7), 496–506.

Kohn, A. (1993/1999). *Punished by rewards: The trouble with gold stars, incentive plans, A's, praise and other bribes.* Boston: Houghton Mifflin.

Kohn, A. (1999). *The schools our children deserve: Moving beyond traditional classrooms and tougher standards.* Boston: Houghton Mifflin.

Kohn, A. (2005). *Unconditional parenting: Moving from rewards and punishments to love and reason.* New York: Atria Books.

Kohn, A. (2006). *The homework myth.* Cambridge, MA: Da Capo Lifelong Books.

Kohn, M. (1977). *Class and conformity: A study in values* (2nd ed.). Chicago: University of Chicago Press.

Kohut, H. (1977). *The restoration of the self.* New York: International Universities Press.

Kolb, D. (1984). *Experiential learning: Experience as the source of learning and development.* Englewood Cliffs, NJ: Prentice-Hall.

Kolb, D. (1985). *Learning style inventory.* Boston: McBer.

Kolb, D. (1999). Experiential learning theory: Previous research and new directions. In R. J. Sternberg & L. F. Zhange (Eds.), *Perspectives on cognitive, learning and thinking styles.* Mahwah, NJ: Erlbaum.

Koltko-Rivera, M. (2003). *Re-discovering the later version of Maslow's hierarchy of needs: Self-transcendence and opportunities for theory, research, and unification.* New York: New York University and Professional Services Group.

Krathwohl, D., Bloom, B., & Masia, B. (1964). *Taxonomy of educational objectives: Handbook 1—Affective domain.* New York: D. McKay.

Kuczynski, L. (2003). *Handbook of dynamics in parent-child relations.* Thousand Oaks, CA: Sage.

Kypros, B. (1989a, April). *Empowering families through an adult education model for parent education.* Paper presented at the Annual Meeting of the American Orthopsychiatric Association, New York.

Kypros, B. (1989b). Facilitating higher order thinking skills in parents through an adult education model for parent education. *The Creative Child and Adult Quarterly, XIV*(3–4), 203–212.

Ladd, G., Profilet, S., & Hart, C. (1992). Parents' management of children's peer relations: Facilitating and supervising children's activities in the peer culture. In R. D. Parke & G. W. Ladd (Eds.), *Family-peer relationships: Modes of linkage* (pp. 215–254). Mahwah, NJ: Erlbaum.

Lake Snell Perry & Associates, Inc. (1999, July-August). *Report on 1000 nationwide interviews.* Washington, DC. For the full report, contact info@preparetomorrowsparents.org.

Lamb, M., & Easterbrooks, M. (1981). Individual differences in parental sensitivity: Origins, components, and consequences. In M. E. Lamb & L. R. Sherrod (Eds.), *Infant social cognition: Empirical and theoretical considerations* (pp. 127–154). Hillsdale, NJ: Erlbaum.

Landerholm, E. (1984). Applying the principles of adult learning to parent education programs. *Lifelong Learning, 6–9.*

Langer, E. (1978). Rethinking the role of thought in social interaction. In J. Harvey, W. Ickes, & R. Kidd (Eds.), *New directions in attribution research. Vol. 2* (pp. 35–58). Hillsdale, NJ: Erlbaum.

Langer, E. (2000). Mindful Learning. *Current Directions in Psychological Science, 9,* 220–223.

Langer, E., & Moldoveanu, M. (2000). The construct of mindfulness. *Journal of Social Issues, 56*(1), 1–9.

Lareau, A. (1989). *Home advantage.* London: Falmer Press.

Lareau, A. (2003). *Unequal childhoods: Class, race and family life.* Berkeley: University of California Press.

Lareau, A., & Shumar, W. (1996). The problem of individualism in family-school policies. *Sociology of Education, 69,* 24–39.

Lerner, J., & Galambos, N. (1986). Temperament and maternal employment. *New Directions for Child Development, 31,* 75–88.

Lerner, R., Rothbaum, F., Boulos, S., & Castellino, D. (2002). Developmental systems perspective on parenting. In M. H. Bornstein (Ed.), *Handbook of parenting: Vol. 2. Biology and ecology of parenting* (2nd ed., pp. 315–344). Mahwah, NJ: Erlbaum.

Levine, B., & Weins, J. (2003). There is another way: A different approach to educational reform. *Phi Delta Kappan, 84*(9), 658–665.

Levine, R. (1988). Human parental care: Universal goals, cultural strategies, and individual behavior. In W. Damon (Series Ed.) & R. Levine, P. Miller, & M. West (Vol. Eds.), *New directions for child development: Parental behavior in diverse societies. Vol. 40* (pp. 3–11).

Lewis, C. (1981). The effects of parental firm control: A reinterpretation of findings. *Psychological Bulletin, 90,* 547–563.

Liff, S. (2003). Social and emotional applications for developmental education. *Journal of Developmental Education, 26,* 28–34.

Lipson, J., Dibble, S., & Minarik, P. (1996). *Culture and nursing care: A pocket guide.* San Francisco: UCFS Nursing Press.

Lopez, M. (2003). *Transforming schools through community organizing: A research review.* Cambridge, MA: Harvard Family Research Project. Retrieved January 30, 2007, from http://www.gse.harvard.edu/hfrp/projects/fine/resources/research/lopez .html.

Lovejoy, M., Graczyk, P., O'Hare, E., & Neuman, G. (2000). Maternal depression and parenting behavior: A meta-analytic review. *Clinical Psychology Review, 20,* 561–592.

Luster, T., & Okagaki, L. (Eds.). (1993). *Parenting: An ecological perspective.* Hillsdale, NJ: Erlbaum.

Luster, T., & Okagaki, L. (Eds.). (2005). *Parenting: An ecological perspective* (2nd ed.). Mahwah, NJ: Erlbaum.

Luster, T., Rhoades, K., & Haas, B. (1989). The relations between parental values and parenting behavior: A test of the Kohn hypothesis. *Journal of Marriage and the Family, 51,* 139–147.

Luster, T., & Youatt, J. (1989, April 27). *The effects of pre-parenthood education on high school students.* Paper presented at the Biennial Meeting of the Society for Research in Child Development, Kansas City, Kansas. (ERIC Document No. 305181)

Lynch, E., & Hanson, M. (1998). *Developing cross-cultural competence.* (2nd ed.). Baltimore: Brookes.

Lynch, E., & Hanson, M. (2004). *Developing cross-cultural competence* (3rd ed.). Baltimore: Brookes.

Maccoby, E. (2000). Parenting and its effects on children: On reading and misreading behavior genetics. *Annual Review of Psychology, 51,* 1–27.

MacPhee, D., Fritz, J., & Miller-Heyl, J. (1996). Ethnic variations in personal social network and parenting. *Child Development, 67,* 3278–3295.

Marcia, J. (1980). Identity in adolescence. In J. Adelson (Ed.), *Handbook of Adolescent Psychology* (pp. 159–187). New York: John Wiley.

Martin, J. (1989). Personal and interpersonal components of responsiveness. In M. H. Bornstein (Ed.), *Maternal responsiveness: Characteristics and consequences.* (pp. 5–14). San Francisco: Jossey-Bass.

Martland, N., & Rothbaum, F. (2006). Thinking critically about the Internet: Suggestions for practitioners. *Child Welfare, 85*(5), 837–852.

Maslow, A. (1969). The farther reaches of human nature. *Journal of Transpersonal Psychology, 1*(1), 1–9.

Maslow, A. (1970). *Motivation and personality* (2nd ed.). New York: Harper & Row.

Masterpaqua, F. (1992). *Educating children for parenting: Evaluation of the Learning about Parenting curriculum.* Unpublished manuscript, Widener University, Chester, PA.

Mattingly, D., Prislin, R., McKenzie, T., Rodriguez, J., & Kayzar, B. (2002). Evaluating evaluations: The case of parent involvement programs. *Review of Educational Research, 72*(4), 549–576.

Mayeroff, M. (1971). *On caring.* New York: Harper & Row.

Mayes, L., & Truman, S. (2002). Substance abuse and parenting. In M. H. Bornstein (Ed.), *Handbook of parenting: Vol. 4. Social conditions and applied parenting* (2nd ed., pp. 329–359). Mahwah, NJ: Erlbaum.

McBride, A. (1973). *The growth and development of mothers.* New York: Harper Colophon Books.

McCaleb, S. P. (1994). *Building a community of learners.* New York: St. Martin's.

McConchie, R. (2004). *Family school partnerships issue paper.* Retrieved February 14, 2007, from http://www.acsso.org.au/fspissuespaper.doc.

McDermott, D. (1997). Parent and teacher plan for the child. *Young Children, 52*(4), 32–36.

McDermott, D. (1999, November 12). *Facilitating the professional and personal lives of the adults in students' lives.* Paper presented at the Annual Conference of the Independent Schools of the Central States, Cleveland, OH.

McDermott. D. (2001). You can't sit at our table. In J. K. Comeau (Ed.), *Family Informa-tion Services professional resource materials.* Minneapolis, MN: Family Information Services, ISSN 1042-0878, 800-852-8112, September, FI/YD, 51–60.

McDermott, D. (2002a). Being your child's advocate. *Independent School, 61*(4), 104.

McDermott, D. (2002b). *Theory and rationale for parenting education in schools.* http:// www.parentingproject.org/theory.htm.

McDermott, D. (2003). *Parents as adult learners: Deconstructing parent involvement and advocacy.* Minneapolis, MN: Family Information Services, ISSN 1042-0878, 800–852–8112, July, FI/PFD, 37–55.

McDermott, D. (2003–2004, Winter). Building better human connections: Parenting/ caring education for children and teens in school. *Childhood Education, 80*(2), 71–75.

McDermott, D. (2006). The complex dimensions of caring in parent, teacher and student relationships. *International Forum on Teaching and Studies, 1*(2), 30–37.

McDermott, D., & Heath, H. (2002, October 17–19). *Preparing tomorrow's citizens today by helping them learn how to care: Education for parenting.* Workshop at the 9th Annual Forum of the Character Education Partnership, Atlanta, GA.

McDermott, D., Heath, H., & Palm, G. (Eds.). (2006). Parenting education and support: theories and advances in the field [Special issue]. *Child Welfare, 85*(5).

McDermott. D., & Segal, J. (1998). *The challenge of developing a school based center for parent growth and development in a JK–12 school.* (ERIC Document No. 426770)

McDonald, L. (1999). *Recruiting inner-city parents into high involvement in school.* Retrieved July 8, 2004, from www.wcer.wisc.edu/FAST/research/ParentInvolvement .htm.

McEwan, E. (1998). *How to deal with parents who are angry, troubled, afraid, or just plain crazy.* Thousand Oaks, CA: Corwin Press.

Meier, D., Kohn, A., Darling-Hammond, L., Sizer, T., & Wood, G. (2004). *Many children left behind: How the No Child Left Behind Act is damaging our children and our schools.* Boston: Beacon Press.

Merriam, S., & Caffarella, R. (1999). *Learning in adulthood.* San Francisco: Jossey-Bass.

Merrow, J. (2002, October 19). Keynote speech at the 9th Annual Forum of the Character Education Partnership, Atlanta, GA.

MetLife Foundation. (2002). *2002 Teacher-parent engagement through partnerships toolkit.* Retrieved February 4, 2007, from http://www.napehq.org/ML-cards.pdf.

Mezirow, J., & Associates. (1990). *Fostering critical reflection in adulthood: A guide to transformative and emancipatory learning.* San Francisco: Jossey-Bass.

Miedzian, M. (2002). *Boys will be boys: Breaking the link between masculinity and vio-lence.* New York: Doubleday.

Minuchin, P. (1985). Families and individual development: Provocations from the field of family therapy. *Child Development, 56,* 289–302.

Minuchin, S. (1974). *Families and family therapy.* Cambridge, MA: Harvard University Press.

Morgaine, C. (1992). Alternative paradigms for helping families change themselves. *Family Relations, 41,* 12–17.

Murphy, D., D'Anna, C., D'Anna, M., Heath, H., & Towey, K. (1994). *Learning to care: A paradigm shift in home, school and community.* (ERIC Document No. 382351)

National PTA. (1995). *Building successful partnerships.* Chicago: The National PTA.

National Standards for Family and Consumer Sciences Education. http://www.doe.state .in.us/octe/facs/natlstandards.htm.

New, R. (1988). Parental goals and Italian infant care. In R. A. Levine, P. M. Miller, & M. M. West (Eds.), *Parental behaviors in diverse societies* (pp. 51–64). San Francisco: Jossey-Bass.

Newberger, C. (1980). The cognitive structure of parenthood: Designing a descriptive measure. *New Directions for Child Development: Clinical Developmental Research, 7,* 45–67.

Newberger, C., & Cook, S. (1983). Parental awareness and child abuse and neglect: A cognitive developmental analysis of urban and rural samples. *American Journal of Orthopsychiatry, 53,* 512–524.

Newman, P., & Newman, B. (1988). Parenthood and adult development. *Marriage and Family Review, 12*(3–4), 313–337.

Noddings, N. (1984). *Caring: A feminine approach to ethics and moral education.* Berkeley: University of California Press.

Noddings, N. (1992). *The challenge to care in schools: An alternative approach to education.* New York: New York Teachers College Press.

Noddings, N. (2006). *Critical lessons: What our schools should teach.* New York: Cambridge University Press.

O'Connor, L. (1990). Education for parenthood and the national curriculum: Progression or regression? *Early Child Development and Care, 57,* 85–88.

Ogbu, J. (1981). Origins of human competence: A cultural-ecological perspective. *Child Development, 52*(2), 413–429.

Ohye, B. (1998). Safeguarding wordless voices in a world of words. In C. Garcia-Coll, J. Surrey, & K. Weingarten (Eds.), *Mothering against the odds: Diverse voices of contemporary mothers* (pp. 134–150). New York: Guilford Press.

Okagaki, L., & Divecha, D. (1993). Development of parental beliefs. In T. Luster & L. Okagaki (Eds.), *Parenting: An ecological perspective.* Hillsdale, NJ: Erlbaum.

Okagaki, L., Frensch, P., & Gordon, E. (1995). Encouraging school achievement in Mexican American children. *Hispanic Journal of Behavioral Sciences, 17,* 160–179.

Osofsky, J., & Jackson, B. (1994). Parenting in violent environments. *Zero to Three, 14*(3), 8–12.

Palacios, J., Gonzalez, M., & Marino, M. (1992). Stimulating the child in the zone of proximal development: The role of parents' ideas. In I. Sigel, A. Migillicuddy-DeLisi, & J. Goodnow (Eds.), *Parental belief systems: The psychological consequences for children* (2nd ed., pp. 71–94). Hillsdale, NJ: Erlbaum.

Palm, G. (2001). Parent education for incarcerated fathers. In J. Fagan & A. Hawkins (Eds.), *Clinical and educational interventions with fathers* (pp. 117–142). New York: Haworth Press.

Palmer, P. (1998). *The courage to teach.* San Francisco: Jossey-Bass.

Palsey, K., Futris, T., & Skinner, M. (2002). Effects of commitment and psychological centrality on fathering. *Journal of Marriage and Family, 64*(1), 130–138.

Parcel, T., & Menaghan, E. (1994). *Parents' jobs and children's lives.* New York: Aldine de Gruyter.

Patri, A. (1923). *Child training* (p. 168). New York: Appleton.

Patterson, G. (1986). Performance models for antisocial boys. *American Psychologist, 41,* 432–444.

Pax Christi. (2001). *Toward a globalization of solidarity.* Retrieved April 27, 2004, from http://www.paxchristiusa.org/news_events_more.asp?id=475.

Philips, S. U. (1983). *The invisible culture: Communication in classroom and community on the Warm Springs Indian Reservation* (pp. 112–115). New York: Longman.

Pickarts, E., & Fargo, J. (1971). *Parent education: Towards parental competence.* New York: Appleton-Century-Crofts.

Pinderhughes, E., Dodge, K., & Bates, J. (2000). Discipline responses: Influences on parents' socioeconomic status, ethnicity, beliefs about parenting, stress, and cognitive-emotional processes. *Journal of Family Psychology, 14,* 380–400.

Pitzer, R. (2000). Authoritative parenting involves balance. *Consortium Connections, 9*(2). Minneapolis, MN: Children, Youth & Family Consortium of the University of Minnesota. Retrieved January 30, 2007, from www.cyfc.umn.edu/family/resources/authpar.html.

Podeschi, R. (1990). Teaching their own: Minority challenges in mainstream institutions. In J. M. Ross-Garden, L. G. Martin, & D. Briscoe (Eds.), *Serving culturally diverse populations.* San Francisco: Jossey-Bass.

Pomerantz, E., & Ruble, P. (1998). The role of maternal control in the development of sex differences in child's self-evaluation factors. *Child Development, 69,* 458–478.

Portes, P. (2005). *Dismantling educational inequality: A cultural-historical approach to closing the achievement gap.* New York: Peter Lang.

Powell, D. (1998, September). Reweaving parents into the fabric of early childhood programs. *Young Children,* 60–67.

Price, A., & Witchterman, L. (2003). Shared family care: Fostering the whole family to promote safety and stability. *Journal of Family Social Work, 7*(2), 35–54.

Professional Data Analysts. (2001/2002). *Evaluations of the Dads Make a Difference curriculum.* Minneapolis, MN. Summary retrieved January 30, 2007, from http://www.dadsmakeadifference.org/ProjEval.html.

PTA. (2000–2006). *National standards for parent/family involvement programs.* Retrieved February 4, 2007, from http://www.pta.org/archive_article_details_1118251710359.html.

Puriefoy, W. (2005). Why the public is losing faith in the No Child law. *Education Week, 24*(39), 34–35.

Reese, L. (2001). Morality and identity in Mexican immigrant parents' visions of the future. *Journal of Ethnic and Migration Studies, 27*(3), 455–472.

Reilly, D., & Soto, J. (1998, May). *The forgotten parent.* Presentation at the 7th Biennial Family Resource Coalition Conference, Chicago.

Repetti, R. (1989). Effects of daily workload on subsequent behavior during marital inter-actions: The roles of social withdrawal and spouse support. *Journal of Personality & Social Psychology, 57,* 651–659.

Repetti, R., & Wood, J. (1997). Effects of daily stress at work on mothers' interactions with pre-schoolers. *Journal of Family Psychology, 11,* 90–108.

Reyes, R. (1995–1996). Storytelling as the life force of an organization. *Family Resource Coaliton Report, 14*(3–4), 32–34.

Ritchhart, R., & Perkins, D. (2000). Life in the mindful classroom: Nurturing the disposi-tions of mindfulness. *Journal of Social Issues, 56*(1), 27–46.

Roberts, C., Wolman, C., & Harris-Looby, J. (2004–2005, Winter). Project baby care: A parental training program for students with emotional and behavioral disorders. *Issues in Education,* 101–103.

Roberts, S., & McCowan, R. (2004). The effectiveness of infant simulators. *Adolescence, 39,* 475–487.

Robertson, D. (1996). Facilitating transformative learning: Attending to the dynamics of the educational helping relationship. *Adult Education Quarterly, 47*(1), 41–53.

Rogers, C. (1973). My philosophy and how it grew. *Journal of Humanistic Psychology, 13*(2), 3–15.

Rogoff, B. (1990). *Apprenticeship in thinking: Cognitive development in social context.* New York: Oxford University Press.

Rohner, R., Kean, K., & Cournoyer, D. (1991). Effects of corporal punishment, perceived caretaker warmth, and cultural beliefs on the psychological adjustment of children in St. Kitts, West Indies. *Journal of Marriage and the Family, 53,* 681–693.

Rolheiser, C., & Wallace, D. (2004). *The Roots of Empathy program as a strategy for increasing social and emotional learning: Program evaluation—final report.* Ontario Institute of Education, University of Toronto. Retrieved February 14, 2007, from http://www.rootsofempathy.org/ontarioCEreportFINAL.pdf.

Russell, A., & Russell, G. (1989). Warmth in the mother-child and father-child relation-ships in middle childhood. *British Journal of Developmental Psychology, 7,* 219–235.

Russell, D. (1990). Type of social support and specific stress: Towards a theory of optimal matching. In B. Sarason, I. Sarason, & G. Pierce (Eds.), *Social support: An interac-tional view* (pp. 319–366). New York: John Wiley.

Ryan, R., & Deci, E. (2003). On assimilating identities to the self: A self-determination theory perspective on internalization and integrity within cultures. In M. R. Leary & J. P. Tangney (Eds.), *Handbook on self and identity* (pp. 253–274). New York: Guilford Press.

Samara, A., & Wilson, J. (1999). Am I invited? Perspectives of family involvement with technology in inner-city schools. *Urban Education, 34*(4), 499–530.

Sameroff, A., & Feil, L. (1985). Parental concepts of development. In I. Sigel (Ed.), *Parental belief systems: The psychological consequences for children* (pp. 83–105). Hillsdale, NJ: Erlbaum.

Sanders, M. (2005). *Building school-community partnerships: Collaborating for student success.* Thousand Oaks, CA: Sage.

Sanders, M., & Wooley, M. (2005). The relationship between maternal self-efficacy, dysfunctional discipline practices and child conduct problems: Implications for parent training. *Care, Health & Development, 31*(1), 65–73.

Sandy, L. (1982). *Teaching child development principles to parents: A cognitive developmental approach.* Unpublished doctoral dissertation, Boston University.

Santelli, B., Turnbull, A., Marquis, I., & Lerner, E. (1997). Parent to parent programs: A resource for parents and professionals. *Journal of Early Intervention, 21,* 73–83.

Sarason, S. (1995). *Parental involvement and the political principle: Why the existing governance structure of schools should be abolished.* San Francisco: Jossey-Bass.

Satir, V. (1976). *Making contact.* Berkeley, CA: Celestial Arts.

Satir, V. (1988). *The new peoplemaking.* Mountain View, CA: Science and Behavior.

Schaefer, E. (1959). A circumplex model for maternal behavior. *Journal of Abnormal and Social Psychology, 59,* 226–235.

Schiffer, J. (2002). *Preparing tomorrow's parents today: How to bring parenting education for children and teens to your schools.* Boca Raton, FL: Prepare Tomorrow's Parents.

Schonert-Reichl, K., Smith, V., & Zaidman-Zait, A. (2004). *Effectiveness of the Roots of Empathy Program in fostering social-emotional development in primary grade children.* Retrieved April 17, 2007, from http://www.rootsofempathy.org/research.html.

Seligman, M. (2002). Positive psychology, positive prevention, and positive therapy. In C. Snyder & S. Lopez (Eds.), *Handbook of positive psychology* (pp. 3–9). New York: Oxford University Press.

Seligman, M. (with Reivich, K., Jaycox, L., & Gillham, J.). (1995). *The optimistic child.* New York: Houghton Mifflin.

Sergiovanni, T. (1993). *Building community in schools.* San Francisco: Jossey-Bass.

Shanook, R. (1990). Parenthood: A process marking identity and intimacy capacities. *Zero to Three: National Center of Clinical Infant Programs, XI*(2), 1–9.

Shartrand, A., Weiss, H., Kreider, H., & Lopez, M. E. (1997). *New skills for new schools: Preparing teachers in family involvement.* Washington, DC: U.S. Department of Education.

Sheldon, S. (2002). Parents' social networks and beliefs as predictors of parent involvement. *The Elementary School Journal, 102*(4), 301–316.

Shick, L. (1998). *Understanding temperament: Strategies for creating family harmony.* Seattle, WA: Parenting Press.

Shirley, D. (1997). *Community organizing for urban school reform.* Austin: University of Texas Press.

Shumow, L., & Lomax, R. (2002). Parental efficacy: Predictor of parenting behavior and adolescent outcomes. *Parenting Science and Practice, 2*(2), 127–150.

Shure, M. (1988). How to think, not what to think: A cognitive approach to prevention. In L. A. Bond & B. M. Wagner (Eds.), *Families in transition: Primary prevention programs that work* (pp. 170–199). Newbury Park, CA: Sage.

Shure, M. (1992). *I can problem solve (ICPS): An interpersonal cognitive problem solving program.* Champaign, IL: Research Press.

Shure, M. (2004). *Thinking parent, thinking child: How to turn your most challenging everyday problems into solutions.* New York: McGraw-Hill.

Siddiqui, A., & Ross, H. (2004). Mediation as a method of parent intervention in children's disputes. *Journal of Family Psychology, 18*(1), 147–159.

Siegel, D. (2005, September 30). *Attachment and self-understanding: Parenting with the brain in mind.* Paper presented at the 24th Annual Conference of the Illinois Association for Infant Mental Health, Chicago, IL.

Siegel, D., & Hartzell, M. (2003). *Parenting from the inside out: How a deeper understanding can help you raise children who thrive.* New York: Penguin.

Sigel, I., & McGillicuddy-DeLisi, A. (2002). Parent beliefs are cognitions: The dynamic belief systems model. In M. H. Bornstein (Ed.), *Handbook of parenting: Vol 3. Being and becoming a parent* (2nd ed., pp. 485–508). Mahwah, NJ: Erlbaum.

Sigel, I., McGillicuddy-DeLisi, A., & Goodnow, J. (1992). *Parental belief systems: The psychological consequences for children* (2nd ed.). Hillsdale, NJ: Erlbaum.

Sikkink, D., & Hernandez, E. (2003). *Religion matters: Predicting schooling success among 5 Latino youth.* Retrieved January 30, 2007, from http://www.nd.edu/~cslr/research/pubs/Sikkink_paper.pdf#search=%22religion%20matters%20by%20Sikkink%22.

Simon, M., & Lambert, H. (1990, November, December). *The growth and development of parents.* CareNetwork.

Simpson, R. (2001). *Raising teens: A synthesis of research and a foundation for action.* Boston: Center for Health Communication, Harvard School of Public Health. Retrieved January 30, 2007, from http://www.hsph.harvard.edu/chc/parenting/raising.html.

Smetana, J. (Ed.). (1994). *Beliefs about parenting: Origins and developmental implications.* San Francisco: Jossey-Bass.

Smith, C., Cudaback, D., Goddard, W., & Myers-Wall, J. (1994). *National extension parent education model of critical parenting practices.* Manhattan, KS: Kansas Cooperative Extension Service. Retrieved January 18, 2007, from http://www.cyfernet.org/parenting_practices/preface.html.

Snell, S., & Rosen, K. (1997). Parents of special needs children mastering the job of parenting. *Contemporary Family Therapy, 19*(3), 425–442.

Spivack, G., & Shure, M. (1974). *Social adjustment of young children: A cognitive approach to solving real-life problems.* San Francisco: Jossey-Bass.

Sroufe, A., Egeland, B., Carlson, E., & Collins, W. A. (2005). *The development of the person* (chap. 9). New York: Guilford Press.

State of Iowa Department of Education. (1994). *Parent involvement in education: A resource for parents, educators and communities.* (ERIC Document No. ED387245)

Steffensmeier, R. (1982). A role model of the transition to parenthood. *Journal of Marriage and the Family, 44,* 319–334.

Steinberg, L. (1996). *Beyond the classroom.* New York: Touchstone.

Steinberg, L., & Levine, A. (1997). *You and your adolescent: Parent's guide for ages 10 to 20* (Rev. ed.). New York: HarperCollins.

Suchman, R. (1972). The child and the inquiry process. In M. Silberman, J. Allender, & J. Yanoff (Eds.), *The psychology of open teaching and learning.* Boston: Little, Brown.

Sutherland, K. (1983). Parents' beliefs about child socialization. In I. Sigel & L. Laosa (Eds.), *Changing families.* New York: Plenum Press.

Swick, K. (1998). *Teacher-parent partnerships.* (ERIC Digest EDO-PS-92-12). Retrieved March 14, 2000, from http://npin.org/library/pre1998/n00381/n00381.html.

Swierk, M., & Moore, K. (2000). *Nurturing brain development.* New York: Glencoe McGraw-Hill.

Taylor, G. (1997). *Curriculum strategies: Social skills intervention for young African American males.* Westport, CT: Praeger.

Taylor, J., Turner, S., Underwood, C., Franklin, A., Jackson, E., & Stagg, V. (1994). Values for life: Preliminary evaluation of the education component. *Journal of Black Psychology, 20,* 210–233.

Taylor, K., Marienau, C., & Fiddler, M. (2000). *Developing adult learners.* San Francisco: Jossey-Bass.

Teti, D., & Gelfand, D. (1991). Behavioral competence among mothers of infants in the first year: The mediational role of maternal self-efficacy. *Child Development, 62,* 918–929.

Thayer-Bacon, B. (1993). Caring and its relationship to critical thinking. *Educational Theory, 43*(3), 323–340.

Thelan, E., & Adolph, K. (1992). Arnold Gesell: The paradox of nature and nurture. *Developmental Psychology, 28,* 368–380.

Thomas, A., Chess, S., Birch, H., & Hertzig, M. (1961). The developmental dynamics of primary reaction characteristics in children. *Proceedings of the Third World Congress of Psychiatry, Vol.1.* Toronto, Canada: University of Toronto Press.

Thomas, R. (1996). Reflective dialogue parent education design: Focus on parent development. *Family Relations, 45*(2), 189–200.

Thomas, R., Cooke, B., & Scott, M. (2005). Strengthening parent-child relationships: The reflective dialogue parent education design. *Zero to three, 26*(1), 27–34.

Thomas, R., & Footrakoon, O. (1998). *What curricular perspectives can tell us about parent education curricula.* Retrieved January 30, 2007, from http://parenthood.library.wisc.edu/Thomas/Thomas.html.

Tinsley, B., Markey, C., Ericksen, A., Kwasman, A., & Ortiz, R. (2002). Health promotion for parents. In M. H. Bornstein (Ed.), *Handbook of parenting: Vol. 5. Practical issues in parenting* (2nd ed., pp. 311–327). Mahwah, NJ: Erlbaum.

Tolan, P., & McKay, M. (1996). Preventing serious anti-social behavior in inner-city children. *Family Relations, 45,* 148–155.

Tomison, A. (1996). *Child maltreatment and family structure.* NCPC Discussion paper #1, Australian Institute of Family Studies. Retrieved January 30, 2007, from http://www.aifs.gov.au/nch/pubs/discussionpaper/discussion1.html.

Tomison, A. (1998). *Valuing parent education: A cornerstone of child abuse prevention.* Issues paper #10. Retrieved January 30, 2007, from http://www.aifs.gov.au/nch/issues10.html.

Tulloch, C., & Omvig, C. (1989). Changing attitudes through parenthood education. *Journal of Vocational Home Economics Education, 7,* 104–113.

Turnbull, A., Blue-Banning, M., Park, J., & Turbiville, V. (1999). From parent education to partnership education: A call for a transformed focus. *Topics in Early Childhood Special Education, 19*(3), 164–172.

Upshur, C. (1988). Measuring parent outcomes in family program evaluation. In H. Weiss & F. Jacobs (Eds.), *Evaluating family programs* (pp. 95–130). New York: Aldine de Gruyter.

Vandell, D., & Wilson, K. (1987). Infants' interactions with mother, sibling and peer: Contrasts and relations between interaction systems. *Child Development, 58*(1), 176–186.

Van der Pas, A. (2003). *A serious case of neglect: The parental experience of child rearing: Outline of a psychological theory of parenting.* Netherlands: Eburon Delft.

Vangelisti, A. (2004). *Handbook of family communication.* Mahwah, NJ: Erlbaum.

Vincent, C. (1996). *Parents and teachers: Power and participation.* London: Falmer Press.

Voight, J., Hans, S., & Bernstein, V. (1996). Support networks of adolescent mothers: Effects on parenting experiences and behavior. *Infant Mental Health Journal, 17,* 58–73.

Vondra, J., & Belsky, J. (1993). Developmental origins of parenting: Personality and relationship factors. In T. Luster & L. Okagaki (Eds.), *Parenting: An ecological perspective* (pp. 1–34). Hillsdale, NJ: Erlbaum.

Vondra, J., Sysko, H., & Belsky, J. (2005). Developmental origins of parenting: Personality and relationship factors. In T. Luster & L. Okagaki (Eds.), *Parenting: An ecological perspective* (2nd ed., pp. 35–71). Mahwah, NJ: Erlbaum.

Vygotsky, L. (1978). *Mind in society.* Cambridge, MA: Harvard University Press.

Wadlington, E. (1995). Basing early childhood teacher education on adult education principles. *Young Children, 50*(4), 76–80.

Walsh, D. (2004). *Selling out America's children: How America puts profits before values—and what parents can do.* Toronto, Canada: Nat Bennett.

Walsh, F. (2002). A family resilience framework: Innovative practice applications. *Family Relations, 51*(2), 130–137.

Wang, X., Bernas, R., & Eberhard, P. (2005). Maternal teaching strategies in four cultural communities: Implications for early childhood teachers. *Journal of Early Childhood Research, 3*(3), 269–288.

Watson, J. (1928). *The psychological care of infant and child, with the assistance of Rosalie Watson.* London: Allen.

Webster-Stratton, C. (1997). From parent training to community building. Families in Society. *The Journal of Contemporary Human Services, 78,* 156–171.

Weikart, D. (1980). Organizing delivery of parent education. In M. Fantini & R. Cardenas (Eds.), *Parenting in a multi-cultural society.* New York: Longman.

Weiss, H. (1988). Family support and education programs: Working through ecological theories of human development. In H. Weiss & F. Jacobs (Eds.), *Evaluating family programs* (pp. 3–36). New York: Aldine de Gruyter.

Weiss, H., Kreider, H., Lopez, M. E., & Chatman, C. (Eds.). (2005). *Preparing educators to involve families: From theory to practice.* Thousand Oaks, CA: Sage.

Weissbourd, B. (1994, May 5). Presentation at the Fifth Conference of the Family Resource Coalition, Chicago.

Wekerle, C., & Wolfe, D. (1993). Prevention of child physical abuse and neglect: Promising new directions. *Clinical Psychology Review, 13,* 501–540.

Wekerle, C., & Wolfe, D. (1998). Windows for preventing child and partner abuse: Early childhood and adolescence. In P. Trickett & C. Schellenbach (Eds.), *Violence against children in the family and the community.* Washington, DC: American Psychological Association.

Wheatley, P. (2002). *Turning to one another.* San Francisco: Berrett-Koehler.

Whitbourne, S., & Weinstock, C. (1979). *Adult development: The differentiation of experience.* New York: Holt, Rinehart & Winston.

White, K., Taylor, M., & Moss, V. (1992). Does research support claims about the benefits of involving parents in early intervention programs? *Review of Educational Research, 62,* 91–125.

White, M., & Koffman, G. (1997). Language usage, social capital, and school completion among immigrants and native-born ethnic groups. *Social Science Quarterly, 78,* 385–398.

White, R. (1959). Motivation reconsidered: The concept of competence. *Psychological Review, 66,* 297–333.

Williams, A. (2002). *Putting parent engagement into action: A practical guide.* Chicago: Family Support America.

Williams, D. (1998). Bringing parents on board. *Catalyst: Voice of Chicago School Reform, 9*(6), 1–15.

Williams, G., III. (1998, October). Toxic dads. *Parenting,* 94.

Wilson, W. J. (1987). *The truly disadvantaged.* Chicago: University of Chicago Press.

Winship, A. (1912). The school's growing service to the home. *Good Housekeeping, 55,* 517.

Winters, W. (1993). *African American mothers and urban schools: The power of participation.* Lexington, MA: Lexington Books.

Wood, D., Bruner, J., & Ross, G. (1976). The role of tutoring in problem solving. *Journal of Child Psychology and Psychiatry, 17,* 89–100.

Wood, W., III, & Baker, J. (1999). Preferences for parent education programs among low socioeconomic status, culturally diverse parents. *Psychology in the Schools, 36*(3), 239–247.

Yust, K., Johnson, A., Sasso, S., & Roehlkepartain, E. (Eds.). (2006). *Nurturing child and adolescent spirituality: Perspectives from the world's religious traditions.* Lanham, MD: Rowman & Littlefield.

Zahn-Waxler, C., Duggal, S., & Gruber, R. (2002). Parental psychopathology. In M. H. Bornstein (Ed.), *Handbook of parenting: Vol. 4. Social conditions and applied parenting* (2nd ed., pp. 295–328). Mahwah, NJ: Erlbaum.

Zero to Three. (1992). *Head Start: The emotional foundations of school readiness.* Washington, DC: National Center for Clinical Infant Programs.

Zigler, E. (1976). *The exploring childhood curriculum.* Newton, MA: Education Development Center, Inc.

Zigler, E. (1999). Testimony to the Connecticut Committee on Children. Retrieved February 14, 2007, from http://www.parentingproject.org/quotes.htm.

Zins, J., Weissberg, R., Wang, M., & Walberg, H. (Eds.). (2004). *Building academic success on social and emotional learning: What does the research say?* New York: Teachers College Press.

INDEX

About the Author

Dana McDermott, PhD, CFLE, is an Assistant Professor at the School for New Learning at DePaul University in Chicago, Illinois. She received her doctorate in Human Development and Social Psychology from Loyola University of Chicago. She is also a nationally certified family life educator. She has worked for more than three decades in the Chicago area, nationally, and internationally in the area of parent and family development. In Chicago, she has been involved in minority parent leadership and in implementing parent education programs for children in K–12 schools and for their parents. She joined the faculty of the School for New Learning in 2002. She teaches classes on parenting in cultural context and parent-school-community relations to both undergraduate and graduate students. Recently she has developed a special, customized Focus Area (Parenting Education and Support) within the School of New Learning's Master of Arts in Applied Professional Studies program. She serves on two national boards: Prepare Tomorrow's Parents, an organization dedicated to promoting and supporting parenting education in schools, and the National Parenting Education Network, dedicated to supporting parenting educators in their work. She consults with schools and parent groups in the areas of parenting, gender relationships, teaching caring, social and emotional development of children, and violence prevention. She is a member of several professional organizations, including the National and Illinois Councils on Family Relations and Psychologists for Social Responsibility.